AF605800

Empirical Perspectives on the Use of Hungarian Nominal Demonstratives

Pragmatic Interfaces

In the last two decades it has become increasingly clear that language and language use cannot be studied separately and independently of each other. This new approach assumes an interaction between grammar (phonology, morphology, lexicon, syntax and semantics) and pragmatics. An analysis of the interfaces between each component of grammar and pragmatics (the 'interface view') can also be applied to hard-pragmatics and soft-pragmatics research. Hard-pragmatics studies the field of language use from philosophical, linguistic and logical points of view, while soft-pragmatics explores phenomena of language use from a social and socio-cultural perspective.

The definitions hard- and soft-pragmatics, adopted around the 1980s, have become somewhat dated since pragmatics has become a field of its own, and so these two trends have merged to some extent. Also, various pragmaticians made important attempts to blend these approaches. Nevertheless, a border between these areas continues to exist: hard-pragmaticians rarely venture into socio-pragmatic issues, and, vice versa, soft-pragmatic studies rarely make use of formal tools of hard-pragmatics.

Pragmatic Interfaces fills an important knowledge gap in the field of pragmatics as the first major publication project devoted to studying grammar–pragmatics interfaces and merging of soft-pragmatics with hard-pragmatics. Through this merging many pragmatic phenomena could be essentially revisited. Pragmatic Interfaces follows an interdisciplinary approach, allowing scholars from different areas of grammar and pragmatics to collaborate.

Published:

A preference hierarchy model of same-turn repair operations in talk-in-interaction
Zsuzsanna Németh

Data and Argumentation in Historical Pragmatics: Grammaticalization of a Catalan Motion Verb Construction
Katalin Nagy C.

Face and Face Practices in Chinese Talk-in-Interaction: A Study in Interactional Pragmatics
Wei-Lin Melody Chang

Implicit Subject and Direct Object Arguments in Hungarian Language Use: Grammar and Pragmatics Interacting
Enikő Németh T.

Impoliteness in Corpora: A Comparative Analysis of British English and Spoken Turkish
Hatice Celebi

Metapragmatics of Attentiveness: A Study in Interpersonal and Cross-cultural Pragmatics
Saeko Fukushima

Politeness Phenomena across Chinese Genres
Edited by Xinren Chen

Empirical Perspectives on the Use of Hungarian Nominal Demonstratives

Enikő Tóth

UNIVERSITY OF TORONTO PRESS
Toronto Buffalo London

Published by University of Toronto Press in 2024
Toronto Buffalo London
utorontopress.com
Printed in the USA

ISBN 978-1-4875-6637-1 (cloth)
ISBN 978-1-4875-6639-5 (EPUB)
ISBN 978-1-4875-6638-8 (UPDF)

Publication cataloguing information available from Library and Archives Canada.

Cover image created with the assistance of DALL·E 2
Cover design: Mark Lee / hisandhers.design

We wish to acknowledge the land on which the University of Toronto Press operates. This land is the traditional territory of the Wendat, the Anishnaabeg, the Haudenosaunee, the Métis, and the Mississaugas of the Credit First Nation.

University of Toronto Press acknowledges the financial support of the Government of Canada, the Canada Council for the Arts, and the Ontario Arts Council, an agency of the Government of Ontario, for its publishing activities.

Canada Council for the Arts
Conseil des Arts du Canada

Funded by the Government of Canada
Financé par le gouvernement du Canada

Canada

Contents

Acknowledgements

Some parts of this book are based on revised materials that have been published before. I would like to thank the editors of *Argumentum*, an open access journal, for their policy of permitting the reuse of materials from published articles. Sections of Chapter 3 are based on the following papers:

- Tóth, Enikő. 2018. A production study on the choice of Hungarian demonstratives. *Argumentum* 14: 110–123.
- Tóth, Enikő. 2020. Some insights on demonstrative use in Hungarian: results of a controlled dialogue game. *Argumentum* 16: 209–229.

My research was supported by the Borbély Szilárd Sabbatical Grant given by the Faculty of Humanities (University of Debrecen). I am also grateful to the Institute of English and American Studies at the University of Debrecen for relieving me of my teaching duties in the spring semester of the 2019/20 academic year. This book is partially based on my habilitation dissertation which I worked on during my sabbatical leave.

My research on demonstratives has also been supported by National Research, Development and Innovation Office of Hungary (NKFIH), grant no. K22_143417.

I wish to thank Péter Csatár from the Department of German Linguistics, University of Debrecen, who I have been working with on Hungarian demonstratives for several years. We have given joint presentations at conferences both in Hungary and abroad, and we have collaborated many times in various research projects. I am also grateful to my colleagues and former colleagues at the Department of English Linguistics, especially to György Rákosi, Tibor Laczkó, Péter Pelyvás and Péter Szűcs, who helped clarify ideas during stimulating and extensive discussions.

My special thanks go to Enikő Németh T., Renate Pajusalu and Gábor Alberti for their insightful comments on previous versions of the manuscript. I am also grateful to the editors of the book series, Enikő Németh T. and Károly Bibok, for their feedback, to George Seel, for proofreading, and to Valerie Hall at Equinox, for guiding me through all the stages of the publishing process.

For their encouragement, I am indebted to my family and friends.

Abbreviations

ABL	ablative
ACC	accusative
ADE	adhesive
ADJ	adjectivalizing
ADR	addressee
ALL	allative
ATTR	attributive
CAUS-FIN	causal-final
COM	comitative
COMP	complementizer
COND	conditional
COP	copula
DAT	dative
DEL	delative
DIM	diminutive
DIST	distal
ELA	elative
ESS-FORM	essive-formal
FORM	formal
FREQ	frequentative
FUT	future
GER	gerund
H	hearer
HNC	Hungarian National Corpus
ILL	illative
IMP	imperative
INE	inessive
INF	infinitive
INS	instrumental
MOD-ESS	modal-essive
NEG	negative
NOM	nominative
NP	noun phrase
POSS	possessive
POSSIB	possibility
PROX	proximal

PRT	particle
PRTC	participle
PST	past
PL	plural
QPRT	question particle
SG	singular
SOC	sociative
SUBJ	subjunctive
SUBL	sublative
SUP	superessive
TRA	translative
1, 2, 3	First person, Second person, Third person

Figures

Tables

Tables

Introduction

The fundamental purpose of this book is to provide an account of the semantics and pragmatics of Hungarian nominal demonstratives while exploring the role of contextual factors that might influence the choice of demonstratives in Hungarian. Thus the work reported here is aimed on the one hand at explaining why a speaker would opt for a given demonstrative form in a particular speech situation, and on the other hand at investigating how the meaning of a demonstrative interacts with contextual clues during the process of reference resolution. The present account addresses these questions from an empirical perspective; it incorporates the results of experimental work and corpus-based analyses. Based on the empirical findings, the book argues that demonstrative reference in Hungarian is a dynamic, highly context-dependent, interactive and hearer-oriented process.

In current research on deixis, there is a rapidly expanding interest in empirical methods; in recent years, the number of observational, experimental and corpus-based studies has increased considerably. There is an ongoing debate on the role of factors that govern demonstrative choice across languages (see, for example, Coventry et al. 2008, 2014 for data on Spanish and English; Jarbou 2010 for Jordanian Arabic; Stevens & Zhang 2013 for English; Peeters et al. 2014, 2015 for Dutch; Reile et al. 2020a, 2020b for Estonian). Previous works related to deixis in Hungarian either represent the traditional descriptive approach (for example, Kugler & Laczkó 2000) or provide a theoretical overview of deictic phenomena in general and demonstratives in particular within a functional-cognitive framework (Laczkó 2010, 2012; Tátrai 2010, 2017). By working with a wider spectrum of data and by the application of various research methods, the present work not only broadens current approaches to the use of Hungarian demonstratives but also contributes to the international debate mentioned above by providing new insights on demonstrative choice in a language that has not been explored by experimental tools before.

Expanding the results of my preliminary investigations (Tóth et al. 2014; Tóth & Csatár 2016), the aim of the book is to develop a deeper understanding of the Hungarian demonstrative system from a novel, empirical perspective. Relying on different types of data gained by the application of diverse methods (including elicitation, corpus-linguistic and experimental methods) leads to more solid empirical foundations and results in a better and more adequate description of the phenomenon under investigation. The work presented in the book enriches our understanding of the semantics and pragmatics of Hungarian nominal demonstratives. It argues that demonstrative reference in Hungarian is a joint action, in which not only the speaker, but the addressee also takes an active role in resolving reference. It is shown that the selection of proximal vs. distal demonstratives, when used exophorically, is only partially governed by physical proximity; the speaker also takes into account the addressee's knowledge about the intended referent, i.e., the nature of the context (contrastive vs. non-contrastive), the presence or absence of visual joint attention, and pointing also influence the choice of demonstratives. The emerging picture can be incorporated into the cross-linguistic typological space by providing a deeper understanding of how different uses of demonstratives (exophoric, contrastive, anaphoric, etc.) relate to each other and what this means in terms of their semantics and pragmatics.

The structure of the book is as follows. Chapter 1 presents the problems demonstratives pose for semantic analysis, then offers an overview of demonstratives from a cross-linguistic perspective. By taking a taxonomic approach, the diverse pragmatic functions and their complex relations are also discussed. Finally, a preliminary description of the relevant Hungarian data is provided.

Chapter 2 offers a critical overview of previous accounts on demonstrative choice per se. After discussing Gundel et al.'s (1993) Givenness Hierarchy, Ariel's (1990/2014) Accessibility Theory, Cornish's (2001) cognitive-psychological theory, and Hanks's (1990, 2009) interactional account, more recent approaches are presented, including the works of Diessel (2012), Diessel and Coventry (2021), Sidnell and Enfield (2017) and Tátrai (2017). The common denominator of these approaches, which mostly focus on the use of English demonstratives, is that they suggest that deictic reference is a collaborative process, where the speaker directs the attention of the addressee towards the intended referent. Also discussed is the proposed analysis of Scott (2013, 2020), who argues in a relevance-theoretic framework that English demonstratives encode procedural meaning, thereby bringing together previous insights about demonstrative reference.

Chapter 2 also provides a brief overview of recent experimental work aimed at challenging the traditional, speaker-centred view on demonstrative selection in general. More specifically, studies carried out by Coventry et al. (2014) and Stevens and Zhang (2013) regarding English, and experiments conducted by Peeters et al. (2014, 2015) focusing on Dutch demonstratives are discussed. Finally, previous experimental work on Hungarian demonstratives (carried out by the author) is presented (Tóth et al. 2014; Tóth & Csatár 2016).

Chapter 3 reports the results of two empirical studies conducted to explore demonstrative practice in Hungarian. First, I collected spontaneous data in a controlled dialogue game setting in order to examine the use of Hungarian nominal demonstratives. The findings indicated that relative distance from the speaker acts as a decisive factor in the choice of (exophoric) demonstratives, but mental accessibility as a factor is discarded. At the same time, the outcome of the qualitative analysis also emphasized that the role of dynamic features of interaction (such as change of perspective, direction of eye gaze) cannot be neglected. The second study investigated the effect of three factors – relative distance, joint visual attention and pointing – on the choice of demonstratives with the help of an online production experiment. The results showed that the selection between proximal and distal demonstratives in Hungarian is influenced by relative distance from the speaker; however, it was also shown that relative distance as a single factor cannot always explain the selection of demonstratives; visual joint attention and pointing are crucial. Moreover, the interaction found between distance and joint attention signalled that it is not enough to examine isolated factors; studying the interactions between individual factors is essential too.

Chapter 4 first explores contrastive uses of demonstratives. By applying the demonstrative questionnaire developed by Wilkins (1999), it examines the role of two factors in demonstrative practice in table-top space: relative distance and contrastiveness. The findings show that in the case of non-contrastive exophoric uses of Hungarian nominal demonstratives in limited space where the speaker and the addressee have the same perspective of their physical surroundings, demonstratives code distance opposition (near and far), namely, the table-top space is divided into a speaker-anchored, interactional proximal region, and a distal region, which governs demonstrative choice. The findings for contrastive uses support the conclusion reached by Tóth et al. (2014), i.e., both proximal and distal demonstratives occurred in the interactional proximal region, thereby providing converging evidence for the generalisation made by Levinson (2018a) that contrastive uses across languages overwrite proximity distinctions.

Another important finding of the elicitation study is that in Hungarian not only *ez/az* 'this/that', but the so-called emphatic or reinforced nominal demonstrative terms *emez/amaz* 'this/that' are also used contrastively. The second part of Chapter 4 investigates the functions displayed by the emphatic demonstratives (*emez/amaz*) by presenting the outcome of a corpus-based analysis of their nominative occurrences in the Hungarian National Corpus. The results demonstrate that although *emez/amaz* are generally considered marginal, they can fulfil a wide range of pragmatic functions. Furthermore, it is also shown that the demonstratives in question are inherently contrastive, that is, the suggestion made by Laczkó (2009) that the core meaning of *emez/amaz* is 'this/that other one' has been confirmed by empirical observations.

Chapter 5 summarizes the findings of this study and outlines some interesting problems left for future research.

CHAPTER 1

Demonstratives – Meaning and Use

1.1 Introduction

It is a basic fact about language use that during everyday communication people frequently refer to objects in their physical surroundings, thereby creating a direct link between language and the real world. Deixis, an intriguing linguistic phenomenon at the semantics/pragmatics interface, is concerned with the study of 'linguistic expressions that are used to indicate elements of the situational and/or discourse context, including the speech participants and the time and location of the current speech event' (Diessel 2012: 2408). Deixis is a pervasive feature of languages; demonstratives, which are prototypical deictic expressions, can be found across all languages and appear very early during language acquisition (Clark 1978; Diessel 1999, 2013; Tanz 1980).

It is a crucial feature of demonstratives that their meaning and use depend heavily on extra-linguistic contextual clues. This fact has important implications; namely, a demonstrative expression cannot be interpreted without analysing the context in which it has been uttered. For example, the referent of the English demonstrative pronoun *this* varies from context to context; therefore, it is not easy to define its contribution to the meaning of the utterance it is part of. According to Enfield (2003: 82), demonstratives constitute 'one of the great puzzles of linguistic science'. Inspired by Bühler's (1934) classic work, deixis and demonstratives have been widely studied both from a philosophical and a linguistic perspective. This chapter provides an overview of different approaches characterising the meaning and use of demonstratives.

1.2 The semantics and pragmatics of demonstratives

1.2.1 The philosophical perspective

Deixis (or indexicality in the philosophical tradition) is the source of many interesting puzzles in the philosophy of language.[1] First of all, indexical expressions, such as *I* and *this*, are problematic, since their meaning is underspecified and their referents cannot be identified without taking into consideration the extra-linguistic context. For instance, *I* always refers to the speaker in the given context at the time of the utterance, which means that the semantic evaluation of any indexical expression heavily depends on the context, i.e. the referent of *I* varies from context to context; it is a context-sensitive expression. This poses a problem for formal theories of meaning. Namely, a sentence involving an indexical expression simply cannot express a proposition (a mapping from possible worlds to truth values derived in a context-independent manner), since the contribution of an indexical expression to the meaning of the sentence depends on the context of utterance. In other words, we need 'contextual resolution of semantically general expressions – in the physical space-time context of the speech event' (Levinson 2004: 101). There are several suggestions to deal with this conundrum in the philosophical literature; one of them is briefly presented here.

Kaplan (1989a) discusses the use of indexical expressions (*I, you, here, now, this*) and differentiates true demonstratives (*this, that*) from pure indexicals (*I, here*). He argues that in the case of the former an associated demonstration is required to determine their referents, while in the case of the latter no such demonstration is necessary, the referent can be identified without receiving any special clue from the speaker. Thus the most essential feature of true demonstratives is that assuming that a speaker utters (1) in a bicycle shop, the use of the demonstrative must be accompanied by a kind of gesture on the part of the speaker (this could be a pointing gesture, an eye gaze or a nod) that identifies the referent in the given context, i.e., the speaker must indicate which object he wants to refer to in the physical environment.

(1) I like *this bike* the most.

Kaplan (1989a) also suggests that a sentence has two semantic values: its content and its character. Content is the proposition expressed by a sentence when it is uttered, while the character of a certain sentence is a mapping from contexts to contents, and this is considered to be the linguistic meaning of the sentence. Within

1 See Levinson (2004) and Wolter (2009) for an extended overview.

the framework of compositional semantics, each constituent of the sentence has both content and character. Consequently, the content of an utterance of a sentence cannot be determined without the context of the utterance. In the case of pure indexicals, such as *I*, Kaplan (1989a) argues that the content is an entity in the given context, i.e., the current speaker, and the linguistic meaning of *I* is specified by its character: a mapping which assigns the current speaker to each context.

Demonstratives behave in a similar fashion; the content of a true demonstrative in a given context is an entity, and formally this means that the character of the demonstrative assigns an entity to each context, the one identified by the demonstration. It is important to note here that besides the linguistically encoded meaning the speaker's demonstration is also essential in identifying the referent. In his later work, Kaplan (1989b) suggests that the speaker's referential intentions are more important than the demonstration itself when demonstratives are interpreted. As we will see later on, this is perhaps one of the most important features that are considered crucial in understanding demonstrative reference in current approaches to deixis. The issue of intentionality in referential acts will be addressed in Chapter 2.

Levinson (2004) states that the philosophical approach outlined above is descriptively inadequate, since deictic expressions often contain both descriptive properties and contextual variables that in turn require pragmatic resolution.[2] An obvious disadvantage of the formal approach is that it cannot explain other (non-indexical) uses of demonstratives, when the accompanying gesture on the part of the speaker is superfluous (cf. the symbolic use of demonstratives described in Section 1.2.3). Green (2011), adopting Bar-Hillel's (1954) approach, states that the complexity of the use of demonstratives not only stems from their context dependence, but also from their being multiply indeterminate.[3] This can be illustrated by the different uses of the English demonstrative *this* (Green 2011: 76):

indexical *this* can thus be intended

(a) deictically to refer to something gesturally indicated,
(b) anaphorically to refer to a just completed bit of discourse,
(c) cataphorically, to refer to a bit of discourse that will follow directly, or
(d) figuratively, to refer to something evoked by whatever is indicated and deictically referred to.

2 Levinson (2004) also mentions further problems that cannot be treated within the formal framework, while Wolter (2009) provides an account of recent developments that have challenged the Kaplanian theory of demonstratives (for a more detailed discussion see Levinson 2004 and Wolter 2009).

3 Different uses of demonstratives will be presented in Section 1.2.3.

Another important point made by Bar-Hillel (1954) is that while interpreting demonstratives, the addressee has to choose from the elements of a set, the set of potential referents, which is always determined by the given context. Hence, the notion of contrast, though not explicitly, also surfaces in the philosophical tradition.[4]

Overall, the formal treatment of indexicality cannot explain the use of deictic expressions and their contribution to utterance interpretation in an adequate manner. This is especially problematic if we consider Bar-Hillel's (1954) claim that more than 90% of declarative sentences uttered by speakers are indexical, and therefore context-dependent.

1.2.2 Some crosslinguistic insights on demonstratives: the typological analysis

As mentioned above, demonstrations are universal across languages. Diessel (1999) analysed deictic expressions from a crosslinguistic perspective, drawing data from 85 languages. Based on his language sample, Diessel (1999) argues that 'all languages have at least two demonstratives that are deictically contrastive: a proximal demonstrative referring to an entity near the deictic centre and a distal demonstrative denoting a referent that is located at some distance to the deictic centre' (Diessel 1999: 2).[5] For example, in English, *this*, *these* are proximals and refer to things that are close to the deictic centre or origo, which is the speaker in the default case; while *that*, *those* are distals and refer to things that are not so close in space.[6] Therefore, in (2), the book being referred to is close to the speaker, while the apple mentioned in (3) is further away from the speaker.

(2) *This* is my favourite book.

(3) Give me *that apple*.

In these utterances, demonstratives refer directly to the extra-linguistic physical context; they allow the interlocutors to 'point' to something in the physical environment, thereby enabling them to orient themselves spatially (O'Keeffe et al. 2011). This use illustrates the most basic pragmatic function of demonstratives, the so-called spatial use.

---

4 The notion of contrast will be discussed in the next section.

5 The observation above is later complemented with the following: 'In some languages, pronominal, adnominal and/or identificational demonstratives are distance-neutral, but adverbial demonstratives are always deictically contrastive' (Diessel 1999: 50).

6 Demonstratives are generally considered to be deictic expressions that can occur either pronominally or adnominally, as in (2) and (3), respectively.

The spatial opposition described above forms a central part of the semantic features in Diessel's (1999) crosslinguistic analysis of demonstratives. According to Diessel (1999), there are two types of semantic features that characterize the meaning of demonstratives: (i) deictic features specify the relative location of the referent regarding its position with respect to the deictic centre and in certain languages they might also encode whether the referent is visible or not, whether it is uphill or downhill, etc., while (ii) qualitative features describe various properties of the referent, for example whether it is animate or inanimate, whether it is human or non-human, female or male, whether it is one entity or a set of entities, etc. Each of these features surfaces in various languages in Diessel's typological analysis.

A crucial difference between the formal approach and the crosslinguistic analysis is whether they consider the spatial contrast to be part of the meaning of the demonstratives or not. When interpreting a given demonstrative in context, the locative information clearly plays a role in identifying the referent, but in the philosophical tradition this is not part of the meaning of the demonstrative itself. Wolter (2009) assumes that the proximity condition related to *this* is a presupposition, but she also mentions that it could also be treated as a conventional implicature. As opposed to this, Diessel's (1999) typological work considers the spatial contrast to be a central semantic feature of demonstratives.

Levinson (2018a) also states that the meaning of demonstratives is 'referentially underspecified', namely, demonstratives 'invite the recipient to use contextual clues to find a definite interpretation' (Levinson 2018a: 6). He also adds that the meaning of demonstratives is necessarily shallow, since the same demonstrative might pick entirely different referents under different circumstances. For example, in the example below, the demonstrative pronoun might refer to an object, such as a piece of cheese that the speaker is smelling, or it might refer to the general impression one gets when entering a certain room.

(4) *This* smells bad. (Levinson 2018a: 6)

In fact, it is the semantic shallow meaning of demonstratives that forces the addressee to rely on various contextual clues to be able to identify the referent under the given circumstances, and that is why their use is usually accompanied by a type of gesture.

Another crucial point made by Levinson (2018a) is that the speaker clearly must have reasons for using a given demonstrative; moreover, important information is also carried by the contrastive items that have not been selected by the speaker. Perhaps the most natural way of invoking a contrast is via spatial demarcation, and then this contrast is highlighted by the traditional proximal/

distal distinction in the characterization of demonstratives. However, this stance runs the risk of oversimplification. For example, in the case of English, Levinson (2018a) argues that 'if *that* is used, the implication is that some crucial properties for the use of *this* did not obtain' (Levinson 2018a: 6). The properties mentioned might be semantic in nature, for example, if *this* specifies proximity, then the use of *that* within the same utterance can create a spatial contrast. This type of usage is illustrated in (5) below:

(5) *This one* (here) is bigger than *that one* (over there). (Diessel 2012: 2419)

In another scenario, when both entities being referred to are located close to the speaker, the same demonstratives might be acceptable, which shows that *that* might be neutral with respect to relative distance from the speaker, and then another kind of contrast is induced between the referents. Consider the example in (6):

(6) *This bracelet* was given to me by my mother, but *that one* by my husband.

It is easy to see that both bracelets in question might be located on the wrist of the speaker, however, distal *that* is appropriately used to refer to one of them.

Demonstratives might invoke different types of contrast in individual languages. For example, in Turkish, the presence or absence of the addressee's visual attention matters; more specifically, *su* indicates that the referent is not yet in the addressee's visual focus of attention, while *o* signals that the referent is already in the addressee's visual focus of attention (Küntay & Özyürek 2006). In a similar fashion, Jarbou (2010) observes that the use of demonstratives in Spoken Jordanian Arabic 'depends on the speaker's perceptions about the addressee's ability to identify perceptible features of a referent in context' (Jarbou 2010: 3095).

There are also languages where contrast is a grammatically encoded feature, usually marked by an affix. For example, in Woleaian a suffix marks a contrastive referent 'when pointing out one member of a group' (Anderson & Keenan 1985: 289, cited by Diessel 1999), as illustrated in (7) below:

(7) Woleaian (Diessel 1999: 53)
mwu(u)-l
that.NEAR.H-CONTRAST
'that one near you'

Another type of contrast is described by Enfield (2009). Relying on the findings of his observational study of the Lao demonstratives *nii4* and *nan4*, Enfield (2009) argues that the former term has a less specific, primitive demonstrative meaning which he defines as 'the (one) that is mutually salient enough in this context for you to know which one I must mean' (Enfield 2009: 36), while the latter has a more specific meaning, which, besides the basic demonstrative meaning just given, also encodes that the entity being referred to is not here.

Turning back to English, Levinson (2018a) claims that *that* has a distal meaning only in spatial opposition to *this*. More specifically, he suggests that the two demonstratives form an informativeness scale, i.e., based on Grice's maxim of quantity (Grice 1975), the use of the less specific term (*that*) implies that the more specific term (*this*) does not apply. Just like any other conversational implicature, this one is also defeasible, which means that the less specific term might be used when the more specific one would be expected. In Levinson's (2000) words: 'This predicts that *that* has a wide distribution, potentially overlapping with *this*, as indeed seems to be the case' (Levinson 2000: 94). Accordingly, analysing two-term demonstrative systems might be perplexing; however, it is clear that speakers in actual situations do choose one of the demonstratives, and one should be able to pin down the semantic features which determine this nonarbitrary choice made by the speaker (cf. Enfield 2009).

As an interim summary, this section emphasized the inherent contrastive nature of demonstratives in two-term demonstrative systems, which was first recognized by Bar-Hillel (1954). Relying on Diessel's (1999) typological work and different characterizations of the English demonstratives *this* and *that*, it can be argued that the semantic representation of demonstratives has to capture the inherent contrast marked by them. From a pragmatic perspective, demonstratives can fulfil a wide range of functions. The various functions of demonstratives have been addressed by taxonomical approaches, and we will turn to these in the following section.

1.2.3 Various uses of demonstratives: taxonomies

Demonstratives are widely used in everyday conversations, and they can fulfil a number of different pragmatic functions. Taxonomies of demonstrative usage not only describe and explain the diverse roles fulfilled by demonstratives in communication, but also explore the various relations between different uses of demonstratives.[7] However, as Levinson (2004) points out, the categories within the taxonomy do not represent complex relations and potential overlaps between the different types of uses. Moreover, as will be discussed later, borderline cases also occur.

---

7 Different pragmatic uses of Hungarian nominal demonstratives will be discussed in Section 1.3.2.

First, deictic and non-deictic uses are differentiated (Levinson 2004). This basic distinction roughly corresponds to the difference between text external or exophoric and text internal or endophoric reference; however, as we will see later, recognitional uses are not strictly speaking endophoric, but they are not exophoric, either. Therefore, the distinction between deictic and non-deictic uses is more adequate, but I will use the labels deictic and exophoric interchangeably.

Within deictic or exophoric uses, speakers orient the addressee in the speech situation by drawing their attention to certain entities. In such cases, the intended referent of the demonstrative can only be identified if the speech event is monitored physically, i.e., the referent can only be established based on the audio, visual, and tactile features of the speech situation (cf. Levinson 1983). Thus in deictic uses the speaker is referring to an entity that is available in the physical context. This can be achieved in two major ways: the use of the demonstrative might either be accompanied by a pointing gesture on the part of the speaker or not. The former use is labelled as gestural. For example, when uttering (8), the speaker is referring to an object in the speech situation and the utterance is probably accompanied by an extra-linguistic gesture (a pointing gesture, a head nod or eye gaze) on the part of the speaker.

(8) Give me *that mug*.

According to Lyons (1977), this is the genuine case of deixis, hence, gestural uses may be treated as prototypical cases of deictic reference.[8] Levinson (2004) divides gestural uses into two subcategories. He differentiates contrastive and non-contrastive cases. Adopting his taxonomy of distinct uses of demonstratives, we will treat contrastive gestural and non-contrastive gestural uses separately. We have already encountered examples of contrastive use above (examples (5) and (6)); another relevant example is given in (9). Non-contrastive uses are exemplified by (8) above.

(9) This garden hose is better than that one.[9]

Within exophoric reference, when there is no accompanying extra-linguistic gesture on the part of the speaker, symbolic uses and transposed uses are set apart. The first category includes cases where the referent is not identified by means of a pointing gesture, but by relying on shared information present in the common ground of the interlocutors. Symbolic uses thus activate contextually available

8 Diessel (1999) argues that such uses are the first to be acquired by children, and cross-linguistically, gestural demonstratives are the least marked in form.

9 https://en.wikipedia.org/wiki/Anaphora_(linguistics)

shared information about the speech situation and the intended referent, but the referent is not necessarily part of the immediate physical environment of the interlocutors. For example, in (10), the speaker, a tourist guide, refers to the city where he and his group of tourists are staying at the time of utterance, and clearly the entire city is not visible in the vicinity.

(10) This city offers beaches, great weather and plenty of entertainment.

As Diessel (1999) notes, symbolic uses also include cases where the referent is not a concrete physical entity. For example, it is possible to refer to emotions in that way.

(11) He was overcome by *this feeling of helplessness.*

According to (Levinson 2018a), transposed uses are characterized by shifting the deictic centre to other participants, often in a different space and time, which can typically be witnessed in narratives. This means that the demonstrative is not anchored in the current situation, but is transferred to the speech situation present in the narrative itself. This type of usage is called deictic projection by Lyons (1977). In such cases the audience either follows the events from the perspective of a character, as in (12), or in the case of first-person narratives, the perspective of the speaker of the narrative event is adopted. The latter case is illustrated by (13):

(12) And he's…you see a scene where he's…coming on his bicycle *this way*. (Himmelmann 1996: 222)

(13) I was looking at *this little puppy* in a cage with such a sad look on its face. (Yule 1996: 13)

Finally, we have to mention a special subtype of deictic use, which includes reference to a physical, usually audible, instantiation of language, as in (14) and (15) below:

(14) Bloop. It sounded like *that*. (Levinson 2018a: 10)

(15) I'm sorry. I didn't hear you. Could you repeat *that*? (Diessel 1999: 101)

Levinson (2018a) labels this type of deictic use as discourse deictic; however, this is not entirely satisfactory, since other authors often reserve the same term for a special type of non-deictic, intratextual reference, where the referent is not part of the physical environment. Therefore, although in general I follow Levinson's (2004) taxonomy, I adopt Lyons's (1977) terminology here and label this phenomenon as pure text deixis.

Other uses of demonstratives are non-deictic. These can be further divided into anaphoric, discourse deictic, and recognitional uses in Diessel's (1999) categorization. Anaphoric and discourse deictic expressions do not refer directly to the extra-linguistic context; instead, they 'refer to elements of the ongoing discourse' (Diessel 1999: 93). In the case of recognitional use the demonstrative signals that the addressee can identify the referent relying on shared knowledge between the interlocutors.

Anaphoric demonstratives co-refer with another noun phrase within the text, which means that they refer to an entity that another term picked out. Within anaphoric uses, a further distinction is made between anaphora and cataphora, depending on the position of the referring term. Anaphora is illustrated by (16); here the demonstrative co-refers with its antecedent, a noun phrase in the previous sentence, and thus does not refer directly to a human being in the speech situation. In the case of cataphora, the demonstrative co-refers with its postcedent.[10]

(16) The cowboy entered. *This man* was not someone to mess with. (Levinson 2004: 108)

Discourse deictic demonstratives are not co-referential with another expression, rather, they refer to parts of the ongoing discourse, as in (17) and (18), where *this* and *that* both refer to a proposition. (17) illustrates anaphoric reference, while (18) is cataphoric:

(17) 'You are wrong.' *That*'s exactly what he said. (Levinson 2004: 108)
(18) I forgot to tell you *this*. Uhm Matt Street phoned while I was out. (International Corpus of English, cited by Diessel 2012: 2426)

Regarding their function, discourse deictic demonstratives 'focus the hearer's attention on aspects of meaning, expressed by a clause, a sentence, a paragraph, or an entire story' (Diessel 1999: 101). For example, *that* in (19) can refer not only to the propositional content of the utterance, but also to its illocutionary force:

(19) A: Peter failed the exam.
B: *That*'s false./*That*'s a lie.

The common feature between exophoric and discourse deictic uses is that the demonstratives pick their referents in the immediate context, either within the physical environment or within the discourse itself. If we compare deictic and anaphoric uses, it is clear that the former points to some entity in the given context,

10 Antecedents and postcedents will be underlined throughout the book.

while the latter establishes a co-reference relation, and it is not the demonstrative itself that identifies the entity under discussion.

The last type of use is called recognitional. In these cases, the referent of the demonstrative cannot be recovered either from the preceding discourse or from the situational context, since the speaker refers to an entity that is familiar to both the speaker and the addressee via shared knowledge and common experience in the past:

(20) Can you recall *that wonderful week we spent in Amsterdam*?

The use of the demonstrative can be considered a kind of instruction to the addressee to find the referent, i.e., the speaker must believe that the addressee will be able to identify the referent based on their shared knowledge; otherwise, he should not have used the demonstrative. To help this identification process, recognitional demonstratives always co-occur with a noun, they are adnominal demonstratives. Recognitional deixis might also create an emotional bond between the participants; such uses often indicate that the speaker and the hearer share the same attitude towards the subject of the discussion. This type of usage is called emotional deixis by Lakoff (1974).

(21) *That Henry Kissinger* sure knows his way around in Hollywood. (Lakoff 1974: 8)

After this survey of different types of demonstrative use (see Figure 1.1), it is important to bear in mind that, as Levinson (2004: 107) claims, 'the relations between these uses are probably more complex than this taxonomy suggests'. For example, deictic and anaphoric use might overlap, as in the example below:

(22) I cut a finger: *this one*. (Levinson 1983: 67)

In this utterance, *this one* and *a finger* co-refer; however, the referent can only be identified by an accompanying gesture in the speech situation.

Nevertheless, it is clear that the wide range of functions performed by demonstratives both within and across languages provides a challenge for a proper

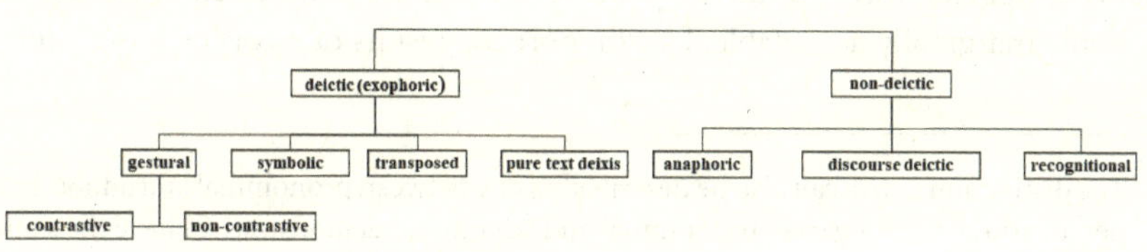

Figure 1.1: Different uses of demonstratives

treatment and analysis. As Scott (2020) claims, accounts that are aimed at a unified treatment of these various uses should be able to answer two questions: (i) What is the core meaning of demonstratives? (ii) How can these different pragmatic uses be derived from that core meaning? In Chapter 2, after a brief outline of the traditional account, I will provide an overview of different theoretical approaches to deictic reference. For the time being, we will consider the pragmatic functions of Hungarian demonstratives.

1.3 Deixis and demonstratives in Hungarian

1.3.1 Overview

The bulk of research on deixis and demonstratives in Hungarian has been carried out in a functional-cognitive framework by Laczkó (2008, 2010), Laczkó and Tátrai (2012) and Tátrai (2017). The aim of this section is to show that Hungarian nominal demonstratives can fulfil each of the diverse pragmatic functions presented in Figure 1.1. Before turning to the individual uses themselves, I briefly describe Hungarian nominal demonstratives.

Hungarian has a two-term demonstrative system; *ez, ezek* 'this, these' are traditionally described as proximals, while *az, azok* 'that, those' are distals. Both terms can be used as independent pronouns or as demonstrative modifiers,[11] and the latter case is called determiner doubling by Egedi (2015), since a definite article is inserted between the demonstrative term and the head noun: *ez az asztal* 'this.NOM the table.NOM = this table', *azokat az asztalokat* 'these.PL.ACC the tables. PL.ACC = these tables'. As shown by the examples, the demonstrative agrees in case and number with the head noun.

For the sake of completeness, it has to be noted here that there are two other nominal demonstrative pronouns in Hungarian, *emez* and *amaz*. These are described in Hungarian descriptive grammars as emphatic pronouns (Kugler & Laczkó 2000), while Kleiber et al. (2018) claim that these forms emphasise distance. Table 1.1 represents only a part of the paradigm of Hungarian nominal demonstrative pronouns,[12] and it is important to note that Kleiber et al. (2018) point out that case-suffixed forms of the emphatic pronouns are considered to be archaic and only marginally acceptable. I will report the results of a corpus-based study

11 The distinction above can also be described as one between pronominal and adnominal demonstratives. Hungarian pronominal and adnominal demonstratives have the same morphological properties.

12 For a detailed analysis of the history and emergence of these forms see Egedi (2015).

Table 1.1: Nominal demonstrative pronouns in Hungarian

	basic			**emphatic**		
case	*nominative*	*accusative*	*dative*	*nominative*	*accusative*	*dative*
proximal	*ez*	*ezt*	*ennek*	*emez*	*emezt*	*emennek*
	'this'	'this.ACC'	'this.DAT'	'this'	'this.ACC'	'this.DAT'
distal	*az*	*azt*	*annak*	*amaz*	*amazt*	*amannak*
	'that'	'that.ACC'	'that.DAT'	'that'	'that.ACC'	'that.DAT'

Table 1.2: The partial system of Hungarian demonstrative pronouns

	proximal	**distal**
nominal	*ez* 'this'	*az* 'that'
	emez 'this'	*amaz* 'that'
adjectival	*ilyen* 'such'	*olyan* 'such'
	ekkora 'this size'	*akkora* 'that size'
	ennyi 'this amount'	*annyi* 'that amount'
adverbial	*itt* 'here'	*ott* 'there'
	ide 'to this place'	*oda* 'to that place'
	ekkor 'at this time'	*akkor* 'at that time'
	így 'like this'	*úgy* 'like that'
	…	…

and discuss the various uses of these so-called emphatic nominal demonstratives in contemporary Hungarian in Chapter 4. This section focuses only on the use of basic demonstratives.

Descriptive grammars of Hungarian assume that demonstrative pronouns (including the adverbials *itt* 'here', *ide* 'to this place') encode spatial relations, expressing positional or directional spatial reference (cf. Laczkó 2010; Kleiber et al. 2018). More specifically, front-vowel demonstratives describe proximal relations, while back-vowel forms indicate distal relations.[13] This generalization holds for the entire class of demonstrative pronouns, which includes adjectival and adverbial pronouns, too. A partial list of these is given in Table 1.2 (see also Kugler & Laczkó 2000; Laczkó 2012; Kleiber et al. 2018):

13 Thus, Hungarian demonstratives follow the pattern observed by Traunmüller (1996) on a language sample of 37 languages, namely, in languages where the difference between proximal and distal demonstratives is vocalic only, the vowel of the distal term appears on the right of the proximal term in the list of [i e a o u].

It is widely accepted that physical proximity to the speaker plays a crucial role in the use of nominal demonstrative pronouns. Consider the following examples:[14]

(23) Mennyibe kerül *ez* *a* *sál* itt/ *ott?
how.much.ILL cost.3SG this the scarf here there
'How much is this scarf here/*there?'

(24) Mennyibe kerül *az* *a* *sál* *itt/ ott?
how.much.ILL cost.3SG that the scarf here there
'How much is that scarf *here/there?'

The incompatibility of a nominal proximal demonstrative with a distal adverbial and vice versa illustrates that the terms in question indeed are associated with a proximity feature. However, we will see later that in certain contexts these features might be overwritten by contextual factors. The next section gives a detailed overview of the various pragmatic functions that can be fulfilled by Hungarian nominal demonstratives.

1.3.2 Pragmatic functions of Hungarian nominal demonstratives

1.3.2.1 Deictic uses

1.3.2.1.1 The role of relative distance

From a cognitive perspective, Boronkai (2010), Laczkó (2008, 2010), Laczkó and Tátrai (2012) and Tátrai (2017) give a comprehensive description of Hungarian demonstratives within a functional-cognitive framework, and Laczkó (2008, 2010) also dedicates special attention to deictic uses of Hungarian nominal demonstratives. Exophoric, gestural and non-contrastive uses of *ez*/*az* as pronominals and demonstrative modifiers are exemplified by (25)–(28) below, while (29) illustrates a symbolic use.

---

14 I adhere to the Leipzig Glossing Rules (Comrie et al. 2008). The list of abbreviations used can be found at the beginning of the book. Due to practical reasons, morphological glosses are kept relatively simple. Category labels are sometimes replaced by a word from English, for example, the proximal demonstrative *ez* is represented as 'this'. Nouns are glossed as their translational equivalent, followed by their case. However, singular number and nominative case are considered to be the default and are not indicated. Verbs are glossed with their translational equivalent, followed by mood, person and number tags, with the exception of the indicative, which is not stated. Verbal particles are transcribed as PRT; their meaning is not spelled out.

(25) *Ezt/* *ezeket* kérem.
this.ACC these.ACC want.1SG
'I want this/these.'

(26) *Ez* *a* *kulcs* nyitja az ajtót
this the key open.3SG the door.ACC
'This key opens the door.'

(27) *Azt/* *azokat* add ide!
that.ACC those.ACC give.IMP.2SG to.this.place
'Give me that/those!'

(28) *Az* *a* *kutya* pisilte le a bicajomat.
that the dog peed.3SG PRT the bike.POSS.1SG.ACC
'That dog has peed on my bike.'

(29) Sok jó étterem van *ebben* *a* *városban.*
many good restaurant COP.3SG this.INE the city.INE
'There are many good restaurants in this city.'

Laczkó (2003, 2010) argues that front- and back-vowel forms indicate proximal and distal relations with respect to the deictic centre, i.e., 'the choice between "near" and "far" is basically determined by where the entity referred to is located in relation to the speaker' (Laczkó 2010: 106). Laczkó (2008, 2010) also considers how demonstratives are processed by the addressee, who has to adopt the speaker's perspective. In essence, the speaker and the hearer can be positioned in two different ways. In the simpler scenario, the speaker and the hearer are located next to each other, and consequently, they share the same perspective. According to Laczkó (2010), the speaker's selection of demonstratives reflects the positions of the entities being referred to. Thus in the case of (30), the proximal term refers to the entity that is close to the speaker and the addressee, while the distal pronoun refers to an object that is further away from both of them.

(30) *Ezt* *a* *dobozt* vidd le a pincébe, *azt*
this.ACC the box.ACC take.IMP.2SG PRT the cellar.ILL that.ACC
viszont hagyd a helyén.
however leave.IMP.2SG the place.POSS.3SG.SUP
'Take this box down to the cellar, but leave that one where it is.'
(Laczkó 2010: 106)

It must be noted that it is not entirely clear where exactly the demarcation line between the proximal and the distal zone lies (if there is such a line at all), i.e., where the speaker would switch from the proximal form to the distal one. I will argue later that the same utterance could be used in an entirely different situation, when the entities in question are located at the same distance from the speaker, in near space.[15] This is not unexpected, since, as Pederson (2012: 2617) points out 'some languages allow distal forms to be used for proximal locations when they are contrastive in some non-spatial way'. Contrastive uses will be addressed in a more detailed fashion in Chapter 4.

In the other scenario, the speaker and the hearer are facing each other; and to identify the referents of demonstratives, the hearer again has to adopt the speaker's perspective. As Laczkó (2010) points out, this process requires more effort on the part of the addressee when he is face-to-face with the speaker. If there are two entities present in the conversational setting, one closer and one further away from the speaker, the speaker has to consider their location with respect to one another when selecting a demonstrative, and the entity located further away acts as a reference point, and is referred to by a distal demonstrative. If there is a third entity that is located at an equal distance from the speaker and the addressee, the choice of the demonstrative referring to this object is again determined with respect to another entity, the reference point. There are two possibilities. On the one hand, the entity in the middle ground is closer to the speaker than the one

15 Laczkó (2008) observes that in this situation the speaker would use two proximal terms. Though (i) is also acceptable when the entities referred to are close to the speaker, this does not mean that (ii) would not be appropriate in the same context:

(i) *Ezt* vidd a pincébe, *ezt* pedig a padlásra.
this.ACC take.IMP.2SG the cellar.ILL this.ACC in.turn the attic.SUBL
'Take this to the cellar, but this one goes to the attic.'
(Laczkó 2008: 328, translation adjusted by me)

(ii) *Ezt* vidd a pincébe, *azt* pedig a padlásra.
this.ACC take.IMP.2SG the cellar.ILL that.ACC in.turn the attic.SUBL
'Take this to the cellar, but that one goes to the attic.'

furthest away, which acts as the reference point, therefore the speaker can use a proximal demonstrative. On the other hand, when the entity positioned closest to the speaker is used as a reference point, a distal pronoun can also be selected to refer to the entity in the middle.

The speaker's and addressee's different construals of space can be illustrated by the following conversational exchange, where both participants refer to the same entity:

(31)	A:	– Ne	*azzal*	írj,	gyerekem,	mondtam	már.
		not	that.INS	write.IMP.2SG	child.POSS.1SG	said.1SG	already
		'Don't write with that one, sweetie, I've told you already.'					
	B:	– Miért	ne	*ezzel*?			
		why	not	this.INS			
		'Why not with this one?'					
		(Laczkó 2008: 328)					

Thus, as Laczkó (2010) observes, the use of demonstratives is determined by relative distance based on the actual construal of space by the current speaker.

As we will see later, the same conversation can also be analysed in a relevance-theoretic framework. Scott (2020) adopts Powell's (2003) analysis and argues that the use of *this/that* is a procedural instruction for the hearer, i.e., the speaker is guiding the hearer in finding the intended referent. Thus '*this* encodes the procedure "find the speaker and then find an object near the speaker"; for *that* the procedure is the same except the hearer expects to find an object far away from the speaker' (Scott 2020: 138). Consequently, the relevance-theoretic approach, just like the previous ones, is also built on the traditional proximal/distal opposition, but it emphasizes that demonstratives encode procedural information.[16] The important point is that the notions proximal/distal are captured relative to a point of reference; thus these are not objective properties of the intended referent; instead, they depend on and vary according to contextual factors. The exchange in (31) above illustrates this, since A and B use different demonstratives to refer to the same entity, relying on their own perspective while guiding the hearer to the intended referent. We will return to the relevance-theoretic analysis of demonstratives in Chapter 2.

---

16 Sidnell (2009) also argues that demonstrative reference is procedural in nature, from a sociocentric point of view; see Section 2.2.1.

1.3.2.1.2 The role of emotion/attitude

Another contextual factor that might influence the choice of demonstratives is mentioned by Laczkó (2008), that of emotion or attitude. She describes these features as the social environment of the speech event, and argues that in the exchange below, where the participants are facing one another, and the intended referent is far from A but close to B, A might use either the proximal or the distal demonstrative, depending on their attitude to the intended referent. More specifically, according to Laczkó (2008, 2010, 2014), the use of the proximal term by A is either a case of deictic projection triggered by 'direction of attention' or indicates the speaker's positive attitude towards the referent.

(32) A: Mi *ez* a kezedben?
what this the hand.POSS.2SG.INE
'What's this in your hand?'
B: Ez egy patkány.
this a rat
'This is a rat.'
(Laczkó 2014: 232)

Similarly, the use of the distal pronoun in (33) either reflects the spatial location of the referent, or it might indicate the speaker's negative attitude, especially with a special intonation.

(33) A: Mi *az* a kezedben?
what that the hand.POSS.2SG.INE
'What's that in your hand?'
B: Ez egy patkány.
this a rat
'This is a rat.'
(Laczkó 2014: 232)

Hence, 'demonstrative pronouns have metaphorical uses in which the proximal form may express positive attitudes (pleasure, affection, interest), whereas the distal form may express negative attitudes (antipathy, rejection, distrust)' (Laczkó 2012: 298; see also Tátrai 2010).

Distal demonstratives can indeed convey the speaker's negative attitude towards the intended referent, as shown more clearly in (34) below:

(34)

Vedd	le	rólam	*azt*	*a*	*mocskos*	*kezedet*![17]
get.IMP.2SG	PRT	me.DEL	that.ACC	the	dirty	hand.POSS.2SG.ACC

'Get that dirty hand of yours off me!'

In this scenario, the addressee is obviously touching the speaker's body, therefore the intended referent, the addressee's hand, is located close to the speaker, so relative distance is overwritten by the negative attitude of the speaker towards the referent.

According to Kleiber et al. (2018), both nominal demonstratives can convey positive or negative attitudes. While there are contexts where this prediction is borne out,[18] such as (35) below, the demonstratives are not always interchangeable, since the proximal form would be unacceptable in (34) above.

(35)

Nézd	már	*ezt/*	*azt*	*a*	*kétballábast.*	Már	megint
look.IMP.2SG	already	this.ACC	that.ACC	the	gimp.ACC	already	again

kapufát	rúgott!
goal.post.ACC	kicked.3SG

'Look at this/that gimp! He has just hit the post again!'

1.3.2.1.3 Referring to (parts of) events

Laczkó (2008, 2010) also describes a special case of spatial deixis, the so-called heterodeixis. This takes place in two-dimensional space, when the point of reference is projected to a photo, a painting, a map or a screen; thus it could be described in terms of transposed use.

According to Laczkó (2010), the nature of the two-dimensional scene, namely, whether it is a motion picture (such as a TV screen) or a static picture (such as a photo), plays an important role in the perception and processing of the virtual

---

17 Tibor Laczkó, personal communication.

18 Demonstratives can also express a positive or negative attitude when used non-deictically:

(i)

Ó,	*ez/*	*az*	*a*	*sármos*	*DiCaprio!*
oh	this	that	the	charming	DiCaprio

'Oh, this/that charming *DiCaprio*!'
(Kleiber et al. 2018: 1034)

(ii)

Ez/	*az*	*átkozott*	*galamb!*	Már	megint	felébresztett	hajnalban.
this	that	damned	pigeon	already	again	PRT.woke.me.3SG	dawn.INE

'This/That damned pigeon! It woke me again at dawn!'

space. A relevant example adopted from Boronkai (2010: 442) is given below, from a Hungarian drama:[19]

(36) VANDA *nézi a tévét. Na, ezek ott a híd*
VANDA watch.3SG the TV.ACC well these there the bridge
alatt... ezek legalább nem törődnek semmivel.
under these at.least no care.3PL nothing.COM
'VANDA (watching TV): So, these people under the bridge … they do not have to care about anything.'

For the sake of completeness, I just mention briefly in passing that the last subtype of exophoric usage, pure text deixis, is also possible, as in the example below:

(37) Nem értettem, amit mondtál. Hogy volt *az az utolsó*
no understood.1SG what.ACC said.2SG how was that the last
szó?
word
'I didn't get what you said. What was that last word?'

Finally, let us consider a type of demonstrative use labelled as event deixis by Laczkó (2010), where demonstratives point to a complex event, theme or physical experience. This can be accomplished by both a pronominal and a demonstrative modifier, as illustrated by (38) and (39), respectively (Laczkó 2010: 109–110).

(38) *Ez* borzalmas.
this awful
'This is awful'

(39) *Ez a meccs* elkeserítő.
this the match exasperating
'This match is exasperating.'

In the case of (38), the participants of the speech event are witnesses of a house fire, watching the firefighters, while in (39) they are at a football match. Thus participants share a physical experience, which can be referred to by the proximal pronoun *ez* 'this', since the time of the event and the time of the utterance coincide. Laczkó (2010) also notes that in the same manner, *ez* can also refer to a recent event, for example, after having watched a movie, while going home, people might discuss the film and use the proximal pronoun:

19 For further details I refer the reader to Boronkai (2010) and Laczkó (2010).

(40)

Jó	kis	film	volt	*ez*.
good	little	film	was	this

'This has been a pretty good film.'

Levinson (2018a) also acknowledges this type of usage, stating that the referents of demonstratives can vary and addressees are invited to work out the intended referent in the actual speech situation, relying on contextual clues. Thus the demonstrative in (38) could refer not only to the event in its entirety, but it can also refer to parts of it, for example, to the heat experienced by the onlookers while they are wondering how firefighters can work in such extreme circumstances. Therefore, the uses mentioned above naturally fall under the term symbolic use in Levinson's (2004) taxonomy.

Another example of event deixis is given below. In (41), *ez* clearly refers to the event described by the previous utterance, since it can be quantified over, as shown by (42), thus it can also be treated as a case of symbolic reference.

(41)

János	szemezett	Marival.	Ez	igencsak	bosszantotta	Évát.
János	flirted.3SG	Mari.COM	this	really	annoyed.3SG	Éva.ACC

'János was flirting with Mary. This really annoyed Éva.'

(Gyuris et al. 2008: 105)

(42)

János	szemezett	Marival.	Ez	igencsak	bosszantotta	Évát,
János	flirted.3SG	Mari.COM	this	really	annoyed	Éva.ACC

mert	azon	az	estén	már	harmadszor	fordult	elő.
because	that.SUP	the	night.SUP	already	third time	turned	forth

'János was flirting with Mary. This really annoyed Éva, since it happened the third time that evening.'

(Gyuris et al. 2008: 106)

1.3.2.2 Non-deictic uses

The next section discusses non-deictic, i.e., anaphoric, discourse deictic and recognitional uses of Hungarian nominal demonstratives.

1.3.2.2.1 Anaphoric uses

As Levinson (1983) notes, in the case of anaphora, it is usually a pronoun that co-refers with another term, but adnominal constructions can also be used anaphorically. Within anaphoric uses, a further distinction is made between anaphora and cataphora, depending on the position of the referring term. Anaphora is illustrated by (43); here the demonstrative co-refers with its antecedent, a noun phrase in the previous sentence. In the case of cataphora, the demonstrative co-refers with its postcedent, as in (44):

(43)

Ja	hogy	<u>a</u>	<u>Ponyvaregényről</u>	van	szó.	Ha	nem
oh	COMP	the	Pulp.Fiction.DEL	COP.3SG	word	if	no

lennék	ilyen	álmos,	most	azonnal	megnézném
COP.COND.1SG	so	sleepy	now	immediately	PRT.watch.COND.1SG

azt	*a*	*filmet,*	annyira	szeretem.
that.ACC	the	film.ACC	that.amount	love.1SG

'Oh, you are talking about Pulp Fiction. If I were not so sleepy, I would immediately watch that movie, I like it so much.'
(Laczkó & Tátrai 2012: 249)

(44)

Ezt	*a*	*filmet*	kellene	megnézned.	<u>A</u>	<u>Blöff</u>	a
this.ACC	the	film.ACC	should	PRT.watch.INF.2SG	the	Snatch	the

legjobb	film,	amit	valaha	láttam.
best	film	that.ACC	ever	saw.1SG

'You should watch this movie. Snatch is the best film I have ever seen.'

In Hungarian, anaphoric tools also include zero anaphora marked by verbal inflection. Anaphoric reference in Hungarian has been widely studied, among others, by Pléh and Radics (1976), Tolcsvai Nagy (2000), Kocsány (1995, 2018), and Farkas and Alberti (2018). Factors that govern anaphora resolution include grammatical function, thematic role, information structure and perspective. It is beyond the scope of this study to give a general overview of these factors. The important point made here is that both the proximal and the distal demonstrative *ez*/*az* can act as anaphors in Hungarian under special circumstances. In what follows, I briefly consider the major factors influencing reference resolution in the case of demonstrative anaphors.

Farkas and Alberti (2018) provide a detailed description of the factors influencing the selection of back-referring forms in Hungarian. The forms themselves are the 3rd person singular pronoun *ő*, the empty phonetic form and the demonstratives *ez* or *az*. The factors are as follows: the animacy feature [+/– HUMAN], grammatical function and information-structural position. The present discussion focuses only on the most essential observations.

The starting point of the analysis is that while *ő* can refer back to animate antecedents, *ez* and *az* take [– HUMAN] antecedents in general, and the use of *ez* is further restricted to 'abstract entities expressed by clauses' (Farkas & Alberti

2018: 21).[20] However, as is described below, distal *az* can also have [+ HUMAN] antecedents. It is a well-known fact about Hungarian anaphors that subject noun phrases as antecedents license zero subject anaphors in the following sentence, as in (45):

(45) A kisfiú észrevette a férfit. ∅ Odament hozzá.
the little.boy noticed.3SG the man.ACC ∅ PRT.went he.ALL
'The boy$_i$ noticed the man$_j$. He$_i$ went over to him$_j$.'

Across sentence boundaries, distal *az* is used as an anaphor when its antecedent is an NP constituent that is not the subject of the first sentence, but *az* occupies the subject position of the second sentence. In the examples below, the antecedents are objects of the verbs. Pronominal *az* can refer back to animate and inanimate noun phrases (Pléh & Radics 1976), as in (46) and (47):

(46) A kisfiú észrevette a kutyát. *Az* odament hozzá.
the little.boy noticed the dog.ACC it over.went he.ALL
'The boy noticed the dog. It went to him.'

(47) A nő elvette a csésze kávét. *Az* megbillent és kifolyt.
the woman PRT.took.3SG the cup coffee.ACC it PRT.tipped.3SG and PRT.spilled.3SG
'The woman took the cup of coffee. It tipped and spilled.'

The important point made here is that the antecedents of distal demonstrative anaphors as subjects are nonsubject constituents in the preceding sentence, while the antecedents of zero anaphors are surface subjects. However, this observation in itself does not account for the data presented below. Compare (48) and (49):

(48) A színésznek tetszett a rendező. ∅ Minden nap új ötleteket adott neki.
the actor.DAT liked.3SG the director ∅ every day new ideas.ACC gave.3SG him.DAT
'The actor$_i$ liked the director. He$_i$ gave him new ideas every day.'

20 This latter use of *ez* will be discussed later, in Section 1.3.2.2.2, as a case of discourse deixis.

(49) A színésznek tetszett a rendező. *Az* minden nap új
the actor.DAT liked.3SG the director that every day new
ötleteket adott neki.
ideas.ACC gave.3SG him.DAT
'The actor liked the director$_i$. He$_i$ gave him new ideas every day.'

To account for this type of data, Pléh (1998) proposes the following rule: the subject anaphor in the second sentence is realized as zero when it co-refers with the psychological subject of the previous sentence, but it is a demonstrative when its antecedent is not the psychological subject of the first sentence.

A further difficulty arises when the neutral word order in (48) is changed, since anaphora resolution might be affected in the case of the demonstrative (Pléh 1982), as shown by (50).

(50) A rendező tetszett a színésznek. *Az* minden nap új
the director appealed.3SG the actor.DAT that every day new
ötleteket adott neki.
ideas.ACC gave.3SG him.DAT
'The actor$_i$ liked the director. He$_i$ gave him new ideas every day.'

Here, the antecedent of *az* is not the patient, but the experiencer. This phenomenon can be explained by the notion of topichood: when the experiencer is not the topic of the first sentence, then *az* can refer back to it, in other words, the role of the distal demonstrative is to mark topic change.

Thus back-referencing in the case of demonstrative anaphors heavily depends on the discourse itself; sometimes distal *az* signals a change of subject, sometimes it marks topic change. Moreover, according to Pléh (1998), this is not a predictive rule, rather, it is a processing strategy.

As Tolcsvai Nagy (2000) notes, referential distance between the antecedent and the anaphor can also play a role. In the default case, the antecedent of a distal demonstrative is always in the immediately preceding clause, as in (51). When there is an intervening clasue between the antecedent and the demonstrative anaphor, as in (52), a lexical NP *a készülék* 'the set' is more acceptable than distal *az*, since the descriptive content of the former provides information that helps the addressee to identify the antecedent, while the use of the distal demonstrative requires extra processing effort on the part of the addressee (Tolcsvai Nagy 2000: 287).

(51) Péter bekapcsolta a tévét. *Az* nem működött.
Péter on.turned.3SG the TV.ACC that no worked.3SG
'Péter turned on the TV. It was out of order.'

(52) Péter bekapcsolta a tévét. Meg akarta nézni a
Péter on.turned.3SG the TV.ACC PRT wanted.3SG watch.INF the
híradót. De ?*az/ a készülék* nem működött.
news.ACC but that the set no worked.3SG
'Péter turned on the TV. He wanted to watch the news. But the set was out of order.'

In emphatic structures, distal demonstrative anaphors play a more prominent role, since zero anaphors cannot receive primary stress, however, personal pronouns are used when the antecedent is animate. Consider the example below, where *az* is in identificational focus:

(53) Abban a dobozban van a piros kréta. *Azzal* írj
that.INE the box.INE COP.3SG the red chalk that.INS write.IMP.2SG
a táblára!
the board.SUBL
'The red chalk is in that box. Use that to write on the blackboard!'

If the referent of the antecedent is located closer to the speaker, the proximal demonstrative can also act as an anaphor:

(54) Itt van a piros kréta. *Ezzel* írj a táblára!
here COP.3SG the red chalk this.INS write.IMP.2SG the board.SUBL
'The red chalk is here. Use this to write on the blackboard!'

This pair of examples demonstrates that the deictic features of the demonstratives are preserved even in anaphoric use.

So far we have not considered anaphoric relations where not the distal, but the proximal demonstrative is the anaphor. Kocsány (2009, 2018) observes that proximal demonstrative plus noun constructions can be used as subject anaphors when the antecedent is a non-topic constituent. It is important to note that the use of the proximal demonstrative is not the default case, as the following examples show (Kocsány 2009: 203–205):

(55) Az épület előtt feltűnt egy taxi. A taxi/ ?*Ez a*
the building in.front.of PRT.appeared.3SG a taxi the taxi this the
taxi lassított, majd megállt.
taxi slowed.down.3SG then PRT.stopped.3SG
'A taxi appeared in front of the building. The taxi/?This taxi slowed down, then stopped.'

(56) Az épület előtt feltűnt egy taxi. *Ez a taxi/*
the building in.front.of PRT.appeared.3SG a taxi this the taxi
Ez az autó azonban nem a megszokott taxi társaság
this the car however no the usual taxi company
emblémáját viselte.
emblem.POSS.3SG.ACC wore.3SG
'A taxi appeared in front of the building. This taxi/This car however was not sporting the emblem of the usual taxi company.'

In (55), the definite article is more appropriate, since the information conveyed by the second sentence fits our general knowledge about the world. In (56), the second sentence describes something unexpected, as indicated by the conjunction *azonban* 'however'. The use of the proximal demonstrative further emphasizes this contrast.

The use of the proximal demonstrative can also be facilitated when the demonstrative phrase expresses new information or a subjective, evaluative comment about the antecedent, as in (57) below:[21]

(57) A házból kifutott egy mérges kis kutya. *Ez a nyavalyás*
the house.ELA PRT.ran.3SG an angry little dog this the annoying
miniatűr emlős egyenesen a bokámat vette célba.
miniature mammal straight.SUP the ankle.POSS.1SG.ACC took.3SG target.ILL
'An angry little dog ran out of the house. This annoying little mammal attacked my ankle straight away.'
(Kocsány 2018: 131)

Proximal demonstrative phrases may also occur in identificational focus position; in that case the use of the demonstrative emphasizes the contrastive function of the focus. For this reason, native speakers prefer the demonstrative to the definite article in the discourse below:

21 For a more detailed analysis I refer the reader to Kocsány (2018).

(58) A rendőrök a bejelentést követő 12 órán belül
the police.PL the report.ACC following 12 hour.SUP within
elfogták a fiatalkorú bűnözőt. *Ez a fiú/ a fiú*
PRT.captured.3SG the juvenile criminal.ACC this the boy the boy
rabolta ki a város három ékszerboltját.
robbed.3SG PRT the city three jewellery.POSS.3SG.ACC
'The police captured the juvenile criminal within 12 hours after the report. This boy/The boy had robbed three jewellers in the city.'
(Kocsány 2018: 125)

Finally, a proximal demonstrative phrase can also take a proposition as its antecedent (Farkas & Alberti 2018; Kocsány 2018: 140):

(59) A Föld kering a Nap körül. *Ez az állapot* évmilliárdok
the Earth revolve.3SG the Sun around this the state year.billions
óta tart.
since last.3SG
'The Earth revolves around the Sun. This state has lasted for billions of years.'

(60) A Föld kering a Nap körül. *Ez a tény* Kepler
the Earth revolve.3SG the Sun around. this the fact Kepler
számításai óta ismert.
calculations.POSS.3SG since known
'The Earth revolves around the Sun. This fact has been known since Kepler's calculations.'

(59) and (60) exemplify discourse deixis, which is to be discussed below, but Kocsány (2018) labels this usage as complex anaphora, since the anaphor, a second or third-order entity in Lyon's (1977) terminology, refers not only to the proposition itself, but rather to a mental construct built by the language user, which is further characterized by the descriptive content of the lexical noun of the anaphor.

Thus Hungarian demonstratives play an active role in anaphoric relations across sentence boundaries. Interpreting these anaphors is not always an easy task, since their use is governed by syntactic, semantic, and pragmatic factors, and the brief overview presented here did not even attempt to describe all of these.

1.3.2.2.2 Discourse deictic and recognitional uses

Discourse deictic demonstratives 'focus the hearer's attention on aspects of meaning, expressed by a clause, a sentence, a paragraph, or an entire story' (Diessel 1999: 101), or, in Levinson's words they refer 'to portions of the unfolding discourse' (Levinson 1983: 62). Depending on the position of the demonstrative and the intended referent – a part of the linguistic context –, we differentiate anaphoric and cataphoric reference, as in (61) and (62), respectively:

(61) … *Ezzel* vége a bizonyításnak.
… this.COM end the proof.DAT
'… This concludes the proof.'

(62) Ismered *ezt* *a* *viccet*? Miért ül a macska a számítógépen?
know.2SG this.ACC the joke.ACC why sit.3SG the cat the computer.SUP
'Have you heard this joke? Why did the cat sit on the computer?'

As is clear from the examples above, in the case of discourse deixis, the proximal demonstrative can have both anaphoric and cataphoric reference in Hungarian. Moreover, it can also act as a special quotative marker:

(63) Az idegen belépett a szobába és *ezt* mondta: Pétert keresem.
the stranger PRT.stepped.3SG the room.ILL and this.ACC said.3SG Péter.ACC look.for.1SG
'The stranger entered the room and he said: "I am looking for Péter."'

Besides referring to the previous or following part of the discourse, it is also possible to refer to the content of the utterance, as in (64) or to the speech act itself, as in (65):

(64) A: Kati eladta a házat.
Kati PRT.sold.3SG the house.ACC
'Kati has sold the house.'
B: *Ez* nem igaz.
this no true
'This is not true.'

(65) A: Kati eladta a házat.
Kati PRT.sold.3SG the house.ACC
'Kati has sold the house.'
B: *Ez* hazugság.
this lie
'This is a lie.'

The example below is taken from the Hungarian National Corpus:

(66) A hajam egyenesen a legjobb és *ezt* tudnod
the hair.POSS.1SG straight.SUP the best and this.ACC know.INF.2SG
kéne már. – *Ez* hülyeség. Te hullámos hajjal is
should already this stupidity you wavy hair.COM too
gyönyörű vagy.
beautiful COP.2SG
'My hair looks best straight and you should already know this. – This is ridiculous. You also look beautiful with wavy hair.'
(doc#2657, personal)

It is worth noting that in Hungarian only the proximal form can act as a discourse anaphor. Nevertheless, as Laczkó (2010) points out, discourse deictic and anaphoric reference might overlap. While in (67) *ezt* 'this.ACC' fulfils a discourse deictic function, the distal demonstrative *azt* 'that.ACC' represents a borderline case between anaphora and discourse deixis:

(67) Péter tegnap vett egy új könyvet. Hazafelé *ezt*/
Péter yesterday bought.3SG a new book.ACC home.toward this.ACC
azt olvasta a buszon.
that.ACC read.3SG the bus.SUP
'Peter bought a new book yesterday. On his way home, he was reading this/that on the bus.'
(Laczkó 2010: 114)

What is more, according to Laczkó (2010), a given statement might be an example of discourse deixis or event deixis (exophoric use), depending on the speech situation. On the one hand, (68) below can be interpreted as an example of event deixis, for example, when encountering an empty fridge in a shared flat. On the other hand, in a different scenario, for example in (69), where the utterance containing the demonstrative is followed by a statement, cataphoric discourse deixis is exemplified.

(68) *Ezt* nem hiszem el.
this.ACC no believe.1SG PRT
'I don't believe this.'

(69) *Ezt* nem hiszem el. Péter és Kati összeházasodtak.
this.ACC no believe.1SG PRT Péter and Kati PRT.married.3PL
'I don't believe this. Péter and Kati got married.'

It is important to note that sometimes it is difficult to differentiate spatial deixis from discourse deixis. A relevant example adopted from Laczkó (2010: 115) is the following:

(70) *Ezt* olvasd el!
this.ACC read.IMP.2SG PRT
'Read this!'

If the speaker is reading a newspaper at the time of speaking, then the demonstrative might refer to the physical entity or it might refer to the content of the newspaper article. Another relevant example is given below:

(71) Frakciónk hétfőn elég hosszan tárgyalta *ezt* *a*
faction.POSS.1PL Monday.SUP quite at.length discussed.3SG this.ACC the
napirendet, ami nyilvánvalóan nem volt meglepő, hiszen elég
agenda.ACC which obviously no was surprising since quite
régóta téma már *ez* *a* *magasház* *kérdés* (Jk.)
for.long.time topic already this the high.house question (minutes)
'Our parliamentary group discussed this agenda at length on Monday, which was not entirely surprising, since this issue of the tower block has been debated for a long time. (Minutes)'
(Laczkó 2008: 343)

Here, both proximal demonstratives perform a complex role. First of all, the items on an agenda are well known to the members; perhaps they have been read out at the beginning of the meeting; therefore, the phrases might refer back to a part of discourse. The phrases might also have cataphoric reference, since the member is putting forward the next item to be discussed. At the same time, the member might be holding the agenda itself, and then this is also a case of spatial deixis.

Finally, we have to mention recognitional deixis in Diessel's (1999) terminology, which is also exemplified in Hungarian. In these cases, the referent is not present in the physical situation, but is evoking memories in the shared experience of the interlocutors.

(72) Emlékszel *arra* *a* *meccsre,* amikor…?
recall.2SG that.SUBL the match.SUBL when
'Do you recall that match when…?'

Recognitional deixis, just as in other languages, always requires demonstrative modifiers; the addressee has to rely on the descriptive content of the noun when identifying the referent. Recognitional uses create a feeling of familiarity between the interlocutors. Interestingly, proximal *ez* also surfaces in such uses:

(73) Tudod, van *ez az új kávézó.* Ettél már ott sütit is?
know.2SG COP.3SG this the new café ate.2SG already there cake.ACC too
'You know, there is this new café. Have you tried their cakes yet?'

This concludes our inventory of the pragmatic uses of Hungarian demonstratives. As we have seen, Hungarian nominal demonstratives occur in each of the uses introduced in Section 1.2.3 (see Figure 1.1). The last part of this chapter presents further (grammatical) functions of Hungarian demonstratives.

1.3.2.2.3 Special functions of Hungarian demonstratives

Finally, there are some special grammatical functions of the Hungarian nominal demonstratives that need to be mentioned; these will be especially important when we turn to the production study, which was aimed at collecting natural data on demonstratives. Across languages, grammatical markers often develop diachronically from demonstratives.[22] According to Diessel and Breunesse (2020), these grammatical markers might be, among others, quotative markers, complementizers, conjunction adverbs, and topic markers. In Hungarian, distal *az* can act as a topic marker, as we will see below.

Szalamin (1988) describes topic-repeating structures involving demonstrative pronouns as follows: 'a clause-initial topic, a verbal argument, is followed by a typically unstressed resumptive pronoun without a pause; the pronoun agrees with the verbal argument in number and case and emphasizes the argument itself' (Szalamin 1988: 91–92).[23] In the generative tradition, Szűcs (2019: 294) describes Hungarian left dislocation as a construction 'whereby some discourse-prominent entity is placed at the left periphery of the clause, with a subsequent co-referential pronoun' and differentiates two subtypes: topic left dislocation and free left dislocation. In both types of left dislocation, there is a resumptive anaphoric pronoun realized by the distal demonstrative *az* 'that'. Topic left dislocation can be illustrated by the following example:

22 For an overview of the grammaticalization of the distal demonstrative *az* in Hungarian, see Dömötör (2012, 2022).

23 'A mondat elején topik szerepet betöltő mondatrész, igei bővítmény áll, amelyet (vele egyeztetett alakban) kiemelő szerepű mutató névmás követ, többnyire hangsúly és beszédszünet nélkül.'

(74) Az orvost, *azt* beengedik Évához.
the doctor.ACC that.ACC PRT.let.3PL Éva.ALL
'The doctor, they let him in to Éva.'
(É. Kiss 2012: 1054)

Here, a discourse-prominent part of the sentence, the topic, is followed by the distal demonstrative; in other words, a resumptive pronoun is associated with a left dislocated definite object. The sentence evokes a contrastive interpretation, which can be paraphrased as 'as for the doctor, he was let in to Éva, but other people, such as her relatives, friends, etc., were not allowed to see Éva.' It is important to note that this example is not only acceptable in speech, it is grammatical in writing, too.

Non-contrastive left dislocation is also possible (Lipták 2012):

(75) Erre Péter *az* fogta magát és elszaladt.
then Péter that took.3SG himself.ACC and PRT.ran.3SG
'Then Péter, he went and ran away.'
(Lipták 2012: 289)

However, Szűcs (2017a) points out that out of context, such sentences are often ambiguous between a non-contrastive and a contrastive topic left dislocation reading. The lack of a comma in writing and a flat intonation in speech favours the non-contrastive reading:

(76) Péter *az* okos volt.
Péter that clever was
'Péter, he was clever.'

Although the resumptive pronoun in left dislocation constructions is usually realized by the distal demonstrative, the proximal form might also occur when the left dislocated element also contains a proximal form, as in (77), adopted from Szűcs (2019: 299), but this utterance can only receive a contrastive interpretation:

(77) Ezt a fiút, *ezt* meghívtuk.
this.ACC the boy.ACC this.ACC PRT.invited.1PL
'This boy, we invited him.'

The proximal pronoun can also be used if the host is a list.

(78) A naptejet, strandpapucsot, törölközőt, *ezeket* már
the sun.lotion.ACC flip.flops.ACC towel.ACC these.ACC already
bepakoltam.
PRT.packed.1SG
'The sun lotion, flip-flops, the towel, these, I have already packed.'

(79) Az ilyen apróbb kihagyásokat, elírásokat, *ezeket* korrigálni lehet
the such smaller omissions.ACC typos.ACC these.ACC correct.INF possible
és kell.
and must
'Such small omissions and typos, these need and must be corrected.'
(Szalamin 1988: 96)

Hungarian resumptive pronouns occur mainly, but not exclusively in speech, they constitute an example of redundancy.[24] Szalamin (1988) and Szűcs (2017a) agree on the fact that the resumptive pronoun is optional in these structures (on the non-contrastive reading). Szűcs (2017b) also notes that the pronoun is preferred when the sentence is minimal (see (74) above) or where there is an intervening relative clause between the topic and the comment, since the presence of the resumptive pronoun helps the processing of the sentence:

(80) Az olyan könyvet, ami túl hosszú, *azt* nem szívesen olvasom.
the such book.ACC that too long that.ACC no willingly read.1SG
'Books that are too long, I don't like reading them.'

In the case of the other type of left dislocation, free left dislocation, the resumptive pronoun is stressed and can occur in identificational focus position, as in (81) below:[25]

(81) A tesztet, *azt* nyomtattam ki (és nem a statisztikát).
the test.ACC that.ACC printed.1SG PRT and no the statistics.ACC
'The test, I printed it (and not the statistics).'

Finally, for the sake of completeness, I will mention two functions of distal *az* that will not be discussed here. First, the distal demonstrative can also occur as the pronominal associate of subordinate clauses cataphorically; for a detailed description see Szűcs (2015).

24 A corpus-based analysis of topic-repeating structures is provided by Veszelszki (2008, 2017).

25 Szűcs (2017a) discusses free left dislocation in depth.

(82) Kati (*azt*) mondta, hogy Péter átment a vizsgán.
Kati that.ACC said.3SG COMP Péter passed.3SG the exam.SUP
'Kati said that Péter had passed the exam.'

Anaphoric reference is also possible:

(83) Hogy kit hívott meg a bulira, *az* titok.
COMP who.ACC invited.3SG PRT the party.SUBL that secret
'It is a secret who he has invited to the party.'

Second, relative clauses in Hungarian have a pronominal associate in the matrix clause, which takes the case that is assigned to the argument it stands for by the matrix predicate (É. Kiss 2002).

(84) *Azt* veszel a piacon, amit akarsz.
that.ACC buy.2SG the market.SUP what.ACC want.2SG
'You can buy at the market anything that you want.'

The grammatical functions of Hungarian nominal demonstratives will be considered again in Chapter 3, where the results of a production study are described.

1.4 Summary

In this chapter, different approaches to demonstratives were presented. After a brief overview of the philosophical tradition, demonstratives were examined from a cross-linguistic perspective and their various pragmatic functions were also introduced. Section 1.3 focused on the use of Hungarian nominal demonstratives and offered a detailed but preliminary description of the relevant data. In the next chapter, I will review several theoretical accounts of demonstrative choice. The theories to be presented include the traditional view, various cognitive procedural approaches, and finally, the findings of recent empirical studies will also be discussed.

CHAPTER 2

Different Approaches to Demonstratives

2.1 Previous approaches to demonstratives

2.1.1 The traditional view

The traditional approach to deixis and demonstratives to be outlined in the following reflects the early treatment of reference. The act of referring itself was considered a relatively straightforward process, where the speaker utters a referring expression that is adequate enough to uniquely identify the intended referent from a set of alternatives (Olson 1970). According to Clark and Bangerter (2004: 27), the most important underlying assumptions of this account are the following:

(i) referring is an autonomous act, done by the speaker,
(ii) referring is a one-step process,
(iii) referring is addressee-blind,
(iv) referring is ahistorical,
(v) the referent is picked from a specific set of alternatives.

Thus when a speaker refers to an object, he does not rely on any kind of knowledge regarding the addressee. More specifically, speakers do not consider the addressees' location and perspective, or the addressees' current knowledge about the speech situation; furthermore, they do not take into consideration previous discourse or the shared beliefs of the interlocutors.

Each of these assumptions has been challenged by the emergence of new theoretical models (for example, Grice 1975; Chafe 1976; Clark et al. 1983), and by the application of new methodologies, such as field observations and experimental studies.[1] In short, Clark and Bangerter (2004) describe referring as a participatory process, where 'speakers may initiate the process of referring, but they count on the active participation of their addressees' (Clark & Bangerter 2004: 45).

Deictic expressions belong to the class of referring terms. Therefore, in early research on deixis, which had been motivated by Bühler's (1934) pioneering work, it was first assumed that demonstratives divide space from the perspective of the speaker, i.e., it was assumed in general that demonstratives describe the location of their referents relative to a so-called deictic centre, or origo, which, in the default case, is the speaker's location in the speech event at the time of the utterance (Fillmore 1971/1997; Lakoff 1974; Lyons 1977; Diessel 1999). Accordingly, it was argued that the choice of demonstratives in two-term systems can be described in terms of spatial opposition, in other words, the use of demonstratives is determined by relative distance from the speaker, i.e., proximal demonstratives are used when the speaker refers to entities that are close, while distal demonstratives are used to refer to entities that are not so close to the speaker. Along the same lines, descriptive grammars usually characterise the English demonstratives *this* and *that* in this manner (cf., for example, Huddleston & Pullum 2002). Overall, a common denominator of these approaches is that they are static, speaker-anchored, and egocentric (Strauss 2002; Hanks 2011; Peeters & Özyürek 2016; Levinson 2018a), since they focus primarily on the role of the speaker; they treat the speaker as the primary reference point and do not consider the addressee's location or their knowledge about the intended referent.

Just as the changing view about reference has been motivated by new research methodologies, the use of demonstratives has recently been studied from an empirical perspective. Relevant research includes observational studies (Enfield 2003, 2009; Burenhult 2003; Jungbluth 2003; Jarbou 2010), corpus-based studies (Gundel et al. 1993; Strauss 2002) and experimental studies (Piwek et al. 2008; Coventry et al. 2008, 2014; Peeters et al. 2014, 2015, Reile et al. 2020a, 2020b).

This chapter offers an overview of recent approaches to reference and demonstrative use. By and large, novel approaches have broadened the horizon and these fresh accounts treat referring as a cooperative, participatory act, where both the speaker and the addressee work together to reach a common goal in interaction. In accordance with that approach, current research argues that the traditional, egocentric view, where only the speaker and distance marking are considered to be crucial, is too simple and cannot adequately describe the use of demonstratives in everyday interactions across languages. Instead, demonstrative choice is treated

1 Clark and Bangerter (2004) offer a comprehensive overview of how the theoretical concept of referring has changed over the past few decades.

as an inferential process where the speaker guides the addressee towards the successful identification of the intended referent.

2.1.2 Cognitive approaches

2.1.2.1 Introduction

As mentioned above, acts of referring in general and demonstrative reference in particular can be perceived as not an egocentric, but an interactional act, where speakers and addressees work together to reach their communicative goal. In what follows, we provide a brief overview of those cognitive theories that describe how the speaker selects a certain referring expression from a set of candidates to guide the addressee in the identification of the referent. The first theory to be presented, Gundel et al.'s (1993) Givenness Hierarchy, assumes that referring expressions are ordered with respect to the cognitive status of the referent, and describes how these cognitive statuses serve as processing instructions to the hearer in finding the intended referent. Similarly, Strauss (1993, 2002) suggests that the choice between *this*, *that* and *it* in American English is guided by the hearer's degree of attention to the referent, while Cornish (2001) argues that deictic reference is a discourse-creative act, governed by social and cognitive interactional principles. The last cognitive theory to be described, Ariel's (1990/2014) Accessibility Theory, proposes that different referring expressions correspond to different degrees of mental accessibility.

2.1.2.2 The Givenness Hierarchy (Gundel et al. 1993)

In a cognitive framework, Gundel et al. (1993) presents a comprehensive analysis of the use of referring expressions. An important feature of this account is that it is aimed at answering the following questions: 'What do speakers/writers know that enables them to choose an appropriate form to refer to a particular object and what do hearers/readers know that enables them to identify correctly the intended referent of a particular form?' (Gundel et al. 1993: 274).

Hence, while trying to account for the overall distribution of referring expressions, the focus is shifted from the speaker to the speaker's assessment of the addressee's current information about the intended referent, i.e., the assumed cognitive status of the referent (cf. Chafe 1976). The novelty of the analysis also lies in the fact that it is supported by empirical data in the form of examples taken from naturally occurring discourse in five different languages.

Gundel et al. (1993) propose a so-called Givenness Hierarchy, a hierarchy of six cognitive statuses of the referent, which governs the speaker's choice among different referring expressions. These cognitive statuses comprise 'assumptions

Table 2.1: The Givenness Hierarchy (based on Gundel et al. 1993: 275)

in focus	activated	familiar	uniquely identifiable	referential	type identifiable
it	*that*	*that N*	*the N*	*indefinite*	*a N*
	this			*this N*	
	this N				

that a cooperative speaker can reasonably make regarding the addressee's knowledge and attention state in the particular context in which the expression is used' (Gundel et al. 1993: 275) and serve as processing signals to the addressee, which generally means that the speaker selects a given referring expression to guide the addressee in reference resolution, that is, to pick the intended referent from a set of potential referents. The hierarchy is represented in Table 2.1.

It has to be emphasized that the statuses themselves are ordered; each cognitive status entails the ones on its right, so the hierarchy represents an ordered scale, the most restrictive status being 'in focus', while the least restrictive is 'type identifiable', that is, the set of potential referents expands as we move from left to right on the scale. For instance, type identifiable in the case of *a dog* means that the addressee is assumed to know the meaning of the head noun, i.e., the addressee can restrict the set of potential referents by assessing the mental representation of the type of entity considered. Uniquely identifiable, which is a necessary and sufficient condition for the appropriate use of the definite article in the phrase *the N*, means that the speaker can pick the intended referent 'on the basis of the nominal alone' (Gundel et al. 1993: 277).

The English referring expressions corresponding to the cognitive statuses in the hierarchy include the demonstratives *this* and *that*, both as pronominals and as adnominals. According to the hierarchy, the intended referent has to be familiar to the addressee, and due to the implicational relations, when a speaker uses *that N*, as in (1), then he signals to the addressee that they are not only familiar with the intended referent, but they can uniquely identify it:

(1) I couldn't sleep last night. *That dog* (next door) kept me awake.[2] (Gundel et al. 1993: 278)

2 This usage is labelled as recognitional use in Diessel's (1999) taxonomy. Namely, the speaker and the hearer's shared background knowledge plays a crucial role in reference resolution.

Hence, when the condition of familiarity is not met, namely, when the addressee does not know that the speaker's neighbour has a dog, then the utterance of (1) is not appropriate, and only the use of the definite article would be acceptable.

In the case of *this*, the referent has to be activated, which means that it is either in the short-term memory of the interlocutors, or it is an element of the extra-linguistic context (cf. the exophoric use of demonstratives). Besides being activated, the referent of *this* and *this N* also have to be speaker-activated,[3] which means that it has to be introduced into the interaction by the speaker, as illustrated by the inappropriateness of *this* in (2):

(2) A: Have you seen the neighbour's dog?
B: Yes, and ??*this dog/that dog* kept me awake last night. (Gundel et al. 1993: 279)

The Givenness Hierarchy also identifies the highest form on the scale that a speaker might choose to refer to an entity in the given interaction. Due to the implicational relations in the scale, this means that if an entity is higher up the scale, then the speaker can choose from the list of referring expressions that occur lower on the scale, i.e., 'a particular form can often be replaced by forms which require a lower status' (Gundel et al. 1993: 294). As the authors point out, the proximal demonstrative therefore can often be replaced not only by *that*, but also by the definite article. However, the choice between these forms is not arbitrary, since a given expression might be more appropriate or might give rise to special effects. These can be accounted for if we consider the interaction between the Givenness Hierarchy and Grice's maxim of quantity (Grice 1975). As noted above, expressions higher up the scale restrict the set of potential referents; therefore, they are more informative than expressions lower down the scale; hence, a scalar implicature arises. In the case of demonstratives, the status of being activated implicates that the referent is not in focus, i.e., the use of a demonstrative pronoun may signal a focus shift. Consider the example below (Gundel et al. 1993: 298):

(3) Anyway going back from the kitchen then is a little hallway leading to a window, and across from the kitchen is a big walk-through closet. On the other side of *that* is another little hallway leading to a window ...

In this excerpt from a personal letter, the kitchen is in focus first, but the use of the demonstrative indicates a focus shift – focus is shifted to the closet. If *that* was replaced by *it*, then there would be no such shift, and the pronoun would still refer to the kitchen.

---

3 Gundel et al. (1993) note that the condition of speaker-activation can be extended to the deictic use of *this*, where *this* refers to entities that are close.

One striking feature of the Givenness Hierarchy is that while it considers *this*, *that* and *this N* to have the same status of being activated, *that N* is less restrictive, its status being familiar. The only difference between *that* and *that N* is the presence or absence of the head noun, which carries descriptive content. Let us consider the following scenario: a man is looking at his wife, who is trying on different dresses. He may utter both (4) and (5) below, but it is hard to explain how the cognitive status of the referent changes from familiar to activated solely because of the general descriptive content of the head noun, when the referent must be equally salient in the context (Zaki 2011: 42).

(4) *That dress* I like.

(5) *That* I like.

It seems counterintuitive that adding the descriptive content, a kind of specification, does not constrain but broadens the set of potential referents. The Givenness Theory can also be challenged for failing to predict a difference between (6) and (7), where the status of the referent is activated in both cases:

(6) Teenagers cost more than babies. *This* is ridiculous.

(7) Teenagers cost more than babies. *That* is ridiculous.

We will reconsider these examples when we discuss Strauss's (2002) account of demonstrative choice in Section 2.1.2.4.

2.1.2.3 Accessibility Theory (Ariel 1990/2014)

Accessibility Theory, developed by Ariel (1990/2014, 2001, 2004), offers a cognitive, procedural account of reference in general. The starting point of the analysis is that referring expressions can refer to different mental entities in different contexts; there is no one-to-one correspondence between form and function. For instance, demonstrative terms might refer to mental entities based on shared knowledge between the speaker and the hearer, to physical entities in the extralinguistic context, or to parts of discourse in the linguistic context. Relevant examples are given below (Ariel 1990/2014: 8):

(8) *This stupid neighbour* is getting on my nerves.

(9) *This stupid neighbour* is getting on my nerves. (referring to John, not Mary, who is passing by)

(10) John has been singing operas all afternoon. *This stupid neighbour* is getting on my nerves!

To account for the different types of reference resolutions observed here, Ariel (1990/2014, 2001) suggests that referring expressions are 'accessibility markers, i.e., expressions cueing the addressee on how to retrieve the appropriate mental representation in terms of degree of mental accessibility' (Ariel 2001: 31). In other words, referring expressions signal for the addressee how easy the retrieval of the intended referent is, i.e., they represent different instructions for the addressee. As stated by Ariel (2001), referring expressions, such as proper names, definite descriptions, and demonstratives, are attributed a different degree of accessibility, which is defined by the factors of relative informativity (lexical information carried by the expression), rigidity (the ability to pick a unique referent), and attenuation (phonological size). The scale of accessibility for English is given below, from low accessibility markers to high accessibility markers (see Table 2.2). It is important to bear in mind that while Ariel (1990/2014) suggests that Accessibility Theory is universal, meaning that referring expressions can be ordered based on their relative accessibility, she maintains that her theory allows language-specific variation, i.e., the hierarchy might be different from language to language.

Table 2.2: Accessibility marking scale (based on Ariel 2001: 31)

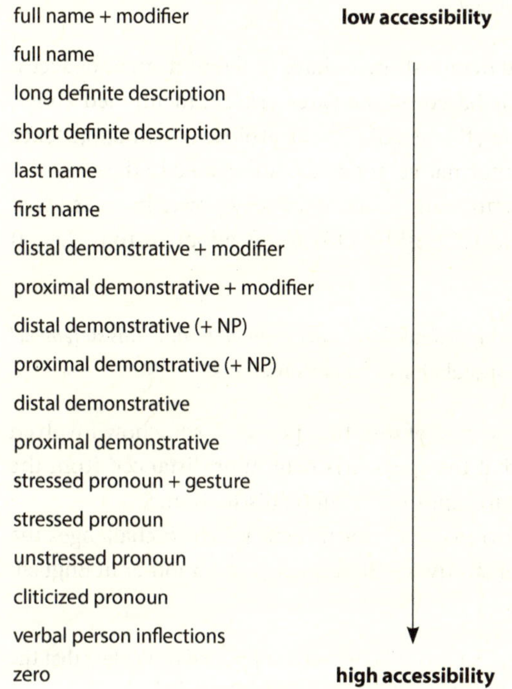

full name + modifier	**low accessibility**
full name	↓
long definite description	
short definite description	
last name	
first name	
distal demonstrative + modifier	
proximal demonstrative + modifier	
distal demonstrative (+ NP)	
proximal demonstrative (+ NP)	
distal demonstrative	
proximal demonstrative	
stressed pronoun + gesture	
stressed pronoun	
unstressed pronoun	
cliticized pronoun	
verbal person inflections	↓
zero	**high accessibility**

Both demonstratives in English are intermediate accessibility markers: the proximal demonstrative *this* marks higher accessibility, while the distal demonstrative *that* is a lower accessibility marker.[4] If the speaker thinks that it is hard to identify the intended referent, then he can add some more information to help the hearer in this process. Therefore, the more information the phrase conveys, the lower its accessibility. For example, the extra information provided in the form of a relative clause in (11) marks lower accessibility.

(11) *That holiday we spent in Cyprus* was really something. (Ariel 1990/2014: 53)

Ariel (1990/2014) also notes that the speaker-activated status associated with *this* in Gundel et al.'s (1993) framework supports the position of the two demonstratives with respect to each other on the scale. Consider the interactions below (Ariel 1990/2014: 52, adopted from Lakoff 1974: 351), where the referent of *this* in (12a) is easily retrievable, therefore it has higher accessibility, as it occurs in the same turn. In (12b), when the referent is in a different turn, *this* is unacceptable:

(12a) A: Dick says that the Republicans may have credibility problems. *This* is an understatement.

(12b) A: Dick says that the Republicans may have credibility problems.
B: **This*/*That* is an understatement.

Thus English proximal and distal demonstratives have different degrees of accessibility, which are supposed to be based on the three criteria mentioned above. However, as Scott (2020) points out, this seems to be an arbitrary distinction, since the English demonstratives are informative, rigid, and attenuated to the same degree. Moreover, this arbitrary distinction lacks explanatory power in cases when both *this* and *that* are grammatical. Consider (13) below adopted from (Lakoff 1974: 346, 350):

(13) The prime minister made his long awaited announcement yesterday. *This statement*/*that statement* confirmed the speculations of many observers.

According to Lakoff (1974), in the case of *this*, the speaker is somehow involved in the topic, but *that* indicates that the speaker is neutral or distanced from the report. Accessibility Theory fails to capture this subtle distinction.

Piwek and Cremers (1996) also make a critical remark, which challenges the relative position of the two demonstratives with respect to one another in English,

---

4 Ariel (1990/2014) also points out that this assumption is supported by the fact that the definite article *the*, a low accessibility marker, has developed from *that*.

and they argue that just the opposite relation might hold by discussing the two examples below (Piwek & Cremers 1996: 839, originally from Fillmore 1975: 71):

(14) I met a friend of yours last night. Well, *this guy* told me some interesting things about you.

(15) Remember the man who sold us those forkball tickets? Well, *that guy* told me....

The first example illustrates the use of indefinite *this*, which introduces a new entity into the discourse. The proximal demonstrative here signals low accessibility; it is not even necessary for the hearer to identify the referent. In contrast, the referent of *that guy* in (15) is easily retrievable and therefore has higher accessibility. These observations contradict the predictions made by Accessibility Theory.

As an interim summary, we have seen that both the Givenness Hierarchy and Accessibility Theory offer a cognitively oriented, general theory of reference by explaining the speaker's choice of referential expressions in terms of the speaker's assessment of the addressee's conceptualization of the intended referent. Moreover, both accounts place different referential expressions on a hierarchy or a scale, the difference being that the Givenness Hierarchy is implicational in nature, while Accessibility Theory offers a scale of referring expressions of varying degrees of mental accessibility. Regarding demonstrative reference, both theories replace the traditional speaker-anchored notion of relative distance with the hearer-oriented notions of cognitive status and mental accessibility. The next section presents a similar, but slightly different account of demonstrative practice in American English.

2.1.2.4 Strauss's (2002) gradient focus model

Strauss's work (1993, 2002) is also aimed at explaining the speaker's choice of demonstrative forms in spontaneous oral discourse based on the results of a corpus-based study of American English. More specifically, Strauss (2002) shows, by analysing the distribution of *this*, *that* and *it* in spoken American English, that the speaker's choice among these forms is influenced by the speaker's presumed knowledge about the addressee's ability to identify the referent and the speaker's assessment regarding the relative importance of the intended referent. She suggests that demonstrative reference indicates gradient focus, where focus means 'the degree of attention the hearer should pay to the referent' (Strauss 2002: 135). Her gradient focus scale is represented in Table 2.3.

In her framework, the use of *this* signals high focus, since it is a tacitly expressed instruction to the addressee that they should pay more attention to the intended referent, usually because it conveys new information and it is usually

Table 2.3: Gradient focus of demonstrative reference (based on Strauss 2002: 135)

	form	**meaning signal**	**hearer** (from the speaker's perspective)	**referent** (from the speaker's perspective)
			new information	important
degree of attention hearer is asked to pay to the referent	*this*	high	↓	↓
	that	medium	↓	↓
	it	low	↓	↓
			shared information	unimportant

important for the speaker, while the use of *that* indicates medium focus, where the referent has intermediate importance in the interaction. At the other end of the scale, we find *it* with low focus, since due to shared knowledge between the interlocutors, the addressee can pay less attention to the intended referent, which is probably not so important for the speaker. Hence, *that* has a kind of intermediate force, it is located somewhere in between *this* and *it*.

Accordingly, the difference between examples (6) and (7) above is that the use of *this* in (6) emphasizes that the referent carries important, new information, which not only represents the speaker's opinion but might signal his intention of elaborating on the topic further, while the selection of *that* in (7) indicates that the referent's information content is not new; it probably indicates the speaker is summarizing his point of view and that this is the end of his turn.

A striking difference between the Givenness Hierarchy and Accessibility Theory, on the one hand, and the notion of gradient focus, on the other, noted by Zaki (2011), is that according to the former accounts, the speaker chooses a given referring expression to guide the hearer to the intended referent, while in the latter, the speaker's aim is to instruct the hearer to pay less or more attention to the referent. This can be illustrated by the example below.

(16) I don't like playing chess. I always lose. I hate *this*.

Here, the proximal demonstrative signals that its referent, the proposition that the speaker always loses, is activated/highly accessible; that is why the speaker opts for the proximal term to guide the hearer to the intended referent. In the framework proposed by Strauss (2002), the speaker invites the hearer to pay more attention to the intended referent, probably because it carries important information. Each of the three approaches relies on related cognitive notions (the attention state of the addressee, the degree of accessibility and the degree of attention paid by the hearer, respectively). However, activation approaches explain the speaker's choice of demonstratives based on the speaker's assessment of the addressee's cognitive state/level of activation of the referent before the utterance is made, while Strauss's gradient focus accounts for the same choice based on what the hearer is expected to do after the utterance is made.

2.1.2.5 Cornish's (2001) discourse model

In this section, we consider the work of Cornish (2001), who, in a cognitive-psychological framework, suggests that the choice between the English demonstrative pronouns is neither an objective process driven by the proximal/distal distinction, nor a matter of attention focus. Instead, he argues that it is a discourse-creative act governed by social and cognitive interactional principles. Cornish (2001) differentiates four different discourse functions of demonstratives. The first three of these correspond roughly to the exophoric, recognitional and discourse deictic categories, but he argues that the most important discourse function is the fourth one, the so-called empathetic or modal deictic reference. He uses the attested example in (17) to illustrate this function (Cornish 2001: 303):

(17) …I'm not going to the Eisteddfod this year. Work doesn't allow *that*. (Interview, BBC Radio 4)

Here, the speaker denies the actuality of the event and guides the addressee to the inference that the referent is outside the speaker's discourse-cognitive space. Cornish (2001) describes this type of usage as modal distancing and argues that the interpretative effect achieved can only be derived from the context of use, it is not part of the encoded semantics of the demonstrative. As Scott (2020) notes, this is an important point, since it implies that it is not enough to label a given occurrence of a demonstrative as exophoric or anaphoric, but, to capture the intended meaning of the speaker, one has to consider the contextual effect created by the interaction between the meaning of the demonstrative and the actual discourse context.

Furthermore, Cornish (2001) assumes that this is the most basic use of the distal demonstrative *that*, which is complemented by the function of *this*: 'the speaker's wish to identify with the referent, placing it within his/her discourse-cognitive sphere' (Cornish 2001: 306). Accordingly, the other three functions of demonstratives (exophoric, recognitional and discourse deictic) work under the same type of discourse-cognitive constraints, and the traditional spatial bias is a by-product of the more basic social-discourse values substantiated by the modal distancing use (for more details, see Cornish 2001). From a certain perspective, Cornish's (2001) theory is similar to Strauss's (1993, 2002) account; he even suggests that the scale of gradient focus can be derived from the more general notion of 'speaker's strong subjective involvement' (*this*), i.e., more attention is required from the hearer, since the referent is important for the speaker; and 'speaker's solidarity and co-alignment with the addressee' (*that*), i.e., the referent is less important for the speaker, therefore the hearer is invited to pay less attention to the referent (Cornish 2001: 309). The major advantage of Cornish's approach over those discussed above is that it attempts to provide a unified picture of the various pragmatic uses of demonstratives.

2.1.2.6 Summary

To sum up, each cognitive theory discussed so far offers a kind of hierarchical or scalar account of the distribution of referring expressions in natural language. Both Givenness Hierarchy and Accessibility Theory are supposed to be universal in nature, but they can also deal with language-specific variation. The novelty of these approaches is that they are procedural accounts and focus on the way the speaker guides the addressee in the retrieval of the intended referent. Therefore, they move beyond the speaker-centred, static approaches. In addition, each theory considered so far makes an effort to broaden its scope, and, in addition to constructed examples, they rely on naturally occurring data. In the next section we turn our attention to demonstrative reference in interaction. The most important characteristic of the interactional approaches to be presented below is that they emphasize not only the dynamic nature of interactional settings, but the dynamic nature of demonstrative reference too.

2.2 Demonstratives in interaction

2.2.1 The sociocentric approach

As we have seen, the traditional distance-based approach to demonstratives has recently been challenged by various cognitive theories. One common denominator of these approaches is that they no longer treat demonstratives as encoding distance; instead, they focus on the process of how the speaker directs the attention of the hearer towards the referent. In fact, it is easy to see that the communicative function of demonstratives is not simply to mark the relative distance from the speaker and to show where the referent is; rather, the speaker wants to specify which entity he is talking about and to help the hearer in the process of referent resolution. This is obvious if we consider the fact that a demonstrative cannot provide a satisfactory answer to a question about the location of an entity. As an illustration, consider the question-answer pair in (18), adopted from Enfield (2009: 30):

(18) A: Where is my book on the French revolution?
B: #*This one.*/#*This book.*

Sidnell (2009) also recognizes that demonstrative reference is procedural in nature, but he considers it not from a cognitive, but from a sociocentric point of view when he argues that it is based on the reciprocity of perspectives between the speaker and other participants. When a speaker intends to carry out a successful referring act using a demonstrative, he has to do it in a way that ensures that both the speaker and the addressee successfully identify the same object, and the interlocutors have to rely on each other to achieve that common goal. To do that, the speaker must consider the knowledge of the addressee about the intended referent. This is in accordance with observing the principle of optimal design, a conversational maxim described by Clark et al. (1983: 246): 'The speaker designs his utterance in such a way that he has good reason to believe that the addressee can readily and uniquely compute what he meant on the basis of the utterance along with the rest of their common ground.' First, the speaker is expected to take into consideration his own beliefs about the knowledge of the addressee and design his act accordingly, second, the addressee takes it for granted that the speaker relies only on such information that he, the speaker believes to be available for the hearer, too. Thus a successful act of referring is 'a collaborative enterprise that requires that speaker and addressee work together' (Peeters & Özyürek 2016: 1), where the role of the addressee is as crucial as the speaker's.

At this point one may reconsider the difference between the act of referring in general and the act of referring by deictic expressions in particular. Sidnell and Enfield (2017: 217) claim that 'reference is a form of shared intentionality in which the cognitive focus of two or more persons is aligned and jointly focused', then argue that deixis differs from other forms of reference, since it is 'a low-cost, highly efficient, minimally characterizing way to accomplish reference' (Sidnell & Enfield 2017: 236). This is the reason deictic expressions are truly universal across languages (Sidnell 2009; Diessel 2012). Moreover, Sidnell and Enfield (2017) state that deictic reference has the following advantages over other forms of referring:

(i) deictic forms are highly appropriate when the speaker intends to refer to an entity that is hard to describe, or does not have a name;

(ii) deictic forms make it possible to avoid a detailed description of the intended referent when such descriptions would be counterproductive to the current purpose of the conversation;
(iii) successful reference by means of deictic forms can demonstrate and strengthen social proximity among participants.

The next section provides a brief overview of two sociocentric approaches to demonstrative reference. First, the ground-breaking work of Hanks (1990) on Maya demonstratives will be introduced, which is based on fieldwork and examines the contextual use of demonstratives. Second, Laury's analysis of the use of Finnish demonstratives in audiotaped everyday conversations (Laury 1997) and Etelämäki's dynamic account of demonstratives in a conversation analytic framework (Etelämäki 2009) will be presented.

2.2.1.1 Hanks's (1990, 2009) pioneering work on Yucatec Maya

Field methods focus on the spontaneous use of language, and accordingly, Hanks (1990) collected data on the actual use of Yucatec Maya demonstratives in real-life communicative settings. Hanks (1990) observed actual conversations in everyday settings, such as the household, the field, the forest, etc. While Hanks focused on the spatial use of demonstratives, his coding scheme does not include the traditional proximal/distal distinction; instead, it urges the introduction of interactional features; for example, Hanks relies on the terms 'immediate' and 'non-immediate', where the former indicates that the referent is closer to the speaker (as opposed to the addressee), while the latter signals that the referent is closer to the addressee and not to the speaker. Within the adverbial system of Yucatec Maya, Hanks (1990) also introduces the inclusive/exclusive distinction to describe the opposition between *waye*' 'here' and *tolo*' 'there'. According to Bohnemeyer (2018: 184), 'this distinction presupposes some kind of perimeter around the speaker, such that *waye*' refers to the inside of that perimeter and *tolo*' to its outside. The perimeter can be defined by the boundaries of, for example, the house, the field, the village, or the state where the conversation takes place. The addressee is normally inside the perimeter as well. *Tolo*' is used in indiscriminate reference to things that are "out there" in the relevant respect.' Thus the analysis of recorded actual conversations shifted the focus of research; the results of Hanks's study emphasized that the exophoric use of demonstratives cannot be captured adequately by relying on only physical proximity to the speaker; instead, the careful analysis of the data showed that social relations are decisive. As Hanks (2009: 21) points out, 'the selection and understanding of deictics relies on the simultaneous articulation of space, perception, discourse, commonsense and mutual knowledge, anticipation, and the framework of participation in which Sprs and Adrs orient to one another.

Any one of these factors can provide the basis for deictic construal, according to the demands of the ongoing relevance structure in which it is produced.'

2.2.1.2 Finnish demonstratives in interaction (Laury 1997, Etelämäki 2009)

Inspired by Hanks' work, Laury (1997) examines the use and meaning of Finnish demonstratives in conversational data and proposes that they are used dynamically to express the speaker's orientation and stance to the intended referent. More specifically, Laury (1997) argues that the main function of demonstratives is to exclude or include the intended referent in the interlocutors' socially and cognitively defined sphere in the interactional context of the speech event. The crucial point is that by using demonstratives speakers not only refer to certain entities in the physical setting in an objective way that is determined by physical proximity, but that demonstratives also function to establish speakers' social spheres, i.e., they 'dynamically create or constitute place and perspective' (Laury 1997: 58), thus demonstratives in Finnish 'not only express context, they also build context. In actual uses of demonstratives, these two functions are simultaneous and inseparable' (Laury 1997: 58–59).

Accordingly, Laury (1997) argues that the Finnish demonstrative *tämä* 'this', which has been traditionally labelled as a proximal term, is used to refer to entities that the speaker focuses on and is manipulating in the actual speech event, i.e., the speaker uses *tämä* to indicate that the intended referent is in their socially defined current sphere, which is 'related to and reflects the speaker's current activities and the social dynamics of the speech situation' (Laury 1997: 70). In turn, the use of *tuo* 'that' signals to the addressee that the intended referent is not in the speaker's sphere, while *se* 'that' is used to refer to entities in the addressee's current sphere.

Thus Laury's (1997) account of Finnish demonstratives also supports the dynamic, interactional view of demonstratives, since it emphasizes that the primary function of demonstratives is to call the attention of the addressee to the intended referent and to mark their accessibility in the dynamically and socially established interactional space.

Etelämäki (2009) develops Laury's (1997) suggestions within the framework of conversation analysis, which analyses dynamic and complex talk-in-interaction, and argues that Finnish demonstratives are used to convey how relevant the intended referent is for the current activity in a given conversational setting. This means that speakers use demonstratives to direct the addressee's attention to the referent or to indicate that the addressee has already enough information to identify the referent for the current purposes of the interaction. In essence, Etelämäki (2009: 43–44) argues that the conversational turn in which *tämä* is used creates the ground against which the referent is identified, thus *tämä* itself presents the referent and indicates that its identification is crucial to understand the current activity. *Tuo* is a means of pointing, used when the interlocutors have shared access to the referents, and identification of the referent is part of the ongoing activity. Finally, *se* is used when the referent is known by both the speaker and the addressee, and its function is only to refer to an already established referent.

2.1.1.3 Summary

As we have seen above, interactional approaches to demonstratives treat deictic reference as a collaborative process, in which not only the speaker, but the addressee also takes an active role in resolving reference, while the speaker directs the attention of the hearer towards the intended referent. Tátrai (2017) also emphasizes that deixis, a context-dependent, attention-directing linguistic operation, is interactional in nature. He argues in a functional-cognitive framework that discourses develop as joint attentional scenes. These include the interaction of the interlocutors, who direct and follow the others' attention while construing a referential scene. This means that the use of prototypical deictic expressions, for example that of demonstratives, provides context-dependent vantage points that help the addressee in processing and understanding the spatial, temporal and socio-cultural relations of the referential act by creating a deictic link between the joint attentional scene and the referential act. Diessel (2012) also argues that demonstratives serve to establish joint attention, which is a triadic relation between the speaker, the hearer and the intended referent. The notion of joint attention is discussed in a more detailed fashion in the next section.

2.2.2 Demonstratives and joint attention

A crucial feature of human communication is the ability to establish triadic joint attention between the speaker, the hearer, and the entity being referred to. Joint attention is a cognitive phenomenon; it can be defined as 'the coordination of orienting between two people toward an object' (Shaw et al. 2017: 268); more precisely, it is a situation 'in which a pair of interlocutors are visually attending to a referent, and both are aware that the other is doing so' (Skarabela et al. 2013: 6; see also Sidnell & Enfield 2017). It is important to emphasize here that it is not enough that both participants in the speech event direct their attention to the intended referent; both participants also have to monitor the other's attention and make sure that it is also directed to the same referent. Therefore, joint attention is established only when there is mutual attention to the intended referent and there is a mutual understanding of the other participant's focus of attention. This is represented in Figure 2.1, reprinted from Skarabela et al. (2013: 7), where I_1 and I_2

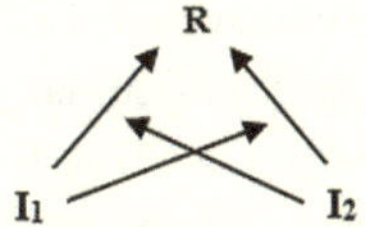

Figure 2.1: Joint attention (reprinted from Skarabela et al. 2013: 7 with permission from Elsevier)

represent the interlocutors, R is the intended referent and the arrows indicate the direction of attention.

The configuration in Figure 2.1 shows that 'reference involves joint attention such that two persons are not only publicly projecting their attention to the same referent, but they are, in addition, mutually aware of the current alignment, and thus sharedness, of their two lines of attention' (Sidnell & Enfield 2017: 221). One special case of shared, triadic joint attention is when one of the interlocutors is holding the intended referent, and, clearly, a pointing gesture on the part of the speaker also aids the establishment of joint attention. Thus the distance of the referent from the interlocutors might vary; the establishment of joint attention requires only that the intended referent is visible for both participants. This is especially important since the notion of joint attention is different from Gundel et al.'s (1993: 279) cognitive status 'in focus', which is defined as a status in which 'the referent is not only in short-term memory, but is also at the current focus of attention'. The difference is illustrated by the following interaction in Inuktitut (Allen 1996, cited by Skarabela et al. 2013: 6)

(19) Mother: Nipittajuurmi qaujimanngilatit?
'You don't know where the Scotch tape is?'
Child: Aah.
'I don't.'
Child: Qariamiikkuk!
'It's in the room.'
Child: Ailaurlaguu?
'Want me to go get it?'

This conversation between a mother and a child shows that the referent might be in focus in Gundel et al.'s (1993) framework, but there is no visual joint attention established between the mother, the child and the intended referent. It is also crucial to emphasize the difference between joint attention and any model of the potential referent that could be part of the common ground of the interlocutors. Hence, joint attention, as outlined above, must be treated as a specific moment in conversation.

In fact, the ability to take part in joint attentional behaviour, which serves as the basis for any successful act of reference and is a crucial component of human communication (Tomasello 1999; Sidnell & Enfield 2017), emerges between 6 and 18 months of age. First, only eye gaze and pointing can direct the attention of other interlocutors; then, with language acquisition, demonstratives become 'the primary linguistic device to manipulate the interlocutors' attention in the speech situation' (Dissel 2012: 2417). According to Diessel (2012), this explains why demonstratives emerge very early, during the one-word stage of language acquisition and it might also be responsible for the high relative frequency of demonstrative tokens in various spoken corpora across languages. For example, English demonstratives are shown to be among the 30 most frequent words in different corpora (see Leech et al. 2001; O'Keeffe et al. 2011; Rühlemann 2007, 2019; Levinson 2018a).

Since joint attention is a triadic action between the speaker, the addressee, and the intended referent, it involves focusing the addressee's attention on a given entity in the current conversational setting. When demonstratives are used to refer, the intended referent has to be selected from a set of alternatives. The encoded semantic meaning of demonstratives offers little information that could help in identifying the intended referent,[5] therefore their use is often accompanied by a type of gesture, such as pointing, body posture, head nod or eye gaze, to effectively establish joint attention in face-to-face interactions. However, other factors, such as some prominent features of the intended referent, could also help the hearer resolve reference. The salience of a given object in a speech situation might arise in different ways. Objects might be salient due to their size, colour or position, they might become salient through the use of a gesture, or simply might achieve a special salience under the given circumstances. For example, when uttering (20) while walking down the street,

(20) My sister has a bike like *that one*.

the speaker might narrow the addressee's attention by pointing, by relying on the bike's bright colour, or by the fact that it has just gone by (Sidnell & Enfield 2017).

The notion of joint attention and the proximal/distal distinction in two-way demonstrative systems contribute to the observation that a crucial feature of demonstratives is that their use always implies a contrast (Cornish 2001). Whenever an interlocutor focuses their attention on an entity, it follows that there must be other entities that remain in the background, out of the focus of attention. The referent

5 When demonstratives are used as modifiers, the lexical content of the NP also helps in identifying the intended referent.

of a demonstrative is always picked from a set of alternatives, and demonstratives fulfil the role of directing the attention of the addressee to the intended referent. As Zaki (2011) notes, this implied contrast is what differentiates demonstratives from other referring expressions, for example from definite descriptions with the definite article or third person pronouns.

In sum, it has been argued above that demonstratives are the most basic linguistic means by which speakers can manipulate the attention of the hearer to the intended referent to align it with their own focus of attention in acts of referring. Establishing joint attention is a collaborative, dynamic act between the speaker and the hearer; thus it contradicts the traditional, egocentric view of referring and challenges the assumption that the function of demonstratives is simply to signal the location of the intended referent.

As we have seen above, the notion of joint attention adequately describes the exophoric use of demonstratives, when their function is to direct the hearer's attention to the intended referent in the physical environment. Diessel (2012) argues that non-deictic uses are built on the same psychological mechanism, i.e., demonstratives serve to focus the addressee's attention on linguistic entities in the discourse context. Thus anaphoric and discourse deictic uses can be explained along the same lines, the only difference being that discourse referents are not visible, and cannot be highlighted by a pointing gesture. In a way, non-deictic uses can be derived from the more basic and fundamental exophoric uses. A strong point of this analysis is that it is language independent, and, since it is built on the cognitive-psychological notion of joint attention, it is suitable to capture cross-linguistic generalizations about demonstrative use.

2.3 The relevance-theoretic approach

Relevance theory (Sperber & Wilson 1986/1995) is a cognitive theory of communication arguing that the ease with which interlocutors arrive at the intended meanings of utterances can be explained if we assume that communication is governed by general psychological-cognitive principles. According to Sperber and Wilson (1986/1995), relevance is the key notion to understand how communication – an intentional, goal-directed activity – works. In everyday life, human beings constantly perceive a considerable number of stimuli, but they avoid cognitive overload by not processing all of these. It is reasonable to assume that there is a kind of general principle that ensures that only those stimuli are processed that result in a positive effect in our cognitive environment, which comprises our assumptions about the world. Processing the input might result in positive cognitive effects in different ways. New information gained while communicating with other people may strengthen an existing assumption; it might contradict an existing assumption and, therefore, result in its elimination; and finally, new information might combine with an existing assumption and result in a contextual implication. Obviously, the mental processing of inputs requires a certain amount of mental effort.

Relevance is a property of the input; it is a function of two cognitive factors: cognitive effects and processing effort. These two factors determine whether a certain input is more relevant than another for a given individual in a given situation. Thus relevance is defined by Wilson and Sperber (2004: 609) as:

Relevance of an input to an individual:

(a) Other things being equal, the greater the positive cognitive effects achieved by processing an input, the greater the relevance of the input to an individual at that time.
(b) Other things being equal, the greater the processing effort expended, the lower the relevance of the input to the individual at that time.

Relevance theory is built upon two basic principles. The Cognitive Principle of Relevance states that 'human cognition tends to be geared to the maximisation of relevance' (Sperber & Wilson 1986/1995: 260). Focusing on communication, this means that interlocutors use their cognitive resources to process stimuli that they think are relevant.

This leads us to the second principle, the Communicative Principle of Relevance, which states that 'every act of ostensive communication communicates a presumption of its own optimal relevance' (Sperber & Wilson 1986/1995: 260). This can be spelled out as follows: 'the utterance is presumed to be the most relevant one compatible with the speaker's abilities and preferences, and at least relevant enough to be worth the hearer's attention' (Sperber & Wilson 2002: 18). The principle also motivates the following relevance-theoretic comprehension procedure, which describes the two-step process that hearers follow when interpreting an utterance (Sperber & Wilson 2002: 18):

Relevance-theoretic comprehension procedure

(a) Follow a path of least effort in computing cognitive effects. In particular, test interpretative hypotheses (disambiguations, reference resolutions, implicatures, etc.) in order of accessibility.
(b) Stop when your expectations of relevance are satisfied.

This implies that once the speaker has produced the most relevant utterance under the circumstances, the hearer can stop processing after applying the least effort to arrive at a relevant interpretation of the utterance. According to Sperber and Wilson (2002), a speaker should formulate his utterance (by choosing appropriate words, structure, intonation, etc.) in a way that satisfies the presumption of relevance, and in that case the first interpretation that satisfies the hearer's expectations about relevance will be the one that the speaker intended to convey. To clarify this point, let us consider the following pair of examples (Scott 2013: 51):

(21) The little boy looks like he is having fun.

(22) The little boy in the blue shirt looks like he is having fun.

The hearer has to follow the two-step process described above. This means that the hearer considers the most accessible referent during the stage of reference resolution. If there is only one little boy present in the physical environment, then the speaker should utter (21) in order to make that little boy the most accessible candidate as the referent of the description as processed by the hearer. However, if there happens to be more than one little boy, then the speaker will add more descriptive content to the definite description, and will utter (22) to narrow down the set of potential referents to the point when the intended referent will be the most accessible one for the hearer. In this second scenario, uttering (21) would not be satisfactory, and it would not have optimal relevance.

Interpretation of utterances within the relevance-theoretic framework is not achieved only by decoding the words and syntactic structure, but, following Grice (1989), inferences also play a role in the process of deriving the intended meaning of the speaker. To work out a meaningful interpretation of an utterance, a hearer has to perform three tasks, which are not sequential in nature (Wilson & Sperber 2004: 615). From the phonetic form of a given utterance a semantic or logical form is derived, which in turn is enriched with the help of pragmatic inferences. These include reference resolution, the resolving of structural ambiguity, and vagueness. As a result of pragmatic enrichment, which is an inferential process, we arrive at the so-called explicature, which is the relevance-theoretic equivalent of the truth conditionally complete proposition. The explicature itself may be enriched again via various inferential processes: the hearer must construct an appropriate hypothesis about the intended contextual assumptions, thereby constructing a context of interpretation, which involves the implicated premises. This process is again driven by the search for relevance. The third subtask concerns the formulation of an appropriate hypothesis about the intended contextual implications, i.e., the implicated conclusions. The speaker's meaning can be derived as a combination of explicatures, implicated premises and implicated conclusions. Each of these is an inferential process and each contributes to the overall relevance of the utterance. As an example, consider the conversation below, based on Clark (2013: 226–27):

(23) A: Do you fancy a cup of coffee?
B: Actually, I'm avoiding drinks with tannin in them at the moment.

When A interprets B's response to his question, we can assume that he derives the following inferences. First, he has to form the explicature carried by B's utterance, namely, he has to decode the words, and via enrichment he arrives at the proposition expressed: B is avoiding tannin-containing drinks. Clearly, this proposition is not the intended meaning; it does not form an appropriate reply to the question. Thus B has to construct the contextual assumptions A intended him to rely on during the interpretation process. Here, these might include the assumption that coffee contains tannins. A might have known this fact before; in that case his assumption is strengthened, and he can use it as an implicated premise, because it is relevant. If A does not know that coffee contains tannins, then he will assume it now and use it again as an implicated premise. Finally, A must consider the contextual implications B wants him to arrive at; that is, he will infer that B does not want to have a cup of coffee.

A final feature of relevance theory that needs to be highlighted for our purposes is the difference between conceptual and procedural meaning. Content words, like *dog*, *table*, *sea*, encode concepts that are represented in the mind of the hearer; and it is this mental representation that surfaces in the explicatures. However, as pointed out by Blakemore (2002), there are other types of words, such as *but*, *so*, which can guide the hearer through the inferential processes that are involved in deriving the overall interpretation, thereby reducing the processing effort of the hearer and resulting in optimal relevance. As an example let us compare the utterances below, discussed by Scott (2020: 19):

(24) Korina is feeling happy. So she is going to the party tonight.

(25) Korina is feeling happy. After all, she is going to the party tonight.

In the case of (24), the hearer is guided to arrive at the conclusion that Korina is going to the party as a consequence of her being happy, while in the case of (25) just the opposite holds, namely, Korina is happy because she is going to the party. The difference can be explained by the presence of discourse markers, which carry information about the inferential processes the hearer is expected to perform. Thus *so* and *after all* encode procedural meaning, which constrains the inferential process, thereby lowering the processing cost for the hearer and reducing the possibility of misunderstanding.

The notion of procedural meaning has recently surfaced in a number of analyses of referring expressions, such as pronouns or definite descriptions (cf. Hedley 2005, Powell 2010). In the next section we will turn to Scott's procedural account of the English demonstratives (2013, 2020) within a relevance-theoretic framework, narrowing the focus of investigation to the spatial uses of demonstratives. As a starting point, let us consider the following examples (Scott 2020: 136):

(26) I'll have a slice of *this cake*.

(27) I'll have a slice of *that cake*.

It is reasonable to assume that if (26) and (27) are uttered in the same situation where there are two cakes, then the demonstratives will refer to different entities in the physical context. In other words, the choice between the demonstratives matters, the utterances themselves express different propositions. It is also important to note that the use of the definite article would be infelicitous within the same speech situation. This fact can be explained if we assume that the use of a demonstrative is motivated, since the choice affects the relevance of the utterance. In procedural terms, the demonstratives guide the reference resolution process.

Scott (2013, 2020) follows Powell's (2010) account by stating that both English demonstratives encode a two-step procedure that guides the hearer in reference resolution. The analysis takes as a starting point the traditional proximal/distal opposition, but it moves beyond it by arguing that proximity and distance are relational terms. Thus the proximal demonstrative encodes the instruction 'find the speaker and then find an object near the speaker', while *that* encodes 'find the speaker and then find an object far away from the speaker' (Scott 2013: 57). The crucial point here is that the proximal/distal distinction is treated as a relational, context-dependent property, which helps the hearer in finding the intended referent, but it is important that it is not an objective property, and it might show flexibility in different speech situations. The resulting variation can be illustrated by the following conversation between a customer and the assistant at the store, where the same referent is picked by proximal and distal demonstratives as the conversation unfolds.

(28) Customer: I would like to buy *that scarf*.
Shop assistant: *This one*?
Customer: Yes, *that one*.
Customer (after having received the scarf): I think *this* will suit my daughter.

The customer uses a distal demonstrative first to guide the attention of the shop assistant to an object that is far away from herself, then the shop assistant reassesses the situation and opts for the proximal demonstrative when instructing the hearer to find a referent that is close to herself, i.e., the choice of the proximal reflects the fact that distance is a relational term. If the shop assistant used the distal demonstrative in the second turn, then confusion would arise. Within the relevant-theoretic framework proposed by Scott (2013, 2020), choosing one of the demonstratives is relevant if it reduces the cognitive effort required on the part of the hearer in identifying the referent. This might be achieved either by 'adding an extra layer of activation to the hearer's mental representation of the intended referent, or by ruling out any non-intended competitors' (Scott 2013: 57).

The choice of the demonstratives above could also be explained within the traditional framework; i.e., the referents of the demonstratives are picked relative to the deictic centre, which is constituted by the actual speaker in the exchange above. Turn by turn, as the current speaker takes over, there is a change in the perspective and the participants can easily adapt to that.[6] However, the traditional approach is too simple, it is not satisfactory in itself; the proximal/distal opposition should be treated as a relative notion, as shown by the following examples taken from Talmy (2000: 25):

(29) *This speck* is smaller than *that speck*.

(30) *This planet* is smaller than *that planet*.

In (29), the referents of the noun phrases are probably minuscule, and they are located close to the speaker, while the referents in (30) are large heavenly bodies, located very remotely from the speaker; hence, according to Kemmerer (1999), the English demonstratives do not encode objectively measurable distances. Kemmerer (1999: 55) also argues that

> the way a speaker uses demonstratives actually reveals more about his or her subjective attitude toward the surrounding spatial world than about the objective features of that world. This is because it is the speaker who determines how the oppositional relations that are abstractly encoded by the terms are applied to distinguish between near and far sectors of space.

Furthermore, he points out that the proximal/distal distinction is not only context-dependent and construed relative to the speaker, but *this* and *that* are also to be interpreted relative to each other, i.e., 'the proximal demonstrative *this* means simply "closer to the deictic centre than *that*" and, conversely, the distal demonstrative *that* means simply "further from the deictic centre than *this*"' (Kemmerer

---

6 Similar exchanges might be problematic for children, as data from language acquisition shows (Tanz 1980).

1999: 52). This implies that English demonstratives are interpreted not only relative to the speech situation and the deictic centre, but 'also relative to one another' (Scott 2013: 57). Similarly, Sidnell and Enfield (2017) suggest that English *this* and *that* are ideal tools for reference, since their underspecified, shallow meaning always interacts with the meaning of the other demonstrative via an inherent contrast; that is, 'each element has a composite meaning, a combination of what it is and what it is not' (Sidnell & Enfield 2017: 218).

Overall, whenever a demonstrative is interpreted, it is not only the deictic centre that has to be identified, but also the type of contrast indicated by the choice of the demonstrative needs to be spelled out. The contrast in question might be realized in spatial terms, but temporal, attitudinal or discourse contrasts might also be implied. In the default case, the deictic centre is the speaker, but it might be switched for example from the speaker to the addressee as in the conversation below (Scott 2013: 58):

(31) Dentist: Does *this one* hurt?
Patient: Yes, it's *that one.*

If we assume that the speaker is the deictic centre, then the traditional approach here would predict just the opposite pattern regarding the choice of demonstratives. As is often the case in similar doctor-patient exchanges, the doctor's perspective is more prominent, so it is his point of view that is relevant, and both participants consider the doctor as the deictic centre.

In summary, Scott (2013, 2020) argues that *this* and *that* encode procedural information, which guides the hearer in the process of finding the intended referent as compared to other potential referents. The hearer finds the intended referent with the least effort, by testing candidates in the order of accessibility, and aborting the process when his expectations are satisfied. If we consider the examples in (26)–(27) again, both utterances would probably be accompanied by some gesture on the part of the speaker, which would indicate where the speaker's attention is directed and what his referential intention is, thereby encouraging the hearer to consider this particular object as a potential referent first.

However, there are also examples where the speaker does not provide any clue in the form of a physical gesture as to his referential intention; the identity of the referent still has to be established. Consider the examples in (32) and (33), which could occur in any academic piece of writing (Scott 2013: 59).

(32) *In this section* we will continue the argument.

(33) *In that section* we will continue the argument.

In the case of the proximal demonstrative, the referent is easily identifiable, *this* is usually interpreted as the current section of the writing, the one the utterance is part of. Considering the referent of *that section*, the speaker intends to refer to one particular section of the text, but, from the addressee's perspective, there is more than one potential referent, and due to the contrastive nature of the demonstratives, these comprise non-proximal ones, i.e. any section might be the referent, except for the current one. According to Scott (2013), following the principle of relevance, the use of *that* is felicitous only when there is a specific section that is more accessible than other potential, non-proximal referents. In Gundel et al.'s (1993) framework the use of *that* has been associated with familiar cognitive status, and it is treated as an intermediate accessibility marker by Ariel (2001). Scott's (2013) analysis, however, is more adequate than any of these approaches, since it offers a unified treatment of gestural and discourse deictic uses, the difference being the way the speaker guides the hearer through the process of reference resolution. In the case of the former, the linguistic meaning is not sufficient in itself, therefore, the speaker offers a clue in the form of a physical gesture (pointing, gaze, body posture, etc.) to help the hearer in the identification of the intended referent. In the case of the latter, no such extra clue is needed, the discourse context and the properties of the intended referent suffice to identify the referent.

The analysis presented above shows how demonstratives encode procedural meaning within a relevance-theoretic framework. According to Zaki (2011: 101),

(a) Demonstratives encode a procedure which directs the hearer to create/maintain a joint level of attention to the intended referent (as opposed to other referential candidates).
(b) Demonstratives encode a (pro)concept of distance.
(c) The interaction of (a) and (b) with context is relevance-driven.

It is important to emphasize here that the notion of distance is treated here as indexical, in the sense that it makes sense only with respect to a scale, a reference point, and in comparison to something, i.e. it is an incomplete concept in itself and requires some inferential work. Furthermore, its 'semantic contribution must be contextually specified for the associated utterance to have a truth-value' (Sperber & Wilson 1998: 185). In addition, demonstratives 'trigger a cognitive procedure directing the hearer to create or maintain a shared level of attention to the intended referent. This cognitive procedure has scope over the concept of distance encoded by the demonstrative, therefore, it gives rise to the contrastive aspect represented by the implication of other referential candidates' (Zaki 2011: 104). Zaki (2011) also argues that the distance encoded by demonstratives can be interpreted not only spatially, but also textually, emotionally, and cognitively. Thus the relevance-theoretic account of demonstratives not only offers a uniform treatment of English demonstrative use, but also brings together previous cognitively oriented assumptions about demonstrative reference.

2.4 Experimental insights

2.4.1 Overview

As mentioned above, the choice between spatial demonstratives has traditionally been assumed to depend on the physical proximity of the referent to the speaker. With the emergence of experimental methods, more and more studies have not only re-examined but also challenged the traditional approach. These works are based on a plethora of designs and often yield mixed and controversial results. The aim of this section is to provide a brief overview of current research on English, Dutch and Hungarian demonstrative practice.

Experimental works on demonstrative practice can be grouped along several dimensions. One major dividing line can be drawn between production and comprehension studies. A related, but more refined grouping could be based on the methodologies applied. Among production studies, we find controlled elicitation tasks (Küntay & Özyürek 2006; Maes and Rooij 2007; Piwek et al. 2008; Peeters et al. 2014), narrative elicitation (Reile 2019), and the so-called memory game paradigm (Coventry et al. 2008, 2014, Reile et al. 2020a). Recently, the comprehension of demonstratives has been investigated in ERP and fMRI studies (Stevens & Zhang 2013; Peeters et al. 2015), while Reile et al. (2020b) conducted an experiment on the interpretation of Estonian demonstrative pronouns and adverbs. A different, but natural classification arises if we consider those studies that support the traditional view and those that argue that the traditional account is insufficient in itself. In this chapter, we provide an overview of recent experimental findings on the choice of demonstratives in different languages along the last feature.

2.4.2 Experimental works supporting the traditional view

2.4.2.1 Coventry et al.'s (2008) experiment

Coventry et al. (2008) explored the use of spatial demonstratives in English in a production study; more specifically, they tested the mapping between perceptual space and demonstrative use with the help of a memory game. Participants received a placement instruction on a card and were asked to place objects on 12 coloured dots arranged in a line on a large conference table; they then returned to their place at the end of the table and named the object while pointing at it using only three words: a demonstrative, an adjective and a noun describing a shape, such as *this green triangle*. Three variables were tested:

(i) distance between the speaker and the object;
(ii) use of tool: participants either used their hands or a 70-cm stick to point at the objects;
(iii) actor: either the participant or the experimenter placed the objects.

The findings of the experiment indicated that relative distance from the speaker matters; speakers opted for the proximal term when referring and pointing at entities within arm's reach. Moreover, it was shown that near space can be extended, i.e., the proximal demonstrative *this* was used not only to refer to objects within arm's reach; speakers also selected the proximal demonstrative when they could point at the object with a stick. Thus the spatial distinction between near and far is not necessarily clear-cut, but might be flexible. Finally, participants used proximal demonstratives more frequently when it was them, and not the experimenter, who placed the objects. Thus the authors conclude that while relative distance from the speaker is crucial, it is not an absolute measure, it can be extended, and contact with the entities being referred to is also important.

Reile et al. (2020a) also tested the effect of egocentric distance on the choice of adnominal demonstratives in Estonian and Võro within the memory game paradigm. Additionally, the role of two interactional factors was also explored; besides the actor parameter (whether the experimenter or the participant interacted with the object) the position of the addressee with respect to the speaker was also varied. The results strengthen the findings of Coventry et al. (2008) regarding relative distance of the referent from the speaker, i.e. in both languages, distal demonstratives were preferred when referring to objects located out of arm's reach. Findings regarding the importance of interactional parameters were less conclusive; contrary to expectations, no effect was detected on the choice of Estonian demonstratives, while in Võro the speaker's interaction with the object referred to and the position of the addressee proved to be weaker factors than egocentric distance.

In a follow-up series of experiments, Coventry et al. (2014) used the same design to reinforce the role of relative distance and actor in the selection of English demonstratives; in addition, they explored several contrasts of object characteristics that have been shown to be lexically marked in the demonstrative systems of several languages. The contrasts tested individually alongside relative distance in subsequent experiments are as follows:

(i) ownership: participants have received four coins at the beginning of their session that they could keep, the experimenter had his own set of coins;
(ii) visibility: objects after placement were either covered by a container or not;

(iii) familiarity is based on the notion of mental accessibility, i.e., on the assumption that familiar objects, such as red squares, come to mind easily, while unfamiliar ones, like viridian nonagons, are less accessible.

The role of relative distance was again reinforced, and each of the other three factors was shown to be important in demonstrative choice in English. This means that the traditional proximal/distal opposition is not satisfactory in itself and demonstrative use is affected by more than a single factor. Coventry et al. (2014: 63) argue that the most important finding is that 'parameters lexicalized in some languages are nevertheless important for the choice of terms in a language that does not make those explicit lexical distinctions'. Moreover, Coventry et al. (2014) also claim that their results, which were obtained in a relatively strictly controlled experimental setting, indicate that demonstrative use is not necessarily tied to interactions and therefore need not always be explained in a rich context; rather, demonstrative practice is a manifestation of a core spatial semantic knowledge. Notwithstanding this, they also acknowledge that while knowledge about the object being referred to was proved to be crucial, other pragmatic factors, such as joint attention or shared background knowledge, cannot be neglected, either.[7]

2.4.2.2 Stevens and Zhang's (2013) experiment

Stevens and Zhang (2013) tackle the same problem in a comprehension study but employ a different design; their experiment is based on the so-called event-related potential (ERP) technique, which tracks neural activity while semantic information is processed. Stevens and Zhang (2013) tested two factors: distance (close to the speaker, close to hearer, and far from both) and gaze (shared gaze or no shared gaze). Participants heard an auditory stimulus (created by a text-to-speech program) containing an English demonstrative while simultaneously looking at an artificial visual scene. Besides the intended referent, a blue cat, the visual scene always included an object at a different location to provide a contrast. The speaker, a woman, was always pointing at the intended referent. The addressee, a man, was either looking in the same direction as the woman or looking in another direction. Subjects had to decide whether the visual scene and the auditory stimulus matched or not.

Stevens and Zhang evaluated both the reaction time of the participants and the ERP data. The analysis of the behavioural data indicated that *this* was felt to be congruent with the scenes where the intended referent was close to the speaker, while *that* corresponded to the other two levels of distance; hence, the

---

7 For a more detailed overview of the series of experiments described above I refer the reader to Coventry (2015).

results support the traditional proximity based approach. However, further analysis found no difference between *this* and *that* in the far conditions when the hearer was looking elsewhere. Thus distance as a factor mattered only in the shared gaze condition, in other words, when joint attention has already been established. On the basis of this finding, the authors propose that 'the role of distance from the speaker is trumped by a more basic requirement of joint attention' (Stevens & Zhang 2013: 41). Hence, demonstrative choice in English is affected by the hearer's gaze, i.e., in demonstrative use 'the speaker is communicating the selection of an object with respect to the hearer's attention' (Stevens & Zhang 2013: 41). These results support Diessel's (2012) claim that the basic function of demonstratives is to establish joint attention; moreover, it can be argued that the proximal/distal opposition of demonstratives directs the hearer's focus in the process of establishing joint attention. In a follow-up experiment, Stevens and Zhang (2014) showed that in English the presence of a pointing gesture on the part of the speaker is also crucial. Their results indicate that participants experienced difficulty identifying the referent without the presence of a pointing gesture.[8] Overall, Stevens and Zhang's (2013, 2014) findings indicate that although distance cannot be discarded, the traditional egocentric view of demonstrative practice needs to be replaced by a more dynamic, multimodal view, where shared gaze and pointing are important factors.

2.4.3 Experimental works challenging the traditional view

2.4.3.1 Cross-linguistic investigations

2.4.3.1.1 Peeters et al.'s (2014) experiment

The experiment of Peeters et al. (2014) explored how speakers refer to entities in their immediate physical environment in Dutch. They used a so-called controlled elicitation task, where participants saw different visual stimuli that elicited the production of referring expressions: demonstratives or NPs with (in)definite articles. Three variables were tested in their study:

- the presence or absence of visual joint attention between the interlocutors to an intended referent;

8 Stevens & Zhang (2014) also tested Japanese native speakers within the same experimental setting. Japanese participants were more successful in trials where there was no pointing clue, which might be a consequence of the more complex demonstrative system of Japanese. Therefore, the authors suggest that different languages may exploit the use of gestures to a different extent in demonstrative reference.

- physical proximity with four levels: close to the speaker, close to the addressee, at middle distance from both speaker and addressee, or relatively far away from speaker and addressee;
- the presence or absence of a pointing gesture.

The visual stimulus was always a photo depicting the speaker, the addressee and the intended referent. The speaker and the addressee were facing each other across a table, and four pictures represented each experimental condition across the trials.

The most important finding of Peeters et al.'s (2014) experiment is that establishing joint attention may be an important factor in the selection of Dutch demonstratives, since participants more often used distal demonstratives when the entity being referred to was in the interlocutors' joint focus of attention. This implies that the speaker takes into account the visual attention of the addressee when selecting a distal demonstrative term, while the use of proximal demonstratives was not affected by the presence or absence of joint visual attention.

Regarding distance, Peeters et al. (2014) found that participants opted for the proximal demonstrative when the entity being referred to was close to the speaker, whereas the distal term was preferred when the referent was located close to the addressee, at middle distance from both interlocutors, or relatively far from the speaker and addressee.

The third factor, the presence of a pointing gesture by the speaker, influenced the use of both demonstrative terms, i.e., both terms were produced more often when there was an accompanying pointing gesture. The authors argue that the function of a pointing gesture therefore may be to demarcate the search space for the addressee. Moreover, they also emphasize the importance of testing the effect of more than one factor within the same experiment, since the selection of demonstratives might be the result of a subtle interplay between various contextual factors.

2.4.3.1.2 Peeters et al.'s (2015) experiment

The aim of Peeters et al.'s (2015) two EEG experiments is to compare the traditional egocentric view on demonstrative choice with the so-called dyad-oriented account (Jungbluth 2003). Jungbluth (2003) suggests that the physical orientation of the speaker and addressee is crucial in Spanish demonstrative use; more specifically, she argues that not only the position of the speaker and the addressee relative to one another (face-to-face, face-to-back, and side-by-side), but also the position of the intended referent relative to the shared space between speaker and hearer is important. In side-by-side conversations, the speaker and the hearer stand or sit next to each other and share the same perspective. In that scenario, the three-term system of Spanish demonstratives encodes relative distance from the speaker; however, according to Jungbluth (2003), even in this case distance is not measurable; the borderlines in between the three regions might be extended and subjectively decided within the speech situation. Face-to-face and face-to-back conversations cannot be adequately described by the speaker-anchored approach. According to Jungbluth (2003), in face-to-face conversations, Spanish speakers always use the proximal demonstrative to refer to an object in the shared space in between the speaker and the hearer. Everything outside this shared space is referred to by a distal demonstrative.

As mentioned above, Peeters et al. (2015) compared the traditional speaker-anchored account with the dyad-oriented account in face-to-face conversations in Dutch. First, a production study was carried out as a pretest, where participants looked at pictures showing the speaker and two objects. The speaker was always pointing at one of the objects (located either close or farther away from the speaker). Objects were sagittally or laterally oriented. The subjects had to adopt the speaker's perspective and provide a demonstrative + noun construct to identify the intended referent, the object to which the speaker was pointing. This method collected data about the linguistic intuitions of the participants. The results supported the traditional view, namely, participants used a proximal demonstrative to refer to the object placed close to the speaker, while a distal demonstrative was used to refer to the far object. These findings are in line with the experimental findings of Coventry et al. (2008) and Stevens and Zhang (2013).

The main experiment was a comprehension study, in which the participants looked at the same pictures; however, this time the addressee's position was also marked. Furthermore, the subjects had to adopt the addressee's perspective while listening to an audio stimulus that contained a demonstrative + noun construction. The EEG of the subjects was recorded. Three variables were manipulated:

(i) the location of the two objects (lateral or sagittal orientation);
(ii) relative distance from the speaker (near or far);
(iii) demonstrative (proximal or distal).

On the basis of the traditional account, both hearing a proximal term when the speaker is referring to the distal object located far from the speaker and hearing a distal term referring to an entity being close should result in higher processing costs. This prediction was not borne out. On the contrary, the findings indicate that it was the orientation of the objects that influenced the comprehension of the demonstratives, namely, lateral orientation induced similar ERPs for both demonstratives, while a more negative wave was found for distal demonstratives in the sagittal condition, and distance did not have an effect at all. Peeters et al. (2015) argue that these results support the dyad-oriented approach, i.e., distal demonstratives are less appropriate to refer to an object in shared space when the interlocutors are face-to-face, and that is why more processing effort was needed during the experiment.

In a second experiment, Peeters et al. (2015) slightly modified their design to explore whether shared space requires the speaker and the (implicit) addressee to be directly facing each other. Hence they aligned the position of the speaker and the addressee in the lateral orientations (thus the speaker was always directly facing the participant, who adopted the role of the addressee) and created a bigger distance in between the participants in the sagittal condition, so relative proximity to the speaker was to be perceived more clearly.

Other things being equal, the results reinforced the findings of the first experiment and offered new insights on the dyad-oriented account. More specifically, in the sagittal arrangement subjects did not show a preference to proximal demonstratives when the speaker was referring to the close object; instead, participants found the proximal demonstrative more appropriate to refer to objects in the shared space between the speaker and addressee, on the condition that no object is located outside this inner space. Once there is another object, when space is not shared (i.e. in the lateral arrangement), a different division of space is created; distal demonstratives are preferred, irrespective of the distance from the speaker.

Overall, the ERP results presented above contradict the predictions of the traditional approach, and, according to Peeters et al. (2015), the findings can be interpreted as favouring a sociocentric approach, which assumes that 'speakers actively take into account the location and bodily orientation of their addressee in interaction' (Peeters et al. 2015: 82). This means that demonstratives are not only anchored to the speaker, but to the addressee as well. To accommodate results obtained for both types of object orientation, it is suggested that demonstrative practice can be described in terms of psychological proximity of the referent, where entities within shared space are psychologically proximal, while objects outside of shared space are psychologically distal. Peeters and Özyürek (2016) also propose that the speaker and the hearer work together to establish which referents are psychologically proximal. This process is built on various contextual clues; for example, visibility or familiarity might increase it, while physical and social boundaries might decrease the psychological proximity of a referent.

The findings of Peeters et al. (2015) do indeed falsify the traditional approach based on relative distance from the speaker; however, only in the case of face-to-face interactions, where the objects are arranged in a sagittal way. Within the same setting, the findings strengthen the dyad-oriented approach, but it would be a challenge to extend this view to all types of arrangements of everyday communication including the speaker, the hearer and at least two potential referents. Nevertheless, it can be concluded that the results presented above pose a challenge for the traditional approach and call for a more refined and more flexible analysis of demonstrative practice, where it is not only the relative distance from the speaker which acts as a determining factor.

We have seen that although the traditional view has been challenged and possibly even refuted under certain circumstances by several experimental studies, spatial distinctions in general cannot be uniformly discarded, especially if one takes cross-linguistic variation into account.

2.4.3.2 Experimental work on Hungarian

2.4.3.2.1. Tóth et al.'s (2014) scripted dialogue study

As outlined in Chapter 1, Hungarian has a two-term demonstrative system; *ez*, *ezek* 'this, these' are associated with the traditional notion of being near the speaker, while *az*, *azok* 'that, those' describe the notion of being far from the speaker. Regarding the choice of demonstratives in Hungarian, Laczkó (2008) points out in a functional-cognitive framework that the traditional factor, physical proximity to the speaker, plays a crucial role. However, as discussed in Section 2.4.3.1, recent cross-linguistic linguistic research proposes that the choice between proximal and distal demonstratives is not so straightforward. Diessel (1999) also states that 'these labels [proximal/distal] are, however, only rough approximations. The meaning of a demonstrative is often more complex' (Diessel 1999: 160).

The use of Hungarian nominal demonstratives in an experimental framework was first explored by Tóth et al. (2014), who investigated three factors that might influence demonstrative choice. In neutral, i.e. non-contrastive contexts, the role of two factors – distance and accessibility – was explored. To investigate a novel but potential determinant, the use of demonstratives in contrastive and neutral contexts was also compared. As mentioned in Chapter 1, Levinson (2004) divides gestural uses of demonstratives into two subcategories, differentiating contrastive and non-contrastive cases. Tóth et al. (2014) extended the scope of contrastive and non-contrastive uses to linguistic contexts, where contrastiveness is explicitly marked, e.g. by using adversative conjunctions or a sentence containing an identificational focus (see É. Kiss 1998 on identificational focus in English and Hungarian). In accordance with the well-known semantic function of identificational focus and relying on Chafe's (1994) definition of contrastiveness, contrastiveness is characterised for the time being by two features:

(i) contrastiveness involves 'a selection of one candidate rather than another from an available set' (Chafe 1994: 77; see also Chafe 1976);

(ii) contrastiveness as a conversational phenomenon often exceeds turn boundaries.

Adopting Luz and van der Sluis's (2011) experimental design, Tóth et al. conducted a production study in the form of an online questionnaire, using the so-called scripted dialogue method developed by Luz and van der Sluis (2011). Participants read a scripted dialogue in a furniture shop setting between the shop assistant (female) and a buyer (male). Their task was to choose between different demonstrative expressions in a multiple-choice online test. By choosing a demonstrative form, they filled in gaps within the dialogue, while they were looking at the schematic representation of a furniture shop setting. They had to adopt the perspective of the current speaker, that of the buyer or the shop assistant. They were located next to each other in the picture, thereby sharing the visual perspective. The layout of the shop was visible throughout the experiment.

It was shown that in neutral contexts distance is indeed decisive, i.e., when referring to entities that were close to the speaker, participants preferred proximal demonstratives, while distal demonstratives were used to refer to entities far from the speaker. The other factor explored in Tóth et al.'s (2014) study in neutral contexts was accessibility, a factor that also questions the purely egocentric view of demonstratives, since it takes into account the addressee's perspective in the given speech situation. The working definition used in the experiment is given below (Tóth et al. 2014: 614):

(i) an entity is associated with low accessibility if, according to the speaker's assessment, the addressee is invited to consider it to be new or unexpected, i.e., an effort is required on the part of the addressee to identify the referent;
(ii) an entity is associated with high accessibility if it is already known to the addressee, i.e., it is in the focus of the joint attention of the speaker and the addressee.

The outcome of the experiment ruled out accessibility as an essential factor in neutral contexts both in Hungarian and Dutch. However, as the authors note, accessibility is not a well-defined notion and experimental findings on the role of accessibility are controversial. For example, while Piwek et al.'s (2008) aforementioned study concludes that accessibility is a crucial factor in Dutch, Tóth et al. (2014) found just the opposite. Regarding Piwek et al.'s (2008) work, Peeters et al. (2014) note that since the distance between the speaker and the entity being referred to was not operationalized clearly, it might be the case that physical proximity and accessibility (i.e. the notion of focus of attention) interacted somehow. Along the same lines, the working definition of accessibility in Tóth et al.'s (2014) study did not explicitly include the hearer's visual focus of attention, and the possible interaction between distance and accessibility was not investigated, either.

Regarding the type of the context, it was shown that in contrastive contexts the pattern of demonstratives is different from the one observed in neutral contexts;

distals were preferred when the referents were close to the speaker. In neutral contexts, the set of potential referents of demonstratives is relatively unlimited, and the choice of demonstratives depends on relative distance from the speaker. As opposed to that, in contrastive contexts, the set of possible referents is much more limited; in most cases there are only two entities that may be referred to, and these are competing to be highlighted. Tóth et al. (2014) concluded that there must be another factor that is responsible for the higher number of distal demonstratives chosen in contexts where distance is constant, i.e., close to the speaker.

2.4.3.2.2 Tóth and Csatár's (2016) experiment: demonstratives in identificational focus

Contrastive contexts were further investigated by Tóth and Csatár (2016), who compared the use of Hungarian demonstratives in neutral and contrastive contexts, the latter being represented by a special subtype of contrastive contexts marked by identificational focus. In an online rating task, participants evaluated the acceptability of a reply to a question in a physical context represented by a picture on a four-point Likert scale (forced choice method). To ensure the maximum reliability of the test, rich contexts were created (Meibauer 2012),[9] namely, the target utterance was always part of a mini dialogue, and it formed an answer to a *wh*-question.

The results provide converging evidence and thereby reinforce the idea that distance plays a crucial role in neutral contexts, i.e., proximals were preferred when the entities being referred to were close to the speaker. However, under the same circumstances, when the entities were close to the speaker, distals received significantly higher ratings when in focus position. Therefore, the findings support the theoretical claim that identificational focus forms a subtype of contrastive context, i.e., identificational focus is one of the linguistic devices that can explicitly mark contrastive contexts.

The findings of the experiments conducted by Tóth et al. (2014) and Tóth and Csatár (2016) regarding the use of Hungarian demonstratives can be briefly summarized as follows:

- the type of context (neutral vs. contrastive) is a major factor;
- in neutral contexts, relative distance from the speaker is a decisive factor;

9 Meibauer (2012) argues that in experiments the use of isolated sentences as stimulus is not satisfactory, i.e. when participants have to rate target items without contextual clues in an experimental setting, they are at a loss. Thus, due to the lack of contextual clues and being uncertain about what to do, participants extend the context evoked by the test material in unpredictable ways, thereby potentially distorting the results. To tackle this problem, the experiment presented here exploited rich contexts when target items were presented.

- in neutral contexts, (mental) accessibility is a weak factor at most;
- in contrastive contexts, distance as a factor cannot explain demonstrative choice;
- identificational focus is one of the linguistic devices that can explicitly mark contrastive contexts.

In short, demonstrative practice cannot be adequately described relying only on the traditional proximal/distal opposition in Hungarian, although physical proximity to the speaker influences demonstrative choice in neutral contexts. At this point of research, it can be concluded that the traditional characterization of demonstrative selection presents an oversimplified picture, and the use of demonstratives in Hungarian cannot be described adequately from a solely speaker-anchored perspective.

2.5 Summary

In this chapter the current state of the art of research on demonstrative usage was presented. First, the traditional account of demonstratives was summarized, then an overview of cognitively oriented theories of demonstrative choice was offered. Although these approaches differ from many perspectives, they do share the basic assumption that referring in general and demonstrative practice in particular can only be described as an interactive, dynamic, highly context-dependent, and hearer-oriented process. As we have seen, experimental results on various languages, including Hungarian, also support the same assumption, i.e. the traditional, distance-based and speaker-anchored account of demonstrative choice is not satisfactory in itself; demonstrative use is affected by more than a single factor and should be treated as a multi-faceted process.[10]

The next chapter offers a more detailed discussion of empirical work on Hungarian, summarizes the findings of a controlled dialogue game that investigated the various pragmatic uses of Hungarian nominal demonstratives and then presents the results of an experimental study aimed at exploring the role of different factors in the selection of Hungarian demonstratives.

10 Diessel and Coventry (2021) present an interdisciplinary overview of current research on deixis and argue that demonstrative reference has social and interactional functions.

CHAPTER 3

Empirical Studies on the Use of Hungarian Demonstratives[1]

3.1 Introduction

In this chapter, I will report the findings of my recent empirical research on the use of the Hungarian nominal demonstratives *ez/az*. The primary aim of the production study presented in Section 3.2 is twofold: (i) to collect samples of spontaneous language use to explore the use of exophoric Hungarian demonstratives in a controlled elicitation task; and (ii) to test the role of two factors, relative distance and accessibility, in the choice of Hungarian gestural demonstratives. Non-exophoric uses of demonstratives are also discussed, since spontaneous interactions provide a good opportunity to analyse demonstrative practice in context. Section 3.3 reports the results of an experiment motivated by Peeters et al.'s (2014) work on Dutch, exploring whether distance, visual joint attention and the presence or absence of a manual pointing gesture influence demonstrative practice in Hungarian. Section 4 contains a brief summary.

3.2 Hungarian demonstratives in interaction – Results of a controlled dialogue game

3.2.1 Methodology

This section presents the findings of a controlled-dialogue game aimed at collecting and examining spontaneous data on Hungarian nominal demonstratives. It has been mentioned in Chapter 1 that the exophoric use of demonstratives is

1 Parts of Chapter 3 have been published as Tóth (2018, 2020).

assumed to be more basic than other types of usages (discourse deictic, etc.),[2] so the work reported here focuses on the use of exophoric demonstratives in Hungarian. However, due to the nature of data collection, non-deictic uses of demonstratives are also represented in the material gathered and will be discussed briefly.

Taking as a starting point Piwek et al.'s (2008) work on Dutch, I collected samples of spontaneous language use via a game in a controlled setting to elicit as many instances of demonstrative occurrences as possible. More specifically, I video recorded conversations between two interlocutors working to reach a common goal in a so-called controlled dialogue game while manipulating LEGO DUPLO blocks in table-top space (Piwek et al. 2008). The recordings were later transcribed.

The recorded conversations revolve around and concentrate on the here and now of the task to be performed. Naturally, participants often refer to the LEGO blocks, to the entities that have a crucial role in achieving their goal. Thus, due to the nature of the task, a relatively high number of demonstrative expressions were elicited. A more detailed description of the game will be given in Section 3.2.3, but some examples taken from the corpus compiled from the task-oriented dialogues are given below.[3] A gestural use of *az* 'that' can be seen in (1), while a discourse deictic use of *ez* 'this' is illustrated by (2):

(1)	Instruktor:	És	most	szedd	le	róla	*azt*	*a*	*kis*
	instructor:	and	now	take.IMP.2SG	PRT	it.DEL	that.ACC	the	little
		kockát		(→).					
		block.ACC		(→)					
	Instructor:	'And now take down that little block (→).'							
	(video8)								

(2)	Instruktor:	[hosszabb utasítást ad]	*Ezt*	így	meg	lehet	csinálni?
	instructor:	[lengthy instruction]	this.ACC	like.this	PRT	possible	do.INF
	Instructor:	[lengthy instruction] 'Can you do this?'					
	(video1)						

The method outlined above has both advantages and disadvantages. First of all, by this type of elicitation method, it is possible to gather a relatively large number of occurrences of the target items quickly, especially compared to traditional observational methods. Although the transcription itself is tedious and time-consuming, one can always watch the corresponding video segment, so contextual clues are not lost. A tremendous benefit of this method over the observation of naturally

2 See for example Levinson (2004).

3 Throughout Section 3.2, '→' indicates a pointing gesture.

occurring speech is that situational variables can be controlled. As a disadvantage, it has to be mentioned that at the beginning of the recording some participants felt self-conscious or were shy, which clearly might have affected their behaviour. Nevertheless, their way of acting became less guarded and more natural as they engaged in solving the task. Overall, the results of the study are limited to a certain extent, since the setting is artificial and the findings cannot be generalized to demonstrative use per se, but the study is still built on data gained from natural communication.

3.2.2 Hypotheses

The analysis focuses on those occurrences of demonstratives that were accompanied by a manual pointing gesture on the part of the speaker; however, other uses of demonstratives will also be discussed to some extent. Following Piwek et al.'s (2008) work on Dutch, I examined two factors: relative distance and (mental) accessibility. Although the empirical setup was limited to table-top space, that is, all LEGO blocks were located relatively close to the participants, it was still possible to explore whether relative proximity of the entities to the speaker affects demonstrative choice. In this section, I introduce the factors under investigation.

The role of relative distance in the choice of gestural demonstratives has been widely studied; however, the exact nature of the notion itself has usually been left unspecified. Kemmerer (1999) presents neuropsychological evidence in favour of the claim that near and far have different perceptual representations, and the brain applies different mechanisms when representing near vs. far space. The distinction stems from the fundamental human need to manipulate objects directly and the need to visually identify and analyse objects in the environment.

Kemmerer (1999) argues that demonstrative systems across languages do not in general encode space in the same manner, since demonstratives 'specify abstract semantic notions that, when combined with the unique pragmatic features of communicative contexts, allow speakers to make a virtually unlimited range of spatial distance contrasts' (Kemmerer 1999: 35). Nevertheless, to operationalize the notion of relative distance in a closed setting, we will treat entities that are located physically within easy arm's reach, i.e., entities that can be touched without effort, as being close, while everything else will be considered to be far regarding the speaker's point of view. It should be noted here that due to the nature of the task, since the participants interacted in table-top space, most of the entities referred to were within easy arm's reach of the speaker.[4] The participants of the game were located next to each other, so their perspective was the same.

The corresponding hypothesis regarding the choice of demonstratives is given below:

Hypothesis 1
Proximal demonstratives are selected to refer to entities that are within easy arm's reach of the speaker, while distal demonstratives are selected to refer to entities that are further away in table-top space.

Turning to the second factor, we have seen in Chapter 2 that accessibility and cognitive status have been analysed by a number of authors (see, among others, Ariel 1990/2014, 2004; Gundel et al. 1993; Strauss 2002). For instance, Ariel (2004) describes accessibility in terms of topicality, distance and competition. She notes that 'mental entities corresponding to discourse topics are highly accessible. So are representations of entities recently mentioned (short distance) and ones that have no competing candidates. Entities that are not topical, that were mentioned a while ago, and that have to compete with other candidates [...] are entertained at a lower degree of accessibility' (Ariel 2004: 99–100). In a similar fashion, Kahneman (2003: 699) identifies accessibility with 'the ease [of mental effort] with which particular mental contents come to mind'. Regarding the use of exophoric demonstratives, Strauss (2002) emphasizes the role of the speaker's presumed knowledge about the addressee's ability to identify the referent and the speaker's assessment regarding the relative importance of the intended referent. She argues that the use of *this* in spoken American English involves a tacitly expressed instruction to the addressee that they should pay more attention to the intended referent, usually because it conveys new information, while the use of *that* indicates that the information carried is more familiar and less important for the hearer as judged by the speaker, therefore the identification of the referent is easier. As Jarbou (2010) points out, these different definitions of accessibility are not necessarily incompatible; in fact, they all describe a kind of verbal pointing, i.e., a common feature is that the speaker wants to draw the attention of the addressee to the intended referent.

Thus, relying on Strauss's (2002) and Ariel's (2004) work, accessibility as a working notion will be defined as follows:

- an entity is associated with *low accessibility* if, according to the speaker's assessment, the addressee is invited to consider it new, unexpected, or

4 Demonstrative reference in elicitation tasks is discussed in a detailed fashion by Wilkins (1999).

important, i.e., an effort is required on the part of the addressee to identify the referent;
- an entity is associated with *high accessibility* if it is already known to the addressee, i.e., less effort is necessary on the part of the addressee to identify the referent.

Accordingly, the second hypothesis to be tested is given below (see also Piwek et al. 2008):

Hypothesis 2

Proximal demonstratives are selected by speakers to refer to entities that are associated with low accessibility, while distal demonstratives are selected to refer to entities associated with high accessibility.

The hypotheses described above were tested only against the data collected on the exophoric use of demonstratives.

3.2.3 Design and participants

Ten pairs of university students participated in the experiment, all native speakers of Hungarian; their average age was 20.5. Subjects were randomly selected, there were 11 male and 9 female participants. They were asked to engage in a so-called controlled dialogue game (Piwek et al. 2008), where they worked with LEGO blocks of the DUPLO series in table-top space. Participants were asked to rebuild a construction, one of them acted as instructor, the other as builder. The two participants were separated by a screen, so that only the instructor had visual access to an example building, and with his help the builder had to rebuild a construction that was visible to both (see Figure 3.1).[5] Their common goal was to set up a building that is identical to the example. To avoid unnatural use of demonstratives, subjects were unaware of the aim of the study. The dialogue games were recorded on video and subsequently transcribed.

5 The instructor was not allowed to touch the LEGO blocks.

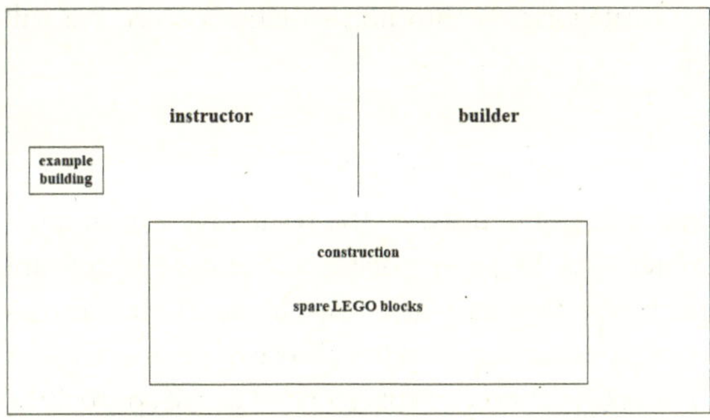

Figure 3.1: The layout of the game

3.2.4 Results and discussion

3.2.4.1 Overall results

Altogether, there were 727 demonstrative expressions in the dialogues obtained; of these 566 were exophoric and 161 were non-exophoric.[6] Exophoric uses were further categorized into gestural (where the speaker is pointing at the intended referent) and symbolic uses (there is no pointing gesture on the part of the speaker). Gestural uses also include cases where the speaker is holding the entity being referred to. The distribution of different exophoric uses over proximal and distal demonstratives is shown in Table 3.1.

Table 3.1: Distribution of exophoric demonstratives

Exophoric uses					
Gestural uses				**Symbolic uses**	
456				110	
ez		***az***		***ez***	***az***
350		106		26	84
holding	not holding	holding	not holding		
115	235	7	99		

6 The categorization of exophoric vs. non-exophoric, more specifically, the distinction between exophoric and anaphoric demonstratives was not always straightforward, since the boundaries between the categories are somewhat blurred (see Levinson 2004). I will discuss the criteria used to tell these categories apart when I turn to the discussion of non-exophoric demonstratives, in Section 3.2.4.5.

I also distinguished different categories within non-exophoric uses. We will turn to these in Section 3.2.4.5.

3.2.4.2 Gestural uses

Table 3.2 displays the distribution of gestural uses.[7] The results have been analysed by computing chi-square statistics. Regarding distance, there is a significant difference between entities located within easy arm's reach (near) and entities positioned further away from the speaker (far) and the choice of demonstratives (proximal vs. distal), hence the first hypothesis is kept ($\chi^2(1) = 112.865, p < 0.001$). The distribution of gestural demonstratives over distance is shown in Figure 3.2.

Thus distance matters, as it influences the choice of Hungarian gestural demonstratives in table-top space: in general, proximals were used when referring

Table 3.2: Distribution of gestural uses over the factors examined

Gestural uses			
456			
ez		***az***	
350		106	
near	**far**	**near**	**far**
316	34	45	61
HA	**LA**	**HA**	**LA**
175	175	46	60

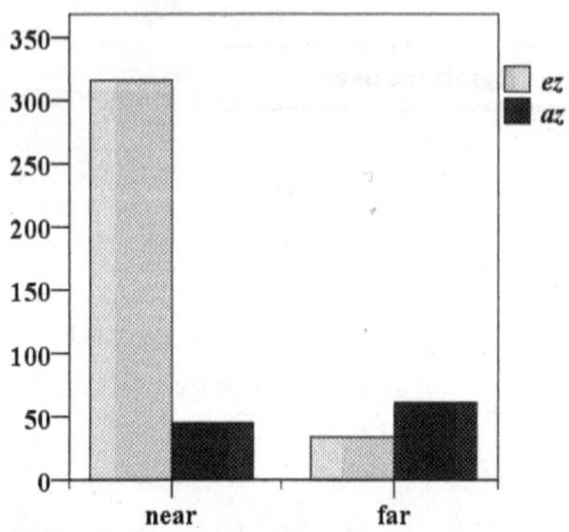

Figure 3.2: Distribution of gestural demonstratives over distance

7 HA stands for high accessibility, while LA stands for low accessibility.

to entities located within easy arm's reach of the speaker, while distals were preferred when referring to entities further away. Similar findings have been reported in a production experiment by Reile (2015) on the use of Estonian demonstrative adverbs.

As I have mentioned, due to the nature of the task, the majority of entities being referred to were located within easy arm's reach of the participants; this explains the high distribution of proximals, which constitute 76.7% of gestural uses.[8] Typically, when the builder was talking about a given part of the structure, or manipulating a block of LEGO, he used the proximal term. In fact, there are many cases where the builder is holding the entity in question; 33% of proximal gestural demonstratives refer to an entity that is being held by the speaker (see Table 3.1).

Kibrik (2011: 510) differentiates five subtypes of pointing as follows:

- out-of-arm-reach, distal pointing;
- within-arm-reach, proximal pointing;
- reaching;
- touching;
- holding, handling.

Kibrik (2011) describes this as a scale of continuum, where the borders between the categories are fluid, but argues that each of these gestures directs the attention of the addressee. The important point is that holding something is a special type of pointing, and since the entities in question are clearly close to the speaker, the use of the proximal form is expected. The other types of pointing from the scale above have all been exemplified in the recorded dialogues.

The use of distals to refer to entities out of arm's reach in this limited space is not unexpected, either. For example, Wilkins (2018) states that Arrernte speakers used distal demonstratives in an elicitation task when referring to the furthest object located on the away axis across a table within 0.7 meters.

Turning to the role of accessibility, there is no significant difference between high or low accessibility and the choice of demonstratives (proximal vs. distal), thus the second hypothesis is rejected ($\chi^2(1) = 1.421$, $p = 0.233$); the choice of proximals versus distals is not dependent upon the accessibility of the referent in Hungarian. As is evident from Table 3.2, speakers used the same number of proximal demonstratives to refer to highly and lowly accessible entities, and distals exhibit a very similar pattern. Results concerning accessibility are controversial in the relevant literature. For example, Piwek et al. (2008) accept the same hypothesis

8 The high proportion of proximals might also indicate that the speakers ignore distance in this close space, but still consider the location of objects relative to one another; the objects being manipulated are definitely closer to them with respect to others.

for Dutch in a similar controlled dialogue game setting, concluding that there is a correlation between low accessibility and gestural proximals and between high accessibility and distals. According to Jarbou (2010), the opposite can be observed in spoken Jordanian Arabic. Many authors note that the notion of accessibility is not well-defined (cf. Burenhult 2003; Hanks 2009). Therefore, further studies may be required that are based on a more exact notion of accessibility, at least in an empirical framework.

As an interim summary, we can conclude that relative distance from the speaker is a crucial factor. However, the results obtained from the data gathered in the controlled dialogue game have to be handled with caution, since all referents were located relatively close both to the instructor and to the builder in table-top space. Nevertheless, both proximal and distal demonstratives were used, and it is also clear from Figure 3.3 that speakers also used proximal demonstratives to refer to entities that were far from the speaker, while distals were also used to refer to entities that were within arm's reach. Some representative cases will be discussed in the next section. Clearly, such examples challenge the traditional view of demonstrative choice and give rise to the assumption that other factors can play a role besides (or instead of) relative distance from the speaker; or there might be an interaction of several factors that determines demonstrative use. Although accessibility as a factor has been discarded above, its role needs to be reconsidered, since it might interact with other factors. This assumption is also motivated by Peeters et al.'s (2014) claim that in Piwek et al.'s (2008) study on Dutch, physical proximity and accessibility (i.e., the notion of focus of attention) must have interacted.

3.2.4.3. The role of distance

In what follows, I will take a closer look at examples in which the traditional near/far opposition cannot adequately explain the use of demonstratives in Hungarian. In each case, I will examine the various contextual factors that might play a role.

First, let us consider an example where a proximal term is used to refer to an entity that is far from both participants:

(3) Instruktor: Utána jön egy ugyanakkora kék, utána pedig *ez*
instructor: after come.3SG one same.size blue after in.turn this
a zöldes kékes (→).
the greenish bluish (→)
Instructor: 'Then comes a blue one, same size, then this bluish-greenish one (→).'
(video6)

The instructor is referring to a block that is located among the spare blocks they can use, out of arm's reach. However, the one he is pointing at is closer to him and to the addressee than the other block of the same kind. Thus there are two blocks of the same kind, which have the same characteristic features in terms of size, shape, colour, etc.; both are located relatively far (out of arm's reach) from the speaker and the addressee, and the speaker is pointing at the one closer to him. In doing so, he evokes a contrast between the two blocks, and by relativizing distance, he successfully guides the attention of the addressee to the intended referent, namely, the addressee can identify the referent. As Kemmerer argues, 'demonstratives do not encode metrically precise degrees of remoteness from the deictic centre, but rather have abstract meanings that are pragmatically modulated by either the discourse context or the referential scenario, thereby allowing speakers to flexibly expand or contract the concentric zones so as to express a potentially unlimited range of distance contrasts' (Kemmerer 2006: 1608). From another perspective, it can also be assumed that the instructor wants to direct the attention of the builder to an entity that is important in Strauss's (2002) framework; consequently, accessibility might overwrite distance.

The next example shows that a distal demonstrative might be used to refer to an entity that is close to the interlocutors. In the example below, the instructor refers to a given part of the construction that is within reach of the participants:

(4)	Instruktor:	Megfordítod	egy	picit,	hogy	*az*	(→)	felém
	instructor:	PRT.turn.2SG	a	little.ACC	COMP	that	(→)	toward.me
		legyen?						
		COP.IMP.3SG						
	Instructor:	'Will you turn it a little, turn that (→) toward me.'						
	(video5)							

In (4), the speaker refers to a particular side of the construction. At the time of speaking, this side is further away than the one facing him, and clearly there is an inherent contrast between the two sides. It has been shown by Tóth et al. (2014) that in contrastive contexts, the distal demonstrative can be used to refer to an entity that is close to the speaker. Thus the contrast evoked here, i.e., the fact that the builder would like to look at that side of the building, not this one, might trigger the use of the distal demonstrative. As an alternative explanation, it could also be argued that the intended referent, the other side, is not visible at the time of speaking. Perceptibility or visibility have been considered as potential factors by Jarbou (2010) and Coventry et al. (2008).

Similarly, the block being referred to is located at the far side of the construction, but still within arm's reach of the speaker in (5). In addition, since the speaker cannot adequately describe the object and uses a 'whatdoyoucallit' expression to refer to it, it might be argued that there is a kind of mental distance between the speaker and the entity:

<table>
<tr><td>(5)</td><td>Instruktor:</td><td>Elcsúszott</td><td>az</td><td>az</td><td>izé</td><td>(→).</td></tr>
<tr><td></td><td>instructor:</td><td>PRT.slipped</td><td>that</td><td>the</td><td>whatever.it.is</td><td>(→)</td></tr>
<tr><td></td><td>Instructor:</td><td colspan="5">'That what-is-it (→) has slipped away.'</td></tr>
<tr><td></td><td colspan="6">(video1)</td></tr>
</table>

The speaker can also create a contrast explicitly, when referring to entities that are located at the same distance, but to distinguish them and to refer to them one by one, the speaker opts for a proximal and a distal term, respectively. In the following example, the entities referred to are within arm's reach of the participants.

<table>
<tr><td>(6)</td><td>Instructor:</td><td>Úgy</td><td>kéne</td><td>állnia,</td><td>hogy</td><td>ez</td><td>(→)</td><td>így</td></tr>
<tr><td></td><td>instructor:</td><td>like.that</td><td>should</td><td>stand.
INF.3SG</td><td>COMP</td><td>this</td><td>(→)</td><td>like.this</td></tr>
<tr><td></td><td></td><td>összeérjen</td><td>azzal</td><td>(→).</td><td></td><td></td><td></td><td></td></tr>
<tr><td></td><td></td><td>PRT.reach.SUBJ.3SG</td><td>that.COM</td><td>(→)</td><td></td><td></td><td></td><td></td></tr>
<tr><td></td><td>Instructor:</td><td colspan="7">'It should be positioned in a way that this (→) adjoins that (→).'</td></tr>
<tr><td></td><td colspan="8">(video1)</td></tr>
</table>

We will return to the notion of contrastiveness in Chapter 4.

A remarkable type of demonstrative use is when the speaker is holding the entity being referred to, but selects a distal demonstrative. The examples in question are peculiar, because they sometimes represent borderline cases between spatial reference and anaphora, as in (7). However, if we consider holding as a subtype of pointing, then the cases in question are to be labelled as exophoric uses. There were seven such examples in the recorded conversations. A closer look at these discourse segments reveals that in each case the speaker is the builder and he is repeating an instruction issued by the instructor. In six of the examples this is almost a word-by-word repetition, and in the remaining one it is a reflection on the instruction, where the builder makes sure that he has managed to find the right block. Two relevant examples are given below:

(7) Instruktor: És *azt* (→) tedd át.
instructor: and that.ACC (→) put.IMP.2SG over
Instructor: 'And put that one (→) there.'
Építő: És *azt* (fogja) tegyem át.
builder: and that.ACC (hold.3SG) put.IMP.1SG over
Builder: 'And I will put that one (holding) there.'
(video4)

(8) Instruktor: Alul a kéket, tehát alul.
instructor: below the blue.ACC so below
Instructor: 'The blue one below, I say, below'
Építő: Ja, *azt az alsó kéket* (fogja) cserélem ki
builder: ah that.ACC the lower blue.ACC (hold.3SG) change.1SG PRT
egy kicsi pirosra.
a small red.SUBL
Builder: 'Ah, I exchange that blue one below (holding) for a small red one.'
(video5)

In the following fragment, the builder again wants to check whether he has understood which entity was meant by the instructor, but this is achieved by using the proximal demonstrative. The object in question is at the same distance from the interlocutors, but the builder is holding it. This is crucial, since Coventry et al. (2008) argue that it matters who is performing the action; namely, they found that English speakers used *this* more often when they themselves were manipulating a given object in an experimental setting.

(9) Építő: Mennyire szedjem le?
builder: how.much.SUBL remove.IMP.1SG PRT
Builder: 'How far do I have to remove it?'
Instruktor: Hát, csak *azt a tetejét.*
instructor: well just that.ACC the roof.POSS.3SG.ACC
Instructor: 'Well, only that roof of it.'
Builder: *Ezt* (fogja)?
this.ACC (hold.3SG)
'This one (holding)?'
(video5)

Interestingly, there are also cases where the speaker himself uses both demonstratives within the same utterance to refer to the same object. It is clear that distance as a factor cannot explain this phenomenon. When analysing the examples below, it is important to know what the speaker is doing at the time of speaking. In that way, the selection of demonstratives can be analysed as a dynamic process. As a starting point, let us consider the following example:

(10) Instruktor: Vedd le a pirosat, mert az itt volt.
instructor: take.IMP.2SG PRT the red.ACC because that here COP.PST.3SG
Instructor: 'Take down the red one, because that one was here.'
Építő: Melyik pirosat, ezt (→)?
builder: which red.ACC this.ACC (→)
Builder: 'Which red one do you mean, this one (→)?
Instruktor: Nem, *azt* (→) ott, *ezt*.
instructor: no that.ACC (→) there this.ACC
Instructor: 'No, not *that one* (→) there, *this one* (→).'
Építő: Ezt a pirosat (→)? De alatta van.
builder: this.ACC the red.ACC (→) but below COP.3SG
Builder: 'This red one (→)? But it is below another one.'
(video8)

It is important to point out that this is not a contrastive example; the intonation and the use of gestures make it clear that the speaker is referring to the same block of LEGO. Jarbou (2010), who observed the use of demonstratives in Jordanian Arabic in spontaneous interactions, argues that in such cases either the perspective of the speaker has changed, or the hearer's attitude towards the referent has been modified. In the example above, the former explanation seems to be more plausible, since the speaker leaned closer to the object in question while producing the utterance. The last utterance by the builder confirms that she managed to identify the intended referent.

The next example illustrates the second option, when, according to the speaker's assessment, the hearer's attitude toward the referent changes. In (11) below, the speaker tries to clarify which block he is referring to. The demonstrative choice by the speaker reflects how he perceives the addressee's ability to recognize the intended referent: the use of the proximal term might indicate, in accordance with the accessibility hypothesis, that the speaker considers the referent to be lowly accessible; therefore, considerable effort is required on the part of the addressee. For that reason, the speaker is trying to guide the addressee in the process of finding the referent, and while doing so, he adopts the hearer's perspective. This is the reason he switches from the proximal form to the distal term (accompanied by a pointing gesture) when he adds further information about the intended referent:

(11) Instruktor: *Ezt* *a* *pirosat* (→) onnan vedd le,
instructor this.ACC the red.ACC (→) from.there take.IMP.2SG PRT
azt *a* *kis* *picit* (→) csak.
that.ACC the little tiny.ACC (→) only
Instructor: 'Take this red one (→) from there, only that little one (→).'
(video6)

3.2.4.4 The role of pointing

The discussion so far has been restricted to gestural demonstratives. However, when we consider exophoric uses in general, a remarkable pattern emerges. By performing the same quantitative test for the relevant data, we find that proximals are often used with an accompanying pointing gesture, while distals occur almost as often with or without a pointing gesture ($\chi^2(1) = 112.129$, $p < 0.001$), as shown in Figure 3.3. The distribution of proximals over gestural and symbolic uses is 93% vs. 7%, while that of distals is 56% vs. 44%. As we will see later on, in another production study (see Section 3.3), participants selected proximal demonstratives significantly more often in the presence of a manual pointing gesture than distals, hence the pattern observed here will be reinforced.

It can also be observed in Figure 3.3 that symbolic uses were more often realized with distal forms; in fact, there were three times as many distal demonstratives as proximals. A similar link has been found in the study by Piwek et al. (2008) on the use of Dutch nominal demonstratives.

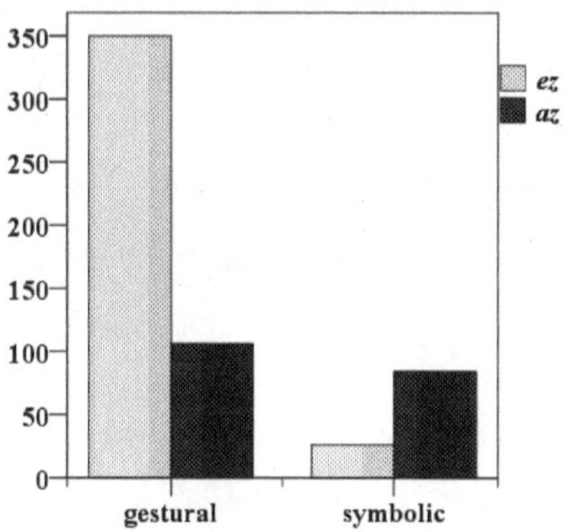

Figure 3.3: Gestural vs. symbolic uses

Table 3.3: Distribution of non-exophoric demonstratives

Non-exophoric uses							
Discourse deictic uses		**Anaphoric uses**		**Resumptive pronouns**		**Other**	
47		71		20		23	
ez	***az***	***ez***	***az***	***ez***	***az***	***ez***	***az***
35	12	15	56	2	18	3	20

3.2.4.5 Non-exophoric uses

Let us now turn to a more detailed analysis of non-exophoric uses. Although these do not form the primary focus of the present work, it is worth studying these examples as well. The frequency of different subtypes is shown in Table 3.3.[9]

Discourse deictic cases identified in the corpus usually refer to an utterance describing an instruction or an action. For instance, in (12), the instructor repeats the instruction they received at the beginning of the game and the builder refers back to it, while in (13), the distal demonstrative refers to an action described in the previous utterance:

(12) Instruktor: nem lehet lebontani az egészet
instructor: no possible take.apart.INF the whole.ACC
Instructor: 'we cannot take the whole apart'
Építő: egyébként éppen *az* lett volna a lényeg
builder: otherwise just that COP.COND.PST.3SG the point
Builder: 'but that would have been the point'
(video12)

(13) Építő: Megnézheted közelebbről is.
builder: PRT.look.POSSIB.2SG closer.DEL too
Builder: 'You can have a closer look.'
Instruktor: Jó, *azt* akarom.
instructor: all right that.ACC want.1SG
Instructor: 'OK, that's what I want.'
(video5)

9 Discourse deictic and anaphoric uses, and the category of resumptive pronouns have been introduced in Chapter 1. The label 'other' includes demonstratives serving as clause associates of subordinate clauses (Szűcs 2015) or as heads of nominal relative clauses (Kenesei 1994).

As mentioned before, it has been pointed out by various authors that there is a fuzzy boundary between exophoric and non-exophoric uses of demonstratives, especially in the case of exophoric and anaphoric reference (see Lyons 1977; Levinson 2004; Laczkó 2008, 2010 on Hungarian). When I categorized the individual occurrences of demonstratives, those cases were labelled as anaphoric in which the demonstrative has an antecedent, and the anaphor serves to maintain an established attention on the referent. Therefore, the occurrences of *az* in (14) and (15) are treated as anaphoric, as the referent of the pronoun is identified via the linguistic context.

(14) Instruktor: Vedd le a pirosat, mert *az* itt volt.
instructor: take.IMP.2SG PRT the red.ACC because that here COP.PAST.3SG
Instructor: 'Take down the red one, because that was here.'
(video8)

(15) Instruktor: Alulról a legalsó fehéret.
instructor: below.DEL the lowest white.ACC
Instruktor: 'From below, the lowest white one.'
Építő: *Azt* vegyem le?
builder: that.ACC remove.IMP.1SG PRT
Builder: 'Shall I take that?'
(video5)

As opposed to that, exophoric reference, especially when there is a pointing gesture on the part of the speaker, is aimed at directing the attention of the addressee to the intended referent. In the example below, gestural reference serves as the antecedent of the distal demonstrative, and hence, spatial deictic reference overlaps with anaphoric reference:

(16) Építő És ez az oldal (→), a másik oldallal szemben?
builder: and this the side (→) the other side.COM opposite
Builder: 'And this side (→), opposite the other one?'
Instruktor: Megnézem *azt* is, stimmel.
instructor: PRT.look.1SG that.ACC too it.is.all right
Instructor: 'I'll have a look at that, it seems right.'
(video2)

In (17), one anaphor is followed by another one, i.e., the antecedent of the first anaphor *arra* 'onto that' is the phrase *egy pirosat* 'a red block.ACC', and then three similar anaphors follow in an elliptical construction:

(17)	Instruktor:	Ezt	a	zöldet	(→)	innen	a	sarokról
	instructor:	this.ACC	the	green.ACC	(→)	from.here	the	corner.DEL
		vedd	le	és	tegyél	helyette	egy	pirosat.
		take.IMP.2SG	PRT	and	put.IMP.2SG	instead	a	red.ACC
		Arra	egy	kéket.	*Arra*	egy	sárgát,	és
		that.SUBL	a	blue.ACC	that.SUBL	a	yellow.ACC	and
		arra	egy	zöldet.				
		that.SUBL	a	green.ACC				

Instructor: 'Take this green one (→) from the corner here and replace it with a red one. Put a blue block on it, then a yellow and finally a green.'
(video2)

In the fragment below, after the anaphoric use of *az*, we find another non-exophoric use; the last utterance by the builder contains a topic-repeating anaphoric resumptive pronoun.

(18)	Instruktor:	Átlátszó	kék,	ami	ott	van	belül.
	instructor:	transparent	blue	that	there	COP.3SG	inside

Instructor: 'The transparent blue that is inside.'

Építő:	*Az*	itt	van	bent,	igen.
builder:	that	here	COP.3SG	inside	yes

Builder: 'That one is inside here, right.'

Instruktor:	Utána	van	egy	sötétkék.
instructor:	after	COP.3SG	a	dark.blue

Instructor: 'Behind that one there is a dark blue one.'

Builder:	Igen,	a	sötétkék	*az*	itt	van.
builder:	yes	the	dark.blue	that	here	COP.3SG

Builder: 'Right, the dark blue, it is here.'
(video4)

In fact, altogether there were 20 occurrences of resumptive pronouns in the corpus. As the example below shows, resumptive pronouns share number and case features with their antecedent.

(19)	Instruktor:	Meg	a	zöldet	*azt*	tedd	vissza.
	instructor:	and	the	green.ACC	that.ACC	put.IMP.2SG	PRT

Instructor: 'And the green one, put it back.'
(video8)

A special use of resumptive pronouns is when there is an intervening clause in between the pronoun and its antecedent; in such cases, the pronoun makes it easier for the addressee to follow the flow of the conversation. This usage is illustrated below:

(20) Építő: Ez a rész, ami itt nekem ilyen különálló, *az*
builder: this the part that here for.me like.this separate that
ott is ilyen különálló?
there too like.this separate
Builder: 'This part that stands alone here on its own, is that on its own there, too?'
(video1)

Especially interesting are those two examples from the corpus where the resumptive pronoun is proximal. According to Szalamin (1988), the proximal demonstrative can function as a topic-repeating resumptive pronoun when the topic itself contains a proximal demonstrative:

(21) Instructor: Ez a kiálló *ez* alul piros.
instructor: this the jutted this below red
Instructor: 'This jutted part, its underside is red.'
(video1)

(22) Instruktor: Ezt a részt (→) *ezt* itt bontsd le.
instructor: this.ACC the part.ACC (→) this.ACC here take.IMP.2SG PRT
Instructor: 'This part (→), take this here apart.'
(video6)

Finally, I will briefly mention two other uses of nominal demonstratives, when they either serve as clause associates of subordinate clauses (Szűcs 2015) or when they occur as heads of nominal relative clauses (Kenesei 1994). In the former case, the pronouns might be subjects, objects, or oblique complements regarding their grammatical function. Associate pronouns are usually realized by the distal demonstrative, but occasionally the proximal demonstrative can also occur as an associate (see Szűcs 2015). In the corpus, only distal demonstratives occurred as clause associates, in 12 examples; two of these are given below.

(23) Instruktor: *Az* a lényeg, hogy van alul, a második
instructor: that the point COMP COP.3SG below the second
szinten egy piros.
level.SUP a red
Instructor: 'The point is that there is at the bottom, on the second level, a red one.'
(video4)

(24) Építő: Ja, *azt* hittem, hogy ezeket fel fogjuk használni.
builder: oh that.ACC believed.1SG COMP these.ACC PRT FUT.1PL use.INF
Builder: 'Oh, I thought that we were going to use these.'
(video3)

The last two examples illustrate relative clauses. Eight distal (adnominal: 3, pronominal: 5) and three proximal demonstratives (adnominal: 1, pronominal: 2) headed relative clauses.

(25) Instruktor: *Ezt,* ami itt elöl van, tedd a másik oldalára.
instructor: this.ACC that here in.front COP.3SG put.IMP.2SG the other side.POSS.3SG.SUBL
Instructor: 'Put the one that is here in the front, to its other side.'
(video8)

(26) Instruktor: … *azon a kockán,* amit a harmadik szintre raktunk
instructor: that.SUP the block.SUP that.ACC the third level.SUBL put.PST.1PL
Instructor: 'on the block that we placed on the third level'
(video4)

3.2.4.6 Individual variation

Ten pairs participated in the experiment, and they followed quite different strategies while performing the task in the controlled dialogue game. As a result, some of them completed the task very quickly, but there were also some lengthy conversations. The number of demonstratives used in individual conversations and the duration of the dialogues are shown in Table 3.4.

In general, as expected, the majority of pairs used a large number of demonstratives, due to the nature of the assignment. However, there was one exception to this general tendency: a pair of two men (video7) worked very efficiently; they completed the task in the least amount of time, and, surprisingly, did not use gestural demonstratives at all. Taking a closer look at the conversation in question, it is revealed that the instructor used quite a lot of definite descriptions, and the builder often pointed at the spare block that he managed to identify based on the information carried by the description, but, contrary to expectations, he did not use a demonstrative to make sure that he picked the right one, as others often did;

Table 3.4: List of the video recordings

			Number of demonstratives used			
Video	**Participants**	**Duration**	**gestural**	**symbolic**	**non-exophoric**	**Total**
1	2 women	14:10	53	15	31	99
2	2 men	9:10	24	5	20	49
3	2 men	10:50	54	8	16	78
4	1 woman, 1 man	14:16	35	19	25	79
5	2 women	15:45	36	16	19	71
6	2 men	19:00	98	15	20	133
7	2 men	5:20	0	1	3	4
8	2 women	20:50	117	9	11	137
9	2 women	7:32	27	8	9	44
10	2 men	6:23	12	14	7	33
Total			456	110	161	727

instead, the instructor often reacted to the pointing gesture using *Így van* 'That's right' to confirm that the builder had succeeded in identifying the referent of the definite description. The utterance used by the instructor contains not a nominal, but an adverbial demonstrative (*így* 'like this'). Analysing adverbial demonstratives lies beyond the scope of the present work. Nevertheless, the following utterance illustrates this type of usage and involves a case of anaphoric reference, too:

(27) Instruktor: A hozzám közelebb lévő legfelső piros,
instructor: the I.ALL closer being uppermost red
(az építő rámutat), így van, *azt*
(the builder points.at.it) like.this COP.3SG that.ACC
vedd le.
take.IMP.2SG PRT
Instructor: 'Take the uppermost one that is nearer to me (the builder is pointing at it), that's right, take that.
(video7)

Regarding the choice between a demonstrative pronominal and a definite description, it can be assumed that the use of a gestural distal pronominal helps to direct the attention of the addressee to the referent in a direct manner; in other words, gestural pronominals signal that the referent is easily identifiable from the set of potential candidates. In contrast to that, processing a definite description might require more effort on the part of the addressee. Nevertheless, the participants in video 7 followed the seemingly more complex strategy and it worked very efficiently.[10]

This assumption is supported by the fact that if we compare the proportions of demonstrative adnominals and pronominals within gestural demonstratives, then it turns out that pronominals were used more frequently, hence the descriptive content of the NP was usually deemed to be superfluous, and the speaker expected the hearer to be able to identify the intended referent with the help of the pointing gesture alone.

Table 3.4 also shows that speakers usually produced more gestural demonstratives than symbolic ones in general, which is not surprising considering the specific demands of the task. This difference is especially remarkable in the case of pair 8 (two women), who produced the highest number of gesturals, 117, while only nine symbolic demonstratives were used. The high number of demonstratives was matched by the length of the dialogue, and similar proportions were detected in the second longest dialogue, 98 and 15, respectively, produced by pair 6 (two men). However, in the latter case there was a misunderstanding regarding the instructions; the members of this pair decided to remove all parts of the construction and then had to restart the task when they were warned that they were not allowed to do that.

Turning to the use of non-exophoric pronouns, we find another interesting difference among the pairs. Namely, some of them did not use topic-repeating pronouns at all; there were three such pairs altogether. However, most pairs produced one or two such pronouns, while the highest number, six, was produced by two women (pair 1). Although the data collected here is not enough to draw any conclusions in terms of individual variation, the data might imply that there are speakers who do not use resumptive pronouns.

3.2.5 Conclusion

The study presented here used data gained from natural conversations that were video recorded in a controlled dialogue game setting where two interlocutors worked to reach a common goal. A detailed quantitative analysis of demonstrative occurrences revealed that the choice between proximal and distal gestural demonstratives in Hungarian is influenced by relative distance from the speaker, i.e., proximals were used when referring to entities located within easy arm's reach of the speaker, while distals were preferred when referring to entities further away. As opposed to that, accessibility, which was defined in terms of the processing

10 For an extensive analysis of different referring expressions in a relevance theoretical framework I refer the reader to Scott (2013, 2020).

effort required on the part of the addressee in identifying the intended referent, was not a decisive factor.

A follow-up qualitative analysis showed that relative distance on its own cannot always explain the selection of demonstratives, hence the use of demonstratives can only be described as a dynamic process affected by the interaction of separate factors. These factors include perceptibility, visibility, pointing, manipulation and change of perspective or attitude. The results obtained in this preliminary study show that further studies based on different methodologies are called for to understand the subtleties of Hungarian demonstrative practice. Finally, since non-exophoric uses of demonstratives were also attested, such uses were also briefly discussed to provide a more complete picture of Hungarian demonstrative use.

3.3 Demonstratives and joint attention – Results of an online production study

3.3.1 Introduction

The results of the controlled-dialogue game described in the previous section indicate that relative distance from the speaker influences the choice of Hungarian demonstratives, while accessibility is not a decisive factor. Notwithstanding this, the qualitative analysis of demonstrative use emphasised the role of pointing, and called attention to the fact that demonstrative practice can be accounted for only when, besides relative distance, other factors are considered. As we have seen, participants in the controlled-dialogue game worked in a table-top space and shared the same perspective. To re-evaluate the results and to broaden the scope of investigation, I carried out an experiment, an online production task.

As mentioned before, from a pragmatic perspective it was first assumed that the choice of demonstratives in two-term systems (proximal vs. distal) is determined by relative distance from the speaker. It was also pointed out in Chapter 2 that recently this traditional view has been challenged by a number of studies, including various empirical studies (see, for example, Piwek et al. 2008; Enfield 2009; Jarbou 2010; Stevens & Zhang 2013; Peeters et al. 2014). Most of these studies emphasize that a crucial feature of the use of deictic expressions is to help the addressee in identifying the location of the referent in the speaker and hearer's joint focus of attention (see also Clark 1996; Diessel 2012). However, it is important to note that there are also experiments which, at least partially, support the physical proximity view.[11] In the studies in question, as will be discussed below, it

11 See Chapter 2, Section 2.4.2.

is argued that while relative distance from the speaker is indeed crucial, there are either other factors to be considered or there is an interaction between various factors. Hence, relative distance from the speaker is treated as one of the decisive factors. For instance, Coventry et al. (2014) state that while there is a mapping between peripersonal vs. extrapersonal place and the selection of demonstratives in English, other factors, such as ownership, visibility and familiarity, are also important, and they conclude that 'demonstrative choice in English is affected by more than a single parameter' (Coventry et al. 2014: 63). In a similar fashion, Stevens and Zhang (2013) showed that many people have strong intuitions about distance being an important factor in the selection of demonstratives. At the same time, they also found in an event-related potential study that the traditional speaker-anchored view of English spatial demonstratives is too simple and emphasized the significance of shared gaze between the speaker and the hearer. More specifically, they proved that when the hearer was clearly not looking at the intended referent, i.e. when the interlocutors did not have a shared focus of attention, the use of demonstratives was intended to manipulate the addressee's focus and thus establish a joint focus of attention.

Peeters et al. (2014) explored how speakers refer to given entities in their immediate physical environment in Dutch. They used a so-called controlled elicitation task, where participants saw different visual stimuli that elicited the production of referring expressions: demonstratives or NPs with (in)definite articles. Three variables were tested in their study:

- joint attention between the interlocutors to an intended referent in line with the previous experimental work described above;
- physical proximity;
- the presence or absence of a pointing gesture.

The most important finding of Peeters et al. (2014) is that establishing joint attention may be an important factor in the selection of Dutch demonstratives, since participants more often used distal demonstratives when the entity being referred to was in the interlocutors' joint focus of attention. This implies that the speaker takes into account the addressee's visual attention when selecting a distal demonstrative term, while the use of proximal demonstratives was not affected by the presence or absence of joint visual attention. It is interesting to note here that Jarbou's (2010) observational study on Jordanian Arabic found just the opposite, i.e., Jordanian Arabic speakers used proximal demonstratives when the speaker believed that the referent had high perceptibility as perceived by the hearer. Regarding distance, Peeters et al. (2014) found that participants opted for the proximal demonstrative when the entity being referred to was close to the speaker, whereas the distal term was preferred when the referent was located close to the addressee, at middle distance from both interlocutors, or relatively far from the speaker and addressee. The third factor, the presence of a pointing gesture by the speaker, influenced the use of both demonstrative terms, i.e., both demonstratives were produced more often when there was an accompanying pointing gesture. The authors argue that the function of a pointing gesture therefore may be to demarcate the search space for the addressee. Moreover, they also emphasize the importance of testing the effect of more than one factor within the same experimental setting, since the selection of demonstratives might be the result of a subtle interplay between various contextual factors.

This section reports the results of an experiment that was motivated by the work of Peeters et al. (2014) on Dutch. I adopted and somewhat simplified the method used by Peeters et al. (2014) to examine whether distance, joint attention, and the presence or absence of a manual pointing gesture influence the selection of demonstratives in Hungarian and to detect possible interactions of these factors.

3.3.2 Hypotheses

Regarding the choice of demonstratives in Hungarian, Laczkó (2008) points out in a functional-cognitive framework that the traditional factor, physical proximity to the speaker, plays a crucial role. This theoretical assumption was supported by the results of the experiments presented briefly in Section 2.4.3.2, which proved that in neutral contexts distance is indeed decisive. However, findings of the same experiments (Tóth et al. 2014, Tóth & Csatár 2016) show that in Hungarian contrastive contexts, distance as an independent factor is outperformed by one or more competing factors, and distance alone cannot explain the choice of demonstratives. Therefore, it is important not only to reinforce the role of relative distance, but to explore the possible interaction of distance and other potential factors. Hence, the study reported here will again try to pin down what kind of influence relative distance from the speaker has on the selection of demonstrative terms.

The second factor to be examined is that of joint attention. As introduced in Chapter 2, joint attention is 'the coordination of orienting between two people toward an object' (Shaw et al. 2017: 268), more precisely 'people have a joint focus of attention if they are attending to the same object and are mutually aware of it' (Bangerter 2004: 415). It is important to emphasize here that it is not enough for both participants of the speech event to direct their attention to the intended referent; in addition, both participants must monitor the other's attention and make sure that it is also directed to the same referent, therefore, joint attention is established only when there is mutual attention to the intended referent and there is mutual understanding of the other's focus of attention. Joint attention is represented in Figure 2.1 in Chapter 2.

As described above, in face-to-face conversations, the speaker's choice of the demonstrative term might be influenced by whether, at the moment of production, the referent is already in the focus of the speaker and hearer's joint attention, or joint attention is still to be created. It is important to emphasize here that situations in which the speaker and the hearer are face to face are more complex and require more processing effort on the part of the participants than those in which the speaker and the hearer are located side by side and share the same perspective of their physical surroundings (for more details on how this affects the creation of joint attention see Laczkó 2008; Laczkó & Tátrai 2012). The different positioning of the interlocutors also influences how relative distance is perceived by the speaker and the hearer. The study reported above explored the simpler setting; therefore, it is crucial to examine the role of distance and its interaction with the presence or absence of joint visual attention in the more complex scenario.

The third factor corresponds to the use of manual pointing gestures. It is widely acknowledged that the use of a demonstrative term in an act of referring is typically accompanied by a pointing gesture (gestural use). However, as Peeters et al. (2014) point out, Piwek et al. (2008) reported that Dutch participants in a controlled dialogue game always used a pointing gesture with proximal demonstratives, but the use of distal demonstratives was not always accompanied by a manual pointing gesture. Regarding Hungarian, in the experiments described briefly in Section 2.4.3.2 (Tóth et al. 2014; Tóth & Csatár 2016), the speaker always made a pointing gesture, which means that the role of pointing and its interaction with other factors in the selection of Hungarian demonstrative terms have not been explored before in an experimental setting.

3.3.3 Materials and methods

The production study reported here is based on the design employed by Peeters et al. (2014). Participants had to look at visual scenes depicting a face-to-face conversational setting between a speaker and a hearer, and there was also an intended referent (that is, an object) present in each setting. In the photos, a speech balloon next to the speaker introduced the target item, and participants had to imagine what they would say in the given situation if they were the speaker. The target items were Hungarian utterances including a gap, for example, *Tegnap vettem … a virágot* 'I bought … [the] flower yesterday',[12] and participants had to select the more appropriate demonstrative term (*ezt* 'this.ACC' or *azt* 'that.ACC') in a multiple choice online test. Figure 3.4 shows an example of a visual scene.

12 As mentioned in Section 1.3.1, the definite article is inserted between the demonstrative and the head noun in Hungarian.

Figure 3.4: A visual scene from the online questionnaire

The target items contained the verbs *vesz* 'buy', *talál* 'find', *süt* 'bake', *köt* 'knit', and the objects being referred to were the following: an orange, a potted flower, a piece of cake, a milk loaf, a wallet, a bunch of keys, a doll and an item of a doll's clothing. There were altogether 32 target utterances, such as *Tegnap sütöttem ... a süteményt* 'I baked ... [the] cake yesterday', *Tegnap találtam ... a kulcscsomót* 'I found ... [the] keyring yesterday', *Tegnap kötöttem ... a babaruhát* 'I knitted ... [the] doll's dress yesterday'. The questionnaire also contained 16 fillers: *Tegnap hímeztem ... terítőt* 'I embroidered ... tablecloth yesterday', where participants had to select either the definite or the indefinite article. The position of the speaker was counterbalanced, i.e., in half of the pictures the speaker (and the speech balloon) appeared on the left-hand side, while in the other half the speaker was on the right-hand side. Test items were presented in a uniform random order for the participants, while the answers appeared in a unique random order for each participant throughout the test.

In total, 101 native speakers of Hungarian completed the online questionnaire; however, 13 of these were discarded, since participants consistently selected either only the proximal demonstrative or just one distal demonstrative altogether. This suggests that perhaps they did not understand the task and, accordingly, did not adopt the speaker's perspective.[13] It is also possible that participants went through the test items too quickly, without making a real effort, which is an obvious disadvantage of this method. These participants also selected the same answer throughout the fillers. Table 3.5 shows the gender and age of the remaining participants.

13 This assumption might explain the fact that the participants in question selected the proximal demonstrative consistently. If they did indeed rely on their own perspective, then all of the entities being referred to were close to them on the screen, even when the objects were actually far from the speaker.

Table 3.5: Participants

Gender	Number	Average age	Age range
Male	19	28	18–67
Female	69	26	19–60
Total	88	27	18–67

As described above, three variables were manipulated in the visual scene: DISTANCE, JOINT (VISUAL) ATTENTION and POINTING. Each of these had two levels. First, adopting Kemmerer's (1999) view on distance, the object being referred to by the speaker was either treated as near the speaker or far from the speaker. In the former case, objects were located within arm's reach of the speaker, within peripersonal space. Everything else outside this domain is extrapersonal from the speaker's point of view, i.e. objects outside arm's reach were considered far from the speaker. Second, following Peeters et al.'s design (2014), there was either joint visual attention or no joint visual attention between the speaker, the hearer, and the entity being referred to. In the latter case, while the speaker was looking at the object, the hearer was looking at the picture on the wall. Third, the speaker was either pointing to the entity being referred to or there was no pointing gesture present on the part of the speaker. Figure 3.4 is an example of the far, no joint attention, pointing condition.

3.3.4 Results

The results for the individual conditions in the case of both types of demonstratives are shown in Table 3.6. A repeated measures ANOVA was carried out on the proportion of proximal and distal demonstratives in order to analyse the data. There was a main effect of DISTANCE for both demonstratives (proximal: $F(1, 87) = 299.76$, $p < 0.001$, $\eta^2 = 0.775$; distal: $F(1, 87) = 289.27$, $p < 0.001$, $\eta^2 = 0.769$), which means that proximal demonstratives were preferred when the entity being referred to was near the speaker in the visual scene, while distal demonstratives were used more often when the object was far from the speaker. Figure 3.5 shows how the mean proportions for both terms were affected by DISTANCE if we ignore all other factors.

There was also a main effect of JOINT (VISUAL) ATTENTION in both cases (proximal: $F(1, 87) = 13.63$, $p < 0.001$, $\eta^2 = 0.135$, distal: $F(1, 87) = 15.468$, $p < 0.001$, $\eta^2 = 0.151$); i.e., participants selected proximal demonstratives significantly more times when the speaker and the hearer were both looking at the entity being referred to (67%) than when there was no joint attention (58%), but just the opposite

Table 3.6: Results

Conditions	*ez* Mean proportion	*ez* SD	*az* Mean proportion	*az* SD
near, joint attention, pointing	96.59	15.71	3.41	15.71
near, joint attention, no pointing	79.26	24.92	20.74	24.92
near, no joint attention, pointing	95.45	14.94	4.55	14.94
near, no joint attention, no pointing	72.16	28.97	27.84	28.97
far, joint attention, pointing	53.69	33.80	46.31	33.52
far, joint attention, no pointing	37.50	31.71	62.50	31.71
far, no joint attention, pointing	41.19	31.49	58.81	32.43
far, no joint attention, no pointing	24.15	31.36	75.85	31.36

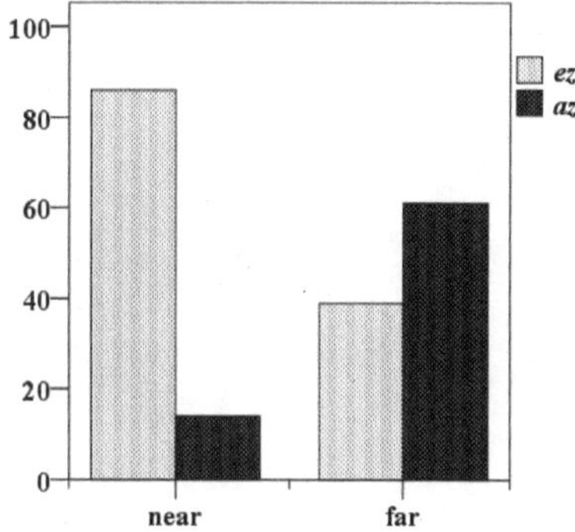

Figure 3.5: Mean proportions of the use of proximal and distal terms as affected by the two levels of DISTANCE

holds for the distal term, since participants selected distal demonstratives more often when there was no joint visual attention (42%) than when there was (33%). However, the effect size shows that this effect is not as substantial as that of DISTANCE. The main effect of JOINT (VISUAL) ATTENTION is represented in Figure 3.6.

The third factor, POINTING, also had a main effect in both cases (proximal: $F(1, 87) = 45.4$, $p < 0.001$, $\eta^2 = 0.343$, distal: $F(1, 87) = 55.788$, $p < 0.001$, $\eta^2 = 0.391$). This means that proximal demonstratives were chosen more often when there was a pointing gesture on the part of the speaker (72%) than when there was no accompanying pointing gesture (53%), and again the opposite is true for the distal term, as shown in Figure 3.7.

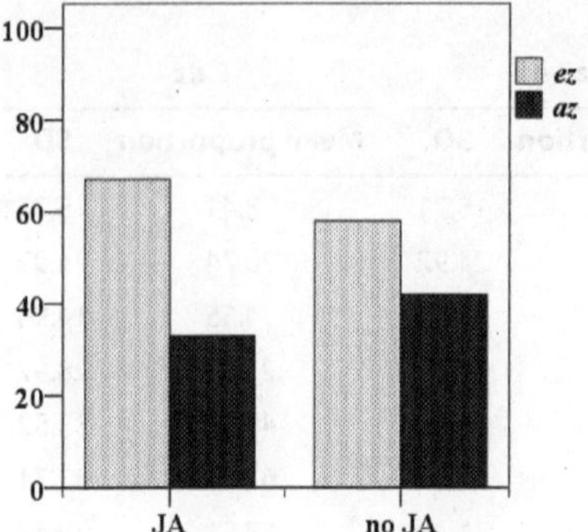

Figure 3.6: Mean proportions of the use of proximal and distal terms as affected by the two levels of JOINT VISUAL ATTENTION

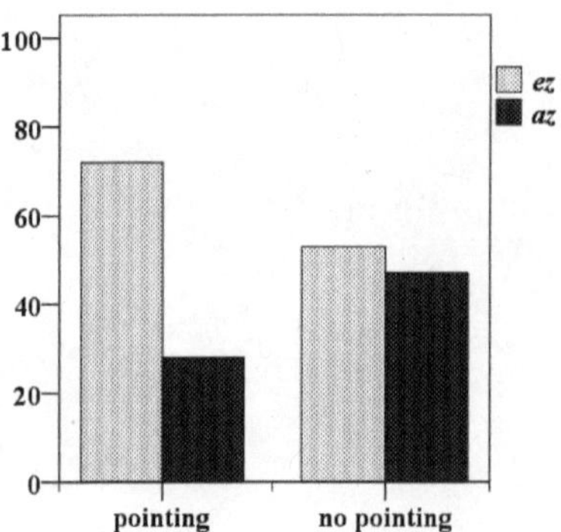

Figure 3.7: Mean proportions of the use of proximal and distal terms as affected by the two levels of POINTING

Finally, a significant interaction of DISTANCE and JOINT (VISUAL) ATTENTION was also detected for both demonstratives (proximal: $F(1, 87) = 9.589$, $p < 0.01$, $\eta^2 = 0.099$, distal: $F(1, 87) = 9.128$, $p < 0.01$, $\eta^2 = 0.095$). However, this interaction is relatively weak, since it is responsible only for 9.9% and 9.5% of the overall variation, respectively. The interactions are represented in Figure 3.8 and Figure 3.9, which show the mean proportions of the use of the proximal and distal demonstratives.

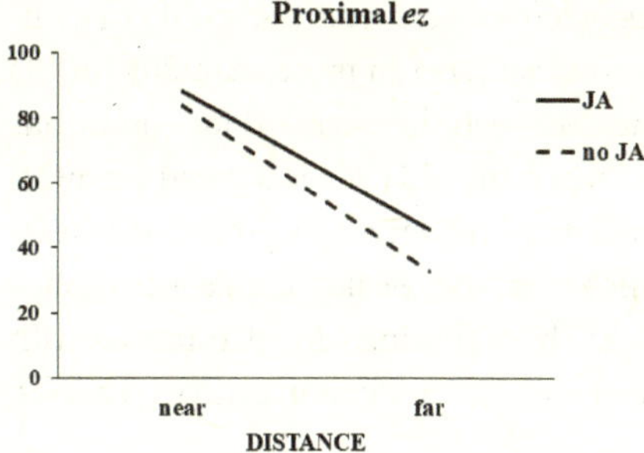

Figure 3.8: The interaction of DISTANCE and JOINT ATTENTION in the case of the proximal demonstrative *ez*

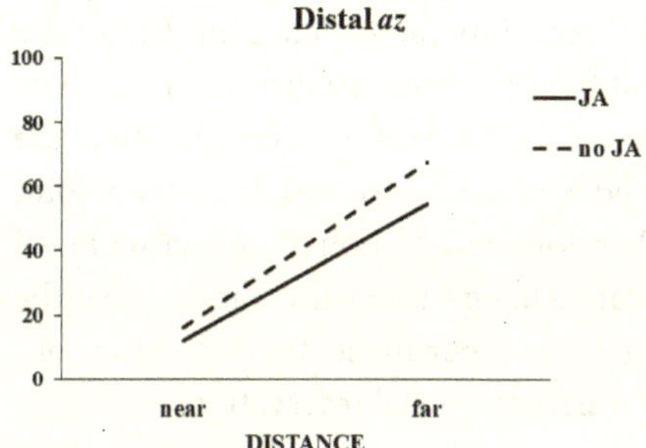

Figure 3.9: The interaction of DISTANCE and JOINT ATTENTION in the case of the distal demonstrative *az*

3.3.5 Discussion

As mentioned before, the use of demonstratives has recently been considered from a novel perspective in the pertinent literature. The choice between demonstrative terms is no longer described as a speaker-anchored, egocentric and addressee-blind phenomenon; instead, demonstrative reference is viewed as a joint action between the speaker and the hearer (cf. Peeters & Özyürek 2016). The experiment presented above tested the role of the traditional speaker-anchored factor of relative distance and that of two novel factors: joint visual attention between the speaker and the hearer to a visible referent and the use of a pointing gesture in the selection of Hungarian demonstrative modifiers in a production task. Besides exploring the effects of these factors, their potential interactions were also examined.

The results obtained support the traditional view, that is, DISTANCE had a strong influence on the choice of both demonstrative modifiers (see Figure 3.5).

This means that when the entities being referred to were near the speaker (within arm's reach), participants selected the proximal term in more than 80% of the cases. There was also a significant difference between the near and far conditions in the case of the distal demonstrative, i.e., when the object was located far away, out of arm's reach from the speaker, the distal demonstrative was preferred. Therefore, the results confirm that relative distance from the speaker is a decisive factor in the choice of Hungarian demonstratives. These findings are also in line with previous experimental findings on the use of Hungarian demonstrative terms (cf. Tóth et al. 2014).

Nevertheless, on the basis of these results, we should not jump to the conclusion that relative distance on its own can explain and motivate the use of demonstrative terms. First, it has to be noted here that from a methodological point of view, the experiment conducted by Stevens and Zhang (2013) collected two types of data: behavioural data in the form of acceptability judgements and EEG data. The analysis relying only on the acceptability judgements confirmed the importance of relative distance in English; however, the ERP results suggested that 'the role of distance from the speaker is trumped by a more basic requirement of joint attention' (Stevens & Zhang 2013: 41). Therefore, in addition to collecting novel types of data on demonstratives, Stevens and Zhang (2013) also showed that the method itself might influence the outcome of an experiment. Therefore, the conclusion about the role of relative distance warrants special reservations.

Second, in the experiment presented above the proximal term was also quite often selected in the far condition, in almost 40% of the cases. This finding might be due to a methodological flaw, that is, if the participants did not take the speaker's perspective, this could have influenced the results. Considering the overall proportions of the two demonstratives regarding distance, the proximal term has a larger overall proportion, which implies that there is no clear-cut near-far, proximal-distal opposition, other factors might also play an important role and may interact with DISTANCE. This assumption will be discussed below.

Turning to the second factor, JOINT (VISUAL) ATTENTION, this also had a main effect in both cases, with proximal terms being more frequently selected when there was a joint visual attention to the object being referred to, while distal terms were preferred when there was a lack of joint visual attention. Furthermore, a weak interaction of DISTANCE and JOINT (VISUAL) ATTENTION was also detected, which seems to indicate that the proximal demonstrative is used when, on the one hand, the entity referred to is near the speaker and, on the other hand, when a triadic joint attention has already been established (see Figure 3.8). In turn, as illustrated in Figure 3.9, distal demonstratives are used when the object is far and there is no joint focus of attention. Similar results have been found for Jordanian Arabic by Jarbou (2010), who showed in an observational study that proximal demonstratives are used when the object being referred to is highly perceptible to the hearer as perceived by the speaker. However, at the same time, the results contradict the experimental findings of Piwek et al. (2008) and Peeters et al. (2014) on Dutch, who found that distal demonstratives in Dutch are preferred when there is joint attention between the speaker, the addressee and the object.

Nevertheless, the method applied in the present experiment has its limitations. It could be argued that distal demonstratives are used to direct the addressee's attention to the object that is not yet in the joint attention of the speaker and the hearer. However, to prove this, more sophisticated experimental designs should be used together with data collected via the observation of naturally occurring speech. Nevertheless, the weak interaction found here signals that it is crucial to examine the interplay of several factors when we try to describe the use of demonstratives.

The last factor tested is POINTING; namely, the study reported here also addressed the question of whether the presence/absence of an accompanying pointing gesture on the part of the speaker affects demonstrative choice or not. This factor also had a main effect. Participants used proximal demonstratives significantly more often in the presence of a manual pointing gesture, while distal demonstratives were selected more often in the absence of a pointing gesture.

Clark and Bangerter (2004) describe two different types of pointing: close and distant pointing. The former is restricted to pointing at entities that are within arm's reach, when the entities can even be touched by the interlocutors. Distant pointing encompasses pointing to entities that are out of arm's reach. They argue that close pointing is more precise than distant pointing, since it is easier to identify the intended referent via the gesture itself. Distant pointing is often accompanied by the use of locative descriptions, which aid reference resolution. Bangerter (2004) showed in an experimental setting in table-top space that interlocutors rely on the use of pointing gestures and deictic expressions when identifying objects within arm's reach, but prefer using locative expressions without a pointing gesture as they refer to entities placed further away from the speaker. He draws two important conclusions: (i) the further away the referent is from the interlocutors, the less reliable pointing becomes; (ii) pointing can effectively replace locative expressions when speakers refer to entities within arm's reach. Bangerter (2004: 418) sums up his findings as follows: 'demonstratives focus attention, by directing the addressee's gaze to the speaker's gesture (Bühler 1965). When a gesture carries the main informational burden of a referring act, speakers need to be sure that the addressees are attending to it. Using a demonstrative accomplishes this.' The large proportion of proximals in the presence of a pointing gesture in the current experiment (see Figure 3.7) is in line with Bangerter's (2004) results; however, the limited possibilities allowed by the use of an online questionnaire only show that pointing is important and must be taken into account when tackling demonstrative choice. Further studies are required to explore the relation between the selection of demonstratives, pointing and joint attention.

3.3.6 Conclusion

In this section, the results of a production study on the use of Hungarian demonstrative modifiers were presented. Participants had to select either the proximal or the distal demonstrative modifier depending on whether the object being referred to was near or far from the speaker, whether there was a joint visual focus of attention between the speaker and the addressee to the referent, and whether there was an accompanying manual pointing gesture present on the part of the speaker. The findings indicate that each of these factors influences the use of demonstrative modifiers in Hungarian and are compatible with similar findings for English (Stevens & Zhang 2013), Dutch (Peeters et al. 2014) and Jordanian Arabic (Jarbou 2010). Further research is needed to explore the interplay of these factors in a more subtle manner.

3.4 Summary

In this chapter, I have presented the results of my recent empirical research on demonstrative choice in Hungarian. The reported work includes a corpus-based quantitative analysis and an online questionnaire study. The empirical findings are in line with the results of Tóth et al. (2014), who argue that demonstrative practice cannot be adequately described relying only on the traditional near/far opposition, although relative distance from the speaker influences demonstrative choice. It has been shown that in addition to distance, other factors, such as joint visual attention and manual pointing, also play a role. At this point of research, it can be concluded that the traditional characterization of demonstrative selection presents an oversimplified picture, and the use of demonstratives in Hungarian cannot be described adequately from a solely speaker-anchored perspective.

CHAPTER 4

Contrastive Uses of Hungarian Demonstratives

4.1 Contrastive uses

As mentioned in Chapter 1, Levinson (2004) divides the gestural use of exophoric demonstratives into two subcategories, differentiating contrastive uses from non-contrastive ones; however, he does not provide a definition of the former. Levinson (2018a: 11) presents the following examples to illustrate the distinction:

(1) *This mug* is larger than *that one*.

(2) It's hard to read in *this light*.

and he also cites a contrastive example by Fillmore (1997):

(3) First take *this pill*, then *that one*. (Levinson 2018a: 32)

In fact, Fillmore (1971/1997) was the first to mention contrastive uses, but later works, including typological studies by Anderson and Keenan (1985) and Diessel (1999), did not address this type of use. It was David Wilkins who first stressed the importance of studying contrastive uses when he developed an elicitation task in order to collect massive data on demonstrative use in general (Pederson & Wilkins 1996), and contrastive use in particular (Wilkins 1999). Cross-linguistically, several authors used the elicitation method developed by Wilkins (1999) to explore contrastive uses of demonstratives. For example, Meira and Terrill (2005) collected data on Tiriyó and Lavukaleve, Margetts (2018) on Saliba-Logea, and Imai (2003) on American English and Japanese among other languages.

Meira and Terrill (2005) describe contrastive uses as situations in which demonstratives contrast more than one referent, while in the case of non-contrastive uses no such contrast can be observed. As the examples above show, the same demonstratives can fulfil both functions in English, but the conditions of use might differ. For example, *that* can be used to refer to a part of the body only in contrastive contexts. Compare:

(4) I hurt *this/*that finger*. (Levinson 2004: 108)

(5) *This finger* doesn't hurt, but *that finger* does. (Meira & Terrill 2005: 1132)

The position of the entities being referred to with respect to the speaker and with respect to one another plays a crucial role in the elicitation studies mentioned above. Imai (2003) argues that contrastive uses emerge only when there are two or more entities at the same distance from the speaker and the speaker uses different demonstrative terms to refer to them. Imai (2003) labels this type of usage equidistant contrast.[1] For example, in English, a speaker can refer to two cups that he is holding in his hand by *this cup* and *that cup*, respectively. Thus English native speakers would accept utterances like *I like this cup more than that one*, when the speaker is holding both objects in his hand, which means that contrast overrides distance. It is important to note that the order of the demonstratives is not arbitrary in English, namely, the proximal term must come first, which is followed by the distal demonstrative, hence *?I like that cup more than this one* would be unacceptable. This is called a serial order (Fillmore 1982) or a sequential order (Imai 2003). However, Levinson (2018a) points out that there are numerous languages where this constraint is not valid, for example, in the case of Yélî Dnye.

Wilkins's (1999) method was aimed at studying contrastive uses only within arm's reach, and accordingly, Imai (2003) also claims that an equidistant contrast can be described only when the entities are close to the speaker, i.e., such a contrast does not occur in the distal region. However, this view can be challenged, since on the one hand there are languages that do not follow this pattern; for example, Bui (2014) reports that contrast can also occur in the distant region between entities that are equidistant from the speaker in Vietnamese. On the other hand, one can also contrast objects that are not equidistant from the speaker, as described, for example, by Margetts (2018).

In general, cross-linguistic research on the contrastive use of demonstratives reveals that such uses might show a considerable difference to non-contrastive uses; therefore, this field of study can shed new light on important features of demonstrative reference. Section 4.2 presents the findings of a contrastive elicitation study I conducted with five Hungarian native speakers adopting the elicitation tool developed by Wilkins (1999). The results of the elicitation task show that, besides the nominal demonstratives *ez/az*, the so-called emphatic demonstratives

1 Thus, cases when a speaker uses two proximal demonstratives to refer to two entities located at the same distance are not considered to be contrastive by Imai (2003).

emez/amaz also surface in contrastive uses. The last section focuses on the use of emphatic demonstratives and attempts to characterise their various deictic functions based on queries run in the Hungarian National Corpus.

4.2 Contrastive uses in Hungarian – An elicitation study

4.2.1 Contrastiveness in Hungarian

As described in Chapter 2, Tóth et al. (2014) explored the contrastive use of nominal demonstratives in Hungarian in an experimental framework. More specifically, Tóth et al. (2014) and Tóth and Csatár (2016) compared the distribution of the Hungarian demonstratives (*ez/az*) in neutral and contrastive contexts and showed that while distance is crucial in neutral contexts, in contrastive contexts, when the objects being referred to are close to the speaker, the distal term (*az*) is used in a significantly higher proportion, i.e., relative distance from the speaker is overwritten by contrastiveness. Hence, Hungarian results fit into the cross-linguistic picture in the case of equidistant contrast. In the experiment, a narrow definition of contrastiveness was implemented, that is, contrastive contexts were explicitly marked by the presence of a coordinating conjunction with a contrastive sense, such as *but* (see the example in (5)) or by identificational focus (see Chapter 2). In what follows, a broader definition of contrastiveness will be employed, illustrated by the examples in (1) and (3) above, and in (6) and (7) below, where contrast simply means that 'one referent is picked out and opposed to another' (Levinson 2018b: 334).

(6) *Ez* *a* *dinnye* kisebb, mint *az.*
this the watermelon smaller than that
'This watermelon is smaller than that.'

(7) *Annak* *a* *telefonnak* nagyobb a memóriája, mint *ennek.*
that.DAT the telephone.DAT bigger the storage.space.POSS.3SG than this.DAT
'That cell phone has more storage space than this one.'

As mentioned in Chapter 1, in addition to proximal *ez* 'this' and distal *az* 'that', there are other less frequently used Hungarian nominal demonstratives, proximal *emez* and distal *amaz*, which are usually called emphatic demonstratives in descriptive grammars. These are either assumed to make a finer distinction within near and far (Tolcsvai Nagy 2001; Laczkó 2006) or to have a reinforcing role to emphasize distance (Kugler & Laczkó 2000). According to Kleiber et al. (2018), *ez* and emphatic *emez*, and *az* and emphatic *amaz* can create the same type of contrast that we have seen in (6) and (7). The intended referents in the examples below are either close, as in (8) or far from the speaker, as in (9):

(8)	*Ez*	*a*	*könyv*	az	enyém,	*emez*	pedig	a	testvéremé.
	this	the	book	the	mine	this	in.turn	the	my.sister.POSS.1SG.POSS

'This book is mine, and this other one is my sister's.'

(9)	*Az*	*a*	*bicikli*	az	enyém,	*amaz*	pedig	a	bátyámé.
	that	the	bike	the	mine	that	in.turn	the	my.brother.POSS.1SG.POSS

'That bike is mine, and that other one is my brother's.'

The elicitation study presented in the following section collected spontaneous contrastive uses of demonstratives in table-top space. The methodology used is described in the next section.

4.2.2 Hungarian demonstratives in table-top space

4.2.2.1 Wilkins' (1999) contrastive elicitation tool

The aim of the task developed by Wilkins (1999) is to elicit contrastive uses of demonstratives in a particular language, that is, to investigate demonstrative practice in a controlled environment, when the speaker contrastively refers to entities in table-top space. During the elicitation sessions the subject and the interviewer are located next to one another, hence they share the same perspective of their physical surroundings. The subject is engaged in a kind of memory game by the researcher, who first shows post-it notes with drawings to the subject, then arranges them face down on the table on the away axis. The subject is then asked about the post-it notes, using questions similar to *Which one is the square?* Sentential frames, such as *This one is the circle* (pointing to a post-it), *but … is the square* can also be used to encourage contrastive uses of demonstratives.[2] The number of the post-it notes (two, three or four) and their arrangements might be varied by the researcher. The answers are noted down and subsequently analysed. Throughout the entire elicitation session, special attention must be paid to the gestures made by the speaker.

I slightly modified Wilkins' (1999) design, as first I wanted to explore the role of relative distance when referring to a single object in table-top space. The subjects

2 For a detailed description of the elicitation tool I refer the reader to Wilkins (1999) and Meira and Terrill (2005).

referred to a small book that was placed further and further away from the participants. The second part of the session focused on contrastive uses; the speakers referred to circle shape memory cards depicting animals (a bear, a frog, and a parrot). The factors investigated are described in the following section.

4.2.2.2 The factors investigated

I intended to examine the role of two factors in demonstrative practice in tabletop space, RELATIVE DISTANCE and CONTRASTIVENESS. The first factor had three levels, which were defined as follows. Based on Kemmerer's (1999) findings, near space is more or less within arm's reach and far space expands outward from that boundary; entities located within arm's reach to the speaker were treated as peripersonal, while everything else was considered far (extrapersonal). Within peripersonal space, I introduced a further distinction between entities the speaker could hold or handle easily and those that were located only within touching distance, at reaching space, thus RELATIVE DISTANCE had three levels:[3]

(i) peripersonal 1: entities located at a distance of 10–20 cm from the speaker, i.e., entities that could be held by the speaker;
(ii) peripersonal 2: entities located at a distance of 50–60 cm from the speaker, i.e., entities that could be touched by the speaker;
(iii) extrapersonal: entities located at a distance of 100–120 cm from the speaker, i.e., entities that were out of arm's reach of the speaker.

The second factor, CONTRASTIVENESS, had two levels:[4]

(i) equidistant contrast: two entities are located at the same distance from the speaker on the across axis;
(ii) non-equidistant contrast: two (or more) entities are located on the sagittal axis, away from the speaker, but still within the same level of distance.

Figures 4.1 and 4.2 illustrate two conditions explored in the elicitation task. When there were only two objects, as in the scenarios depicted in Figures 4.1 and 4.2, the speakers could mention the objects as they preferred, that is, the order of mention was not manipulated. As opposed to this, when three entities were located on the away axis, subjects were asked to mention the object that was closest to them first, the middle one next and the one that was the furthest away last.

---

3 The distinction between the peripersonal 1 and peripersonal 2 categories can further be motivated by Enfield's notion of engagement area, which is defined as 'the place, which is, at moment t, the conceived site of a person's currently dominant manual and attentional engagement' (Enfield 2003: 89).

4 See Wilkins (1999), Imai (2003).

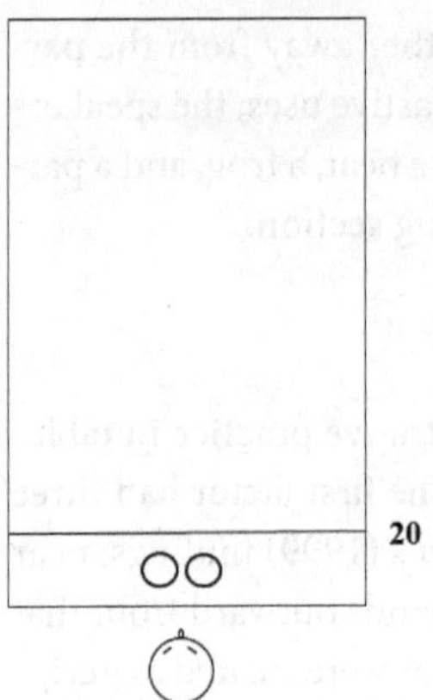

Figure 4.1: Equidistant contrast within peripersonal 1 space

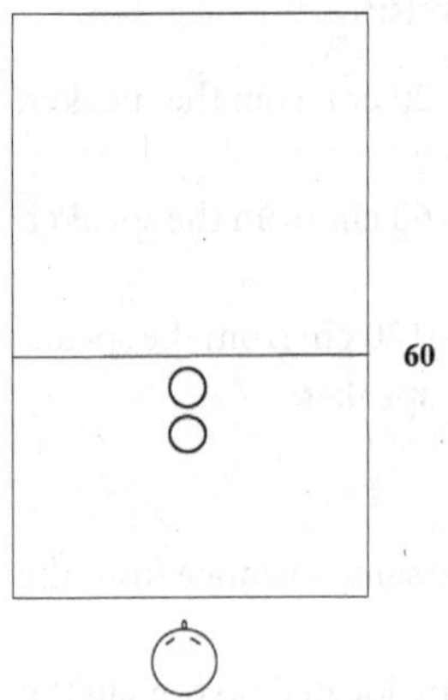

Figure 4.2: Non-equidistant contrast within peripersonal 2 space

Throughout the elicitation sessions, I took notes of the demonstratives used in a prepared answer sheet, paying attention both to the gestures made by the subjects and, when it was relevant, to the order of mention. I also used clarification questions when necessary, for example, *Could you have used X instead of Y when you referred to the card with the bear?*

4.2.2.3 Participants

Five native speakers of Hungarian, three women and two men, participated in the elicitation study, aged between 29 and 49. Each of them was born and raised in the Tiszántúl region, in the northern-eastern part of the country. As mentioned above, the speaker and the researcher were both sitting at the head of a table during the elicitation sessions.

4.2.2.4 Results

4.2.2.4.1 Non-contrastive uses

Results for the non-contrastive uses, when speakers referred to one object in table-top space are shown in Table 4.1. The aim of this task was to examine whether relative distance from the speaker affects the choice of demonstratives. The participants produced utterances like *I have already read this book.*

The data elicited indicates that speakers indeed preferred the proximal demonstrative when they referred to one object located in the peripersonal zone. In the peripersonal 1 condition, each speaker used the proximal form; moreover, several subjects even touched or took the intended referent in their hands.

As can be seen in Table 4.1, at the second level of RELATIVE DISTANCE, when objects were located at a distance of 50–60 cm from the speaker, both demonstratives were acceptable. Three participants opted for the proximal demonstrative, and two of them chose the distal term. The use of the demonstratives was always accompanied by a pointing gesture. One of the subjects pointed out that in the presence of a manual pointing gesture, the distal demonstrative is more acceptable; however, when he changed his position and leaned closer to the intended referent, and finally also touched it, he preferred the proximal form. Thus it is reasonable to assume that spatial zones do not have a clear-cut demarcation line; instead, there is a gradual transition from one to the other. Furthermore, the presence or absence of a pointing gesture on the part of the speaker, the type of gesture, the speaker's body posture and the change of position are also crucial.

At the third level of distance, when the entities referred to were well beyond arm's reach, the speakers unequivocally selected the distal form, and the use of the demonstrative was always accompanied by a manual pointing gesture.

Table 4.1: Non-contrastive uses

	most natural	**less natural**	**unacceptable**
extrapersonal	*az*		*ez*
peripersonal 2	*ez*	*az*	
peripersonal 1	*ez*		*az*

4.2.2.4.2 Contrastive uses

Before the memory game, I asked the participants to imagine that they were at the dentist, and they had to show which of their teeth hurt. Each subject pointed to one of their teeth and uttered (10):

(10) *Ez* *a* *fogam* fáj.
this the tooth.POSS.1SG hurt.3SG
'This tooth hurts.'

I also asked them to think about how they would exactly identify their hurting tooth if there was another one that might be the source of pain. Four speakers reacted by uttering (11) while they pointed to the tooth in question:

(11) *Ez* *a* *fogam* fáj, *ez* nem.
this the tooth.POSS.1SG hurt.3SG this no
'This tooth hurts, this one doesn't.'

One subject used the distal demonstrative *az* to identify the tooth that did not hurt:

(12) *Ez* *a* *fogam* *fáj,* *az* nem.
this the tooth.POSS.1SG hurt.3SG that no
'This tooth hurts, that one doesn't.'

However, another participant labelled the utterance in (12) as totally unacceptable. The acceptability judgements of the utterances in (10)–(12) indicate that Hungarian and English license different demonstratives when reference is made to parts of the body (cf. examples (4)–(5) in Section 4.1).[5]

---

5 One of the subjects noted in a spontaneous manner that if the dentist tapped on their tooth asking whether it was the one that hurt, they would reply using the distal form:

(i) Dentist: *Ez* *a* *foga* fáj?
this the tooth.POSS.3SG hurt.3SG
'Does this one hurt?'
Patient: Igen, *az.*
yes that
'Yes, it's that one.'

This example is not unknown in the literature; for instance, it is discussed by Scott (2013). If we assume that the speaker acts as the deictic centre in both utterances, then, according to the traditional approach just the opposite pattern regarding the choice of demonstratives is expected. As is often the case in similar doctor-patient exchanges, in

Table 4.2 presents the results of the first memory game, when the speakers referred to two entities located on the away axis. The rows of the table mirror the placement of the objects in table-top space, that is, within the peripersonal 2 condition in the first column, speakers preferred the use of proximal demonstrative *this* to refer to the object that was closer to them, which was followed by the distal term to refer to the object placed further away. The following utterance illustrates this type of use:

(13) Szerintem *ez* *a* *maci,* *az* pedig a papagáj.
according.to.me this the bear that in.turn the parrot
'I think this is the bear, and that is the parrot.'

As is clear from the table, the use of two proximal terms in the peripersonal 2 condition was less natural.[6]

The results displayed in Table 4.3 represent the task in which the speakers referred to three entities that were arranged on the sagittal axis. In this case, I asked the participants to refer to the object that was closest to them first.

Table 4.4 presents the results of the equidistant contrastive uses, with the speakers always referring first to the entity that was on their left-hand side. It is worth noticing that in Tables 4.3 and 4.4 the emphatic demonstratives also occurred

Table 4.2: Contrastive uses: non-equidistant contrast with two referents

	most natural	**less natural**			**unacceptable**	
extrapersonal	*az*	*az*	*amaz*	*amaz*	*ez*	
	az	*ez*	*emez*	*az*	*az*	
peripersonal 2	*az*		*ez*		*ez*	*az*
	ez		*ez*		*az*	*az*
peripersonal 1	*ez*		*az*		*ez*	
	ez		*ez*		*az*	

(i), the doctor's perspective is more prominent, so it is their point of view that is relevant, and both participants consider the doctor as the deictic centre.

6 Two subjects pointed out that it is also possible to refer first to the entity that is further away from the speaker, but only the distal demonstrative can be used. The corresponding utterance is given below:

(i) *Az* a papagáj, *ez* meg itt a maci.
that the parrot this and here the bear
'That is the parrot, and this is the bear.'

Table 4.3: Contrastive uses: non-equidistant contrast with three referents

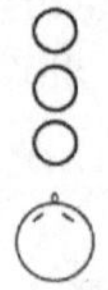

	most natural	less natural	unacceptable
extrapersonal	*az*	*amaz amaz amaz*	*ez*
	az	*az emez az*	*ez*
	az	*ez ez az*	*ez*
peripersonal 2	*az*	*ez amaz*	*az*
	ez	*ez az*	*az*
	ez	*ez ez*	*az*
peripersonal 1	*ez*	*amaz*	*az*
	ez	*emez*	*az*
	ez	*ez*	*az*

Table 4.4: Contrastive uses: equidistant contrast with two referents

	most natural	less natural	unacceptable
extrapersonal	*az az*	*ez az*	*ez ez*
		az amaz	
peripersonal 2	*ez az*	*ez ez*	*az ez*
		az az	
peripersonal 1	*ez az*	*ez ez*	*az az*
			az ez

marginally; two participants used these forms spontaneously. I also asked the opinion of the other speakers. They said that although they find these forms acceptable, they would not use them. A detailed analysis of the results presented above is provided in the following section.

4.2.2.5 Discussion

4.2.2.5.1 Non-contrastive uses

Based on the data collected by elicitation, it can be observed that in the case of non-contrastive exophoric uses of Hungarian nominal demonstratives in limited space where the speaker and the addressee have the same perspective of their physical surroundings, demonstratives code distance opposition (near and far) in an egocentric manner: proximal *ez* refers to entities that are located close to the speaker, within reaching space; distal *az* refers to entities that are out of arm's reach. Thus the table-top space is divided into a speaker-anchored, interactional proximal region, and a distal region. This is represented in Table 4.5. The dotted

Table 4.5: Spatial oppositions coded by Hungarian nominal demonstratives in table-top space

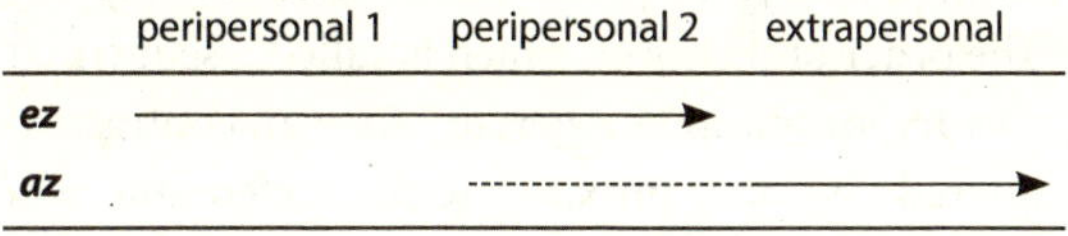

line shows acceptable, but less natural uses of *az* 'that'. So, we find a small overlap in the regions where the two demonstratives are used, which indicates that there is no clear-cut boundary between these regions.

The use of the proximal term is unavoidable when the speaker refers to an entity within the peripersonal zone. The use of the distal term signals to the addressee that the conditions regarding the location of the intended referent for uttering the proximal term are not met, hence, the entity referred to is in the extrapersonal or, possibly, in the peripersonal 2 zone.

It is important to note here that Coventry et al. (2008) showed in a production experiment that near space can be extended when a tool, for example, a 70-cm stick is used to point to the intended referent during the referential act. Therefore, the boundaries of the spatial regions mentioned above are not rigid, but flexible, and the use of a pointing tool, or as we have seen, the change of body posture can have an impact on the selection of demonstratives.

Nevertheless, the results reported above have limitations. First, the elicitation task took place in an artificially created restricted space, where only one entity was displayed on the table. In everyday communication settings, the intended referent can be salient for various reasons, it must always be selected, based on contextual clues, from a set of entities that are competing for the attention of the addressee. In any referential act, the speaker selects the demonstrative term in a way that maximally helps the addressee in identifying the intended referent. The referential acts in the elicitation task were extremely limited as compared to the ones that can be observed in spontaneous interactions.

The scope of the study could be extended, though, for example, by changing the position of the speaker and the addressee, or by broadening the interactional space (cf. Wilkins 2018, Reile et al. 2019). It is also desirable to compare and reassess the findings of the present work with the outcome of other research methods, such as observation, to get a clearer understanding of the demonstrative processes at hand.

4.2.2.5.2 Contrastive uses

As mentioned before, contrastive uses of Hungarian nominal demonstratives were explored within a memory game paradigm, where speakers referred to two or three objects displayed in different settings in table-top space. In addition to the basic nominal demonstratives *ez*/*az*, two subjects spontaneously used the emphatic demonstratives *emez*/*amaz*. The order of mention, which is called a sequential order by Imai (2003), proved to be important in Hungarian, since, in contrastive uses, distal forms were always uttered only after proximal terms. Referential acts almost always included a manual pointing gesture on the part of the speaker. Results concerning equidistant and non-equidistant contrast are presented in Tables 4.2–4.4.

When two entities are arranged in table-top space, the findings for both levels of CONTRASTIVENESS support the conclusion reached by Tóth et al. (2014), i.e. both proximal and distal demonstratives occurred in the peripersonal 1 and peripersonal 2 regions, within reaching space, in the case of contrastive uses; but the distal demonstrative was not acceptable in the peripersonal 1 zone in the case of non-contrastive uses. The results obtained by different research methods provide converging evidence for the generalisation made by Levinson (2018a), who claims that 'contrastive uses of demonstratives tend to neutralize proximity distinctions' (Levinson 2018a: 37), i.e., RELATIVE DISTANCE is no longer a decisive factor in the selection of demonstratives.

When subjects had to refer to three entities, that is, in the non-equidistant contrast condition, proximal *ez* and distal *az* were used exclusively in the peripersonal 1 and the extrapersonal condition, respectively (see Table 4.3). Thus the effect of CONTRASTIVENESS here is weaker with respect to reference to two entities. Special attention needs to be paid to the occurrence of the emphatic demonstratives, *emez*/*amaz*. As mentioned in Section 4.2.1, Kleiber et al. (2018) note that *ez*/*emez* and *az*/*amaz* can create a contrast, as illustrated by (8) and (9) above. The attested examples corroborate this assumption; the demonstratives in question only surfaced in the case of contrastive uses. In the case of non-equidistant contrast, see Table 4.2, and especially when reference is made to entities located in the extrapersonal region, in addition to *ez*/*az*, the use of *emez*/*amaz* is also acceptable, though less natural. It is reasonable to assume that the function of distal *amaz* is to direct the attention of the addressee to an entity that is located further away with respect to another entity that is closer to the speaker and that was identified by the use of *emez*. The emphatic demonstratives *emez*/*amaz* also occurred in the peripersonal 1 condition when three entities were referred to (see Table 4.3), which provides further evidence that *emez*/*amaz* are contrastive in nature.

4.2.2.6 Conclusion

This section reported the findings of an elicitation study based on the Contrastive Demonstrative Questionnaire developed by Wilkins (1999) aimed at investigating the contrastive use of Hungarian nominal demonstratives. The data collected suggest that in the case of non-contrastive uses physical proximity to the speaker was crucial regarding the choice of demonstratives in table-top space, but in the case of contrastive uses the pattern of demonstratives changed, relative distance from the speaker was neutralized, and distal demonstratives occurred even when speakers referred to entities within easy arm's reach. The emphatic demonstratives, *emez/amaz* 'this/that' were also spontaneously used during the task. Though the demonstratives in question are considered marginal, it can be assumed that they have an inherently contrastive function in present day Hungarian. This assumption will be explored by corpus-linguistic tools in the following section, where I present a corpus-based study aimed at exploring and comparing the use of *emez/amaz* in the Hungarian National Corpus.

4.3. A corpus-based study on the use of *emez/amaz*

4.3.1 Previous research on *emez/amaz*

From a diachronic perspective, Egedi (2014, 2015)[7] argues that *imez/amaz* 'this/that' are reinforced demonstratives, which were first attested in the 15th century (Late Old Hungarian). From an etymological perspective, they are derived by syntactic fusion from *íme* and *ám* 'look, behold' + basic forms: *ez/az* (Benkő 1993; Egedi 2014, 2015). The function of the first members of the composite forms included calling attention to something, emphasizing something or creating a contrast between two or more things. Later *imez* was replaced by the present-day form *emez*, which was first attested in 1628. The distributional frequency of *imez/amaz* is relatively low across historical corpora; nevertheless, the attested forms display the following characteristics: morphologically, there is a proximal/distal contrast, syntactically, they were used both adnominally and pronominally, but the latter form was much more frequent. As adnominals, they did not show number and case agreement with the head, but pronominal forms were inflected. In Middle Hungarian, these forms also occurred in the so-called determiner-doubling construction, although attested examples are quite rare. From a semantic perspective, they preserved the original meaning of the reinforcing element, i.e., their meaning could be paraphrased as 'this X here', and 'that X over there', respectively. Regarding their use, their function was restricted; for example, they never occurred in anaphoric contexts. D. Mátai (1999: 451) notes that they could emphatically point

7 See also D. Mátai (1999), Dömötör (2008).

to an entity while creating a contrast with another entity identified by a definite description or a pronoun, as in (14) below:

(14) *Imez vennek* mosam en meg labat te kedeg az masyknak.
this elder.DAT wash.1SG I PRT foot.POSS.3SG.ACC you in.turn the other.DAT
'I wash this elder's foot, you wash the other's.'
(Virginia-Kódex: 60)

According to Egedi (2015), the distal form was also used in contrastive listings or emphasizing contexts, but most frequently it surfaced in the so-called recognitional use.

In contemporary Hungarian, *emez/amaz* are less frequently used than *ez/az*. Regarding their form, the pronominal form is more persistent.[8] It is widely accepted in Hungarian descriptive grammars that *ez/emez* are proximals, while *az/amaz* are distals, since generally front-vowel forms describe proximal relations, while back-vowel forms indicate distal relations. However, in the pertinent literature there are two opposing views regarding the role of *emez/amaz*: on the one hand, Laczkó (2009) and Pete (2012) claim that there is no difference between *ez/emez* and *az/amaz* regarding proximity; thus essentially there is only a two-way distinction in the Hungarian nominal demonstrative system. In addition, Kleiber et al. (2018) note that by using *ez* and *emez* 'this other', and *az* and *amaz* 'that other', we can compare two entities, which are either close to the speaker, as illustrated by (15) which is uttered while looking at a picture book, or far from the speaker, as in (16) which is uttered by the shop assistant in a bike shop:

(15) *Ez az állat* növényevő, *emez* meg húsevő.
this the animal herbivorous this and carnivorous
'This animal is herbivorous, and this other is carnivorous.'

(16) *Az a bicikli* kontrás, *amaz* pedig tárcsafékes.
that the bike back.pedal.ADJ that in.turn disc.brake.ADJ
'That bike has a back-pedal brake, and that other has a disc brake mechanism.'

Thus according to Kleiber et al. (2018), the basic use of *emez* and *amaz* is contrastive.

On the other hand, Tolcsvai Nagy (2001) and Laczkó (2006) state that *ez/emez* and *az/amaz* make a finer distinction within near and far, respectively.

8 A corpus-based frequency analysis will be presented in Section 4.3.2.

More specifically, they suggest that *ez* and *emez* divide the proximal region further, their referring function being paraphrasable as 'this one here' and 'this one nearby', while *az* and *amaz* make a similar distinction in the far region, referring to 'that one there' and 'that one over there'. Thus the following demarcation of space emerges, representing incremental distance from the speaker: *ez – emez – az – amaz.*

Interestingly, the *Explanatory Dictionary of Hungarian (A magyar nyelv értelmező szótára,* henceforth *ÉrtSz.*) provides just the opposite distinction with respect to *ez/emez,* stating that the reinforced form refers to an entity that is closer to the speaker as compared to the one referred to by *ez. Emez* can also be contrasted with *amaz,* in which case it refers to an entity that is closer to the speaker, as below:

(17)	Ne	*amazt*	add,	hanem	*emezt.*
	not	that.ACC	give.IMP.2SG	but	this.ACC

'Don't give me that, give me this.'
(*ÉrtSz.*)

Laczkó (2009) and Kleiber et al. (2018) suggest that the core meaning of *emez/amaz* could be described as 'this/that other one', which implies that their referents can be picked only relative to another entity, that is, they occur in contrastive constructions, emphasizing the contrast itself.

According to the *ÉrtSz.*, in the case of anaphoric reference,[9] the antecedent of *emez* is the last mentioned referring expression:

(18)	Egy	uzsorást	látunk,	aki	bosszút	akar	állni	egy
	a	usurer.ACC	see.1PL	who	revenge.ACC	want.3SG	stand.INF	a

kalmáron,	mert	*emez*	megvetőleg	bánt	vele	s
merchant.SUP	because	this	contemptuously	treated.3SG	he.COM	and

népével.
people.POSS.3SG.COM

'We see a usurer who wanted to take revenge on a merchant, since the latter has treated him and his people contemptuously.'
(Ambrus Zoltán as cited in the *ÉrtSz.*)

The anaphoric use of *amaz* is illustrated in the *Comprehensive Dictionary of Hungarian* (*A magyar nyelv nagyszótára,* henceforth *NSz.*). The antecedent is the NP mentioned first:

9 It is worth noting here that *emez/amaz* never surface in anaphoric contexts in historical corpora.

(19) Elöl jött Vica, a szürke lipicai, mögötte egy sárga
in.front came.3SG Vica the gray Lippizaner behind.it a chestnut
színű, nagytestű igásló, *amaz* játékosan nyargalt a lapulevelek
coloured large carthorse that playfully galloped.3SG the burdocks
felé, de ez a sárga csak fáradtan bóklászott, és csak
toward but this the chestnut just tiredly walked.3SG and only
néha ügetett.
sometimes trotted.3SG
'Vica, a dark Lippizaner, was leading, followed by a large chestnut carthorse. The former was playfully galloping towards the burdocks, but the chestnut was walking tiredly, trotting only occasionally.'
(Mohás Lívia as cited in the *NSz.*)

The aim of this chapter is to explore the distribution of the reinforced nominative demonstrative pronouns (*emez*/*amaz*) and their pragmatic uses in the Hungarian National Corpus (HNC). It is important to note that I do not intend to give a formal analysis; instead I explore and, as a result, present an overview of typical uses of the reinforced demonstratives, relying on corpus-based data.

4.3.2 Hungarian reinforced demonstratives in use

4.3.2.1 The Hungarian National Corpus

The Hungarian National Corpus is a general representative corpus of present-day Hungarian containing examples from written and spoken language. It is divided into five subcorpora by region and into five subcorpora by register. The queries were executed on each register of the Hungarian regional variant, whose composition is given in Table 4.6. Three of the five registers comprise written texts; these account for almost 80% of the Hungarian regional variants. The remaining parts,

Table 4.6: The Hungarian National Corpus, Hungarian region (Oravecz et al. 2014: 1721)

Register	size (million words)	Sources
journalism	71	news media
literature	35.5	Digital Literary Academy
(popular) science	20.5	Hungarian Electric Library
official	19.9	laws, parliamentary debates
personal	17.8	internet forums
Total	164.7	

the personal and official subcorpora, might be considered good approximations of spontaneous language use.

Clearly, corpus-based research in pragmatic investigations has to face the problem that much of the contextual information is missing from the corpus. Nonetheless, as Rühlemann (2007) notes, deixis constitutes a special area of linguistic inquiry, since several aspects of the situational context manifest themselves in deixis. Hence, corpus-based queries might provide useful information about demonstrative use per se. The research questions addressed by the corpus-based work reported here are the following:

- What is the basic syntactic function of *emez*/*amaz*? Do they occur both as pronominals and adnominals in present-day Hungarian?
- Is the distribution of *emez*/*amaz* different across registers?
- What are the most typical pragmatic uses of *emez*/*amaz*?
- Is there evidence that *emez*/*amaz* make a finer distinction between near and far, as suggested by Tolcsvai Nagy (2001)?
- Do *emez*/*amaz* have a special contrastive function?

In what follows I will describe the emerging data patterns and the analyses I carried out while addressing these questions.

4.3.2.2 Categorization and frequency data

The primary aim of the corpus queries was to explore the various pragmatic (exophoric and non-exophoric) uses of *emez*/*amaz* in present-day Hungarian. To be able to analyse the findings manually (and to save time and effort), I restricted the queries to singular, nominative cases of the demonstratives in question. This decision has been motivated by the fact that a simple frequency query in the Hungarian Webcorpus (Halácsy et al. 2004; Kornai et al. 2006) results in 1161 hits for *emez*, out of which 646 are singular nominative forms, these making up 55.64% of the occurrences. There are 3835 hits for *amaz*, with 2112 singular nominative forms; their frequency is 55.07% of the total number of hits. Therefore, it is reasonable to assume that the restricted queries would capture roughly the same proportion of uses in HNC, and that analysing these uses is sufficient for the purposes of this study.[10]

Each hit in the subsequent queries of *emez*/*amaz* was identified and classified with respect to syntactic function (pronominal or adnominal) and type of use (exophoric, anaphoric, discourse deictic, recognitional, phraseologism, other). The

10 Additionally, as Kleiber et al. (2018) note, case-suffixed forms of the reinforced pronouns are considered to be archaic and only marginally acceptable.

different types of use are based on the taxonomy presented in Chapter 1, Figure 1.1, except for the terms 'phraseologism' and 'other'. Phraseologisms are defined by Gries (2008: 6) as 'the co-occurrence of a form or a lemma of a lexical item and one or more additional linguistic elements of various kinds which functions as one semantic unit in a clause or sentence and whose frequency of co-occurrence is larger than expected on the basis of chance'. This is a relatively broad definition, but it suffices for the aim of the present paper. Henceforth phraseologisms will be labelled as fixed phrases; these will be discussed briefly in Section 4.3.5. The label 'other' refers to those uses of demonstratives that do not fit any of the categories mentioned so far. Within this category, the demonstrative usually serves as the head of a relative clause. Such uses fall out of the scope of the present paper and will not be analysed.

It has to be noted here that one has to proceed with caution when analysing frequency data across various corpora to compensate for the differences in the size of the given corpora. For that reason, to get an overall picture of the distribution of *emez/amaz* in the Hungarian regional variant of the HNC across registers, first their normalized frequencies per million words are presented (Biber et al. 1998; Rühlemann 2007). This means that the number of occurrences for each demonstrative is divided by the size of the individual subcorpus (which is given in Table 4.6 in million words). Later on, a more detailed analysis of various uses will rely on the raw frequencies themselves.

As a starting point, Table 4.7 represents the normalized frequencies of singular nominative forms of *emez/amaz* across registers, i.e., Table 4.7 and Figure 4.3 show how frequent a given word form is out of 1 million words in each subcorpus. If we compare the normalized frequencies of *emez* and *amaz* per million words, it is apparent that *amaz* is consistently more frequent than *emez*; i.e., in each register, *amaz* has far more occurrences than *emez*. This is in line with Egedi's (2015) observations about demonstrative use in Old and Middle Hungarian in general, namely, distal demonstratives occurred more frequently in the Old Hungarian Corpus and in the Middle Hungarian Historical Corpus of Hungarian Private Language investigated by Egedi (2015). The margins are remarkably wide for all but one of the subcorpora: in the journalism corpus *amaz* occurs only twice as many times than *emez*, while, for example, in personal language use we find four times as many occurrences of *amaz*. This particular feature of the distribution of *emez/amaz* will be analysed in a more detailed fashion when the exophoric and non-exophoric uses of the two demonstratives are discussed.

It is worth noting that both *emez* and *amaz* are most widely used in the literary subcorpus, while the personal subcorpus has the second highest number of normalized frequencies for both demonstratives. The latter result is especially interesting, since the personal subcorpus, which is based on discussions of internet

Table 4.7: Normalized frequencies per million words in the HNC across registers

Register	*emez*	*amaz*
journalism	1.141	2.183
literature	9.944	28.056
(popular) science	2.244	9.317
official	0.251	2.362
personal	4.045	17.989

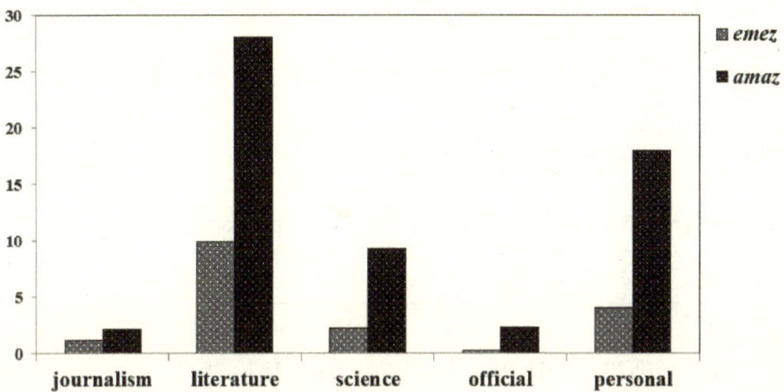

Figure 4.3: Normalized frequencies of *emez/amaz* in the HNC across registers (per million words)

forums, is considered a good approximation of spontaneous language use, so this finding indicates that both *emez* and *amaz* are present in contemporary spoken Hungarian, too.

4.3.2.3 Syntactic functions

Frequency data about the syntactic functions of the demonstratives under scrutiny is given in Tables 4.8 and 4.9 below. The overall picture shows that both demonstratives can occur as pronominals and adnominals, in accordance with Egedi (2015)'s observations on Old and Middle Hungarian. Egedi (2015) also emphasizes the fact that *emez* and *amaz* only rarely occurred in the so-called determiner-doubling construction, since there are only a few such attested examples in Middle Hungarian, probably due to rule generalization or analogy. The same pattern is exhibited in contemporary Hungarian; there were only three determiner-doubling constructions regarding both *emez* and *amaz* (nominative cases).

Egedi (2014) points out that *emez* and *amaz* are only used as pronouns in Standard Modern Hungarian. This claim is not supported by the data, since adnominal

Table 4.8: Syntactic functions of *emez* (nominative case)

	journalism		literature		science		official		personal	
emez	pr	ad	pr	ad	pr	ad	pr	ad	pr	ad
exophoric	0	1	30	12	0	2	0	1	3	3
anaphoric	51	28	173	56	28	7	3	0	41	6
discourse deictic	0	1	2	72	0	8	0	0	7	12
recognitional	0	0	0	0	0	0	0	0	0	0
fixed phrase	0	0	13	0	0	0	1	0	0	0
other	0	0	5	0	1	0	0	0	0	0
Total	51	30	223	140	4	1	29	17	51	21

Table 4.9: Syntactic functions of *amaz* (nominative case)

	journalism		literature		science		official		personal	
amaz	pr	ad	pr	ad	pr	ad	pr	ad	pr	ad
exophoric	12	0	51	0	2	2	1	0	4	1
anaphoric	98	11	528	109	91	5	2	0	131	25
discourse deictic	0	0	0	17	0	5	0	0	0	11
recognitional	0	10	0	95	0	65	0	0	0	55
fixed phrase	18	0	78	0	2	2	44	0	105	0
other	0	6	0	118	17	0	0	0	2	4
Total	128	27	657	339	112	79	47	0	242	96

forms are also found in each subcorpus. On the whole, the ratio of pronominal vs. adnominal use is the following: in the case of *emez*, 63% of the occurrences are pronominal and 37% adnominal; in the case of *amaz* the ratio of pronominal vs. adnominal uses is 69% vs. 31%. Thus the pronominal form is more common in general. However, it is worth noting that the type of usage also matters. Exophoric and anaphoric uses favour the pronominal form, but the adnominal form is the dominant one in discourse deictic and recognitional uses. As we will see later, the presence of the lexical noun in adnominal constructions cannot be described as superfluous, since it often helps the addressee in identifying the referent by adding descriptive content. Admittedly, adnominal uses might sometimes be considered marked and archaic in nature; nevertheless, their occurrence in each subcorpus, and their prevalence in the discourse deictic and recognitional uses indicate that they are still present in contemporary Hungarian.

4.3.3 Pragmatic uses

4.3.3.1 Introduction

In this section, I will describe and analyse the different exophoric and non-exophoric uses of *emez/amaz*. Tables 4.10 and 4.11 display the raw frequencies of singular nominative forms of *emez* and *amaz*, respectively, with a breakdown into the registers and the attested demonstrative functions.[11] It is crucial for the purposes of the present study to analyse spontaneous language use, so the number of occurrences in the personal corpus is broken down into occurrences in three

Table 4.10: Raw frequencies of *emez* (nominative case) in the HNC

					personal				
emez	**journalism**	**literature**	**science**	**official**	forum	social media	spoken	**Total**	**%**
exophoric	1	42	2	1	3	2	1	52	9.17
anaphoric	79	229	35	3	15	30	2	393	69.32
discourse deictic	1	74	8	0	15	3	1	102	17.99
recognitional	0	0	0	0	0	0	0	0	0
fixed phrase	0	13	0	1	0	0	0	14	2.47
other	0	5	1	0	0	0	0	6	1.05
Total	81	363	46	5	33	35	4	567	100

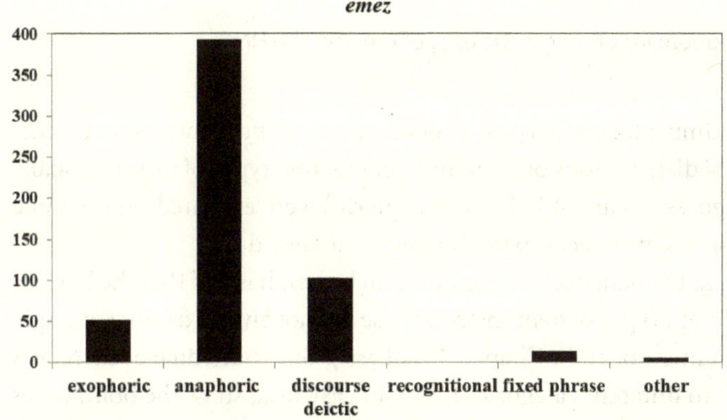

Figure 4.4: Raw frequencies of pragmatic uses of *emez* in the HNC

11 I have manually removed duplicates.

Table 4.11: Raw frequencies of *amaz* (nominative case) in the HNC

					personal				
amaz	**journalism**	**literature**	**science**	**official**	forum	social media	spoken	**Total**	**%**
exophoric	12	51	4	1	0	3	2	73	4.23
anaphoric	109	637	96	2	68	84	4	1000	57.90
discourse deictic	0	17	5	0	1	0	10	33	1.91
recognitional	10	95	65	0	26	28	1	225	13.03
fixed phrase	18	78	4	44	13	22	70	249	14.42
other	6	118	17	0	2	4	0	147	8.51
Total	155	996	191	47	110	141	87	1727	100

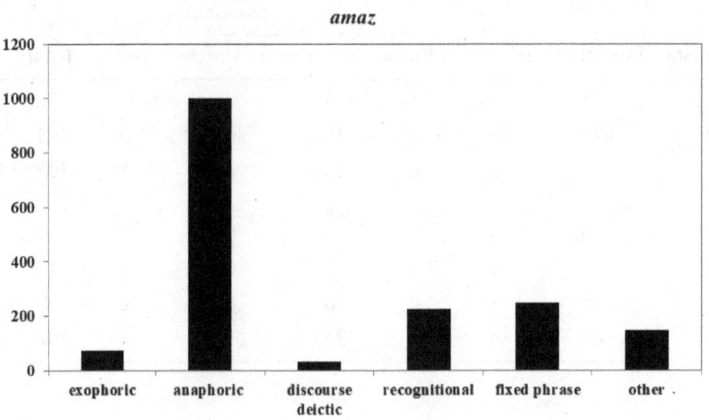

Figure 4.5: Raw frequencies of pragmatic uses of *amaz* in the HNC

subcorpora, including a forum corpus, a social media corpus, and a spoken corpus. The individual distributions of *emez* and *amaz* across types of use are visually represented in Figures 4.4 and 4.5. Since the queries were executed on the same subcorpora, it makes sense to compare the raw frequency data.

Before turning to the data itself, it should again be emphasized that the boundaries between different types of demonstrative use are not always distinct enough. It has already been mentioned in Chapter 1 that assigning individual occurrences of demonstratives to different categories is not an easy task, since the boundaries of the individual categories might be fuzzy, or there might be an overlap between categories. Therefore, it is not always possible to make a decision with absolute certainty. Among others, Levinson (1983: 67) points out that 'clearly the proliferation of different kinds of usage of deictic terms is a source of considerable potential confusion to the analyst'. I followed the same guidelines here as the ones outlined in Section 1.3.2,[12] with one exception.

Non-gestural uses include symbolic uses where no gesture is required on the part of the speaker for the successful identification of the referent by the hearer. The prototypical example could be *This city has many good restaurants*, where the interlocutors can quickly and effortlessly identify the referent of the demonstrative phrase. Another type of non-gestural usage is the so-called transposed use, labelled by Lyons (1977) as deictic projection, when the deictic centre is shifted and the situation is described from the point of view of a speaker in a narrative setting. In such cases the narrator describes an imaginary setting, but he situates the addressee within this imaginary physical environment. Diessel (1999: 95) argues that such uses 'can also be accompanied by a pointing gesture, just like demonstratives that are anchored in the immediate speech situation. The referents are physically absent, but they do exist in the universe of discourse, and speakers point to them as if they were there.' As mentioned above, a large portion of the corpus is based on written sources, many of these being written narratives. Therefore, demonstrative references in narratives, i.e., cases of deictic projection, will be treated here as examples of gestural uses.

A first glimpse at the data reveals that *amaz* not only occurs more frequently, but can also fulfil a wider variety of functions than *emez*. In what follows, I will consider the different types of demonstrative use one by one, provide further details about the distributions and produce some illustrative examples.

4.3.3.2 Exophoric uses

Within the category of exophoric uses, gestural uses of demonstratives rely heavily upon contextual clues, since an accompanying pointing gesture on the part of the speaker is required. Thus it is often sufficient to use only a pronominal to achieve the communicative goal, although the speaker might provide additional cues relying on the descriptive content of the noun. In general, in the case of demonstrative reference, the speaker is guiding the hearer through the process of identifying the referent by narrowing down the set of potential referents. The use of a gesture makes this process highly efficient, i.e., in most cases the use of a pronominal form suffices. For instance, in (20) below, which represents deictic projection, the speaker would probably use some physical gesture to point out and thereby identify the referent that is close to him:

12 Anaphoric uses include cases of anaphora and cataphora.

(20) Tisztességes polgárok lakóházai állnak itt. *Emez* itten éppen az
respectable citizens house.POSS.PL stand.3PL here this here in.fact the
enyém.
mine.
'Respectable citizens' houses stand here. This one here is mine.'
(doc#1935, literary)

In certain situations, a more detailed description of the referent might be required. Such cases involve using a demonstrative plus noun construction, as in the following example, where *amaz ablak* 'that window' without doubt refers to an object located further away from the speaker, due to the nature of the action:

(21) Kétszer elsütheted. Itt a másik töltés is, nesze. Odamégy
twice shoot.POSSIB.2SG here the other bullet too look PRT.go.2SG
amaz ablak alá. És durr!
that window under and crack
'You can shoot twice. Look, here is the second bullet. Go over there to that window. And crack!'
(doc#760, literary)

In the example below, the entity referred to must be close to the speaker, he may even be holding it. The descriptive content of the NP emphasizes the uniqueness of the referent.

(22) Ami maradt: *emez egyetlen könyv.*
what remained.3SG this single book
'The one left behind: this single book.'
(doc 1635, literary)

A special subtype of exophoric use occurs when speakers refer to entities in the situational context that do not have a physical realization in the immediate environment. However, successful reference resolution still relies on contextual information about the time and place of the speech event that is well known to the participants. This usage typically requires an adnominal phrase:

(23) Tisztelt Képviselőtársak és tisztelt Vendégeink, akik
esteemed fellow.representatives and esteemed guests.POSS.PL.1PL who
a testület részéről megtiszteltek minket *emez éjjeli órán*!
the board behalf.DEL PRT.honoured.3PL us.ACC this night.ATTR hour.SUP
'Fellow members and esteemed guests who have honoured us on behalf of the board at this late hour with their presence.'
(doc#2174, official)

(24) Hogy már futásnak eredjek, kiszaladnék *emez*
COMP already running.DAT start.SUBJ.1SG PRT.run.COND.1SG this
országból.
country.ELA
'I should start running away, I should leave this country.'
(doc#2042, literary)

The most interesting question regarding exophoric reference is whether the corpus provides some evidence in favour of the claim that *emez*/*amaz* create a further distinction within near and far. Clearly, the exact characteristics of the physical environment are not available in these cases; still, we can try to draw some tentative conclusions based on the corpus findings.

Laczkó (2009), relying on a limited set of attested data from the HNC, argues that *emez* picks out an entity that is relatively close to the speaker, but this entity is always profiled with respect to another entity that is also close to the speaker, although it is not possible to decide which one is closer to the speaker. Hence, the use of *emez* only implies that there is another entity that is also situated close to the speaker. First, let us reconsider the example in (20), repeated here as (25):

(25) Tisztességes polgárok lakóházai állnak itt. *Emez* itten éppen
respectable citizens house.POSS.PL stand.3PL here this here in.fact
az enyém.
the mine.
'Respectable citizens' houses stand here. This one here is mine.'
(doc#1935, literary)

In line with Laczkó's (2009) suggestion, the speaker here draws the attention of the addressee to a given entity out of a set of similar entities, and thus immediately evokes a contrast between the referent and the other members of the set.

Regarding the co-occurrence of two proximal forms, *ez* and *emez*, Pete (2012) claims, in accordance with the relevant dictionary entry of the *ÉrtSz.*, that *emez* can refer to an entity that is located closer to the speaker than the one being referred to by the other proximal form, *ez*. In the examples below we see cases of deictic projection. (26) is a first-person narrative, while in (27) and (28) the events are narrated by another character. However, it is not possible to decide whether the entities are equidistant from the speaker or one of the entities being referred to is closer to the speaker in the imaginary setting; in fact, the only important thing is that there is an alternative, i.e., there is at least another entity present in the physical environment and the potential referents are competing to be in the joint focus of attention of the interlocutors.

(26) Ne zavarj kérlek éppen egy meggybordó autó
not disturb.IMP.2SG please right.now a cherry.red car
fékcsövét kell elvágnom s hiába van
brake.pipe.POSS.3SG.ACC have.to PRT.cut.INF.1SG and in.vain COP.3SG
a térdemen a könyv az istennek se tudom
the knee.POSS.1SG.SUP the book the god.DAT not know.1SG
mellik az. Ez itt vagy *emez*?
which that this here or this
'Please don't disturb, I have to cut the brake pipe of a red car, and although I have the book on my knees, I cannot decide which one it is. This one or this other one?'
(doc#1001, personal forum)

(27) Szegfűgomba – mondja a férfiú –, ehető. Ez meg
marasmius says the man edible this and
begöngyölt szélű cölöpös. Mérgező, nagyon veszélyes. *Emez* egy
common roll-rim poisonous very dangerous this a
változata, szintén cölöpös; könnyen felismerhető.
variant.POSS.3SG also roll-rim easily recognizable
'This is a marasmius, says the man, it is edible. This one is a common roll-rim, it is poisonous and very dangerous. This other one is one of its variants, a type of roll-rim, too, it can be recognized easily.'
(doc#712, literary)

(28) Nekem háromféle tujám van – mutatja készségesen a
I.DAT three.type thuja.POSS.1SG COP.3SG show.3SG willingly the
választékot egy kedves idős hölgy a palotai piacon.
supply.ACC a nice elderly lady the Palota.ATTR market.SUP
– Ez egy lazább szétterülősebb fajta, mi csak nyugatinak
this a looser flatter type we only western.DAT
nevezzük, ez az öblösebb a keleti, *emez* meg a
call.1PL this the thicker the eastern this and the
nemesített.
domesticated
'I have three types of thuja – a nice elderly lady is showing the stock at the Palota market. – This belongs to a larger, flattened type, we call it western thuja, this thicker one is called eastern thuja, and this other one is domesticated.'
(doc#1091, journalism)

Thus these examples support Laczkó's (2009) assumption that the basic function of *emez* is to call attention to an entity located close to the speaker in relation to (at least) another entity that is also close to the speaker; and accordingly, the meaning of *emez* can be paraphrased as 'this other one'.

As the examples above show, *ez* and *emez* quite frequently occur together, and there seems to be a preferred order of mention: *ez* usually precedes *emez*, as in (26)–(28) above. However, we have to keep in mind that the examples above are contrastive in the broader sense of the term, where one entity is picked out and compared to another one. Under this broad definition of contrastiveness, the following segment is also contrastive: the speaker picks out three entities and describes the differences between them, but the order of mention is different.

(29) Az ott egy kis Maulpertsch, valami mennyezetkép vázlata,
that there a small Maulpertsch some ceiling.fresco sketch.POSS.3SG
emez egy ál-Cranach, ez a parányi meg egy
this a fake-Cranach this the tiny and a
Bosch-hamisítvány.
Bosch-forgery
'That one over there is a small Maulpertsch, it is the sketch of a ceiling fresco, this other one is a fake Cranach, and this tiny one is a Bosch forgery.'
(doc#331, literary)

It is clear that the entity depicted by distal *az* is located further away from the speaker, and the other two are close to the speaker, but there is no clue regarding their relative position to one another. The same example is cited by Laczkó (2009:

240), who claims that the order of mention might indicate that *emez* denotes the object that is closer to the speaker, but admits that this assumption cannot be proved based on the context. The important point is that the order of mention is not entirely fixed when we consider broadly defined contrastive contexts, but there seems to be a preferred order of mention, where *emez* follows *ez*.[13]

If we consider narrowly defined contrastive uses, where contrastiveness is explicitly marked linguistically, we find that there is a serial order of mention. Unfortunately, I have not found narrowly contrastive examples in the corpus, but my own intuitions support the assumption that there is a fixed serial order in these cases. Consider the pairs of examples below. (30) and (32) can be uttered out of the blue in the right conversational setting where many books are present, but (31) and (33) are marked. The latter are acceptable only when they form an answer to a question. For example, if the participants of the speech event are looking at some books at a book fair, (31) can serve as a reply to the question *Ezt olvastam el, és te?* 'I've read this one, and you?'.[14] The fact that the demonstratives occur in identificational focus, as indicated by the position of the verbal particle, also emphasizes the contrast.

(30) Ezt olvastam el, nem *emezt*.
this.ACC read.PST.1SG PRT no this.ACC
'I have read this, not this other one.'

(31) ?*Emezt* olvastam el, nem ezt.
this read.PST.1SG PRT no this.ACC
'I have read this other one, not this.'

(32) Nem ezt viszem el, hanem *emezt*.
no this.ACC take.1SG PRT but this.ACC
'I won't take this one, I'll take this other one.'

(33) ?Nem *emezt* viszem el, hanem ezt.
no this.ACC take.1SG PRT but this.ACC
'It is not this other one I'll take, but this one.'

Nevertheless, the preferred order of mention does not provide any information about the locations of the entities being referred to; the referents might even be equidistant from the speaker. Hence, the question whether *emez* creates a further

13 See also Section 4.3.4.
14 I am grateful to Enikő Németh T. for noting that (31) and (33) are also acceptable and for providing the context described above.

distinction within 'near' is left open. In summary, the examples found in the HNC support Laczkó's (2009) and Kleiber et al.'s (2018) suggestion about the core meaning of *emez* as 'this other one'.

Turning to *amaz*, the emerging picture is slightly different: it can be argued that *amaz* makes a further distinction within 'far' with respect to *az*, and refers to objects that are located further away from the speaker. The order of *az* and *amaz* is fixed in these broadly contrastive examples, so this is a serial order in Fillmore's (1982) terminology.

(34) Honnan a francból jön az a fény a puszta
where.from the hell.ELA come.3SG that the light the prairie
közepén? És az a fény? És *amaz*?
middle.SUP and that the light and that
'Where the hell does that light come from in the middle of the puszta? And that one? And that one further away?'
(doc#2777, personal forum)

(35) A part közepe táján a tudós ránézett a
the riverbank middle.POSS.3SG around the scientist PRT.looked.3SG the
cédulára. Ha az ott az erőmű, *amaz* meg az északi
note.SUBL if that there the power.station that and the northern
összekötő, akkor az lesz a kocsma – mondta.
road then that COP.FUT.3SG the pub said.3SG
'In the middle of the riverbank, the scientist looked at the note. If that one there is the power station, and that one over there is the northern road, then that one must be the pub' – he said.
(doc#1087, journalism)

At the same time, *amaz* can also be used to emphasize that there is another alternative, and can refer to the entity competing to be in the centre of joint attention, meaning 'that other one there':

(36) ÓDÓ ATYA Melyik volt?
Ódó father which COP.PST.3SG
Father Ódó 'Which one did you mean?'
KOLUMB ATYA Ahol úszik ott az a nagy!
Kolumb father where swim.3SG there that the big
Father Kolumb 'It's swimming there, the big one there!'
ÓDÓ ATYA Nagyobb volt az annál!
Ódó father bigger COP.PST.3SG that than.that
Father Ódó 'It was much bigger than that!'
KOLUMB ATYA Akkor *amaz.*
Kolumb father then that
Father Kolumb 'Then that one over there.'
(doc#1512 literary)

Finally, here is an example where the exophoric use of the four demonstratives is illustrated within the same narrative context. Again, it is not the location of the entities that is highlighted; more importantly, the entities being referred to are compared and contrasted with one another:

(37) Furcsálkodva néztünk körül a pompás régiségkereskedésben,
curious.GER looked.1PL around the gorgeous antique.store.INE
amelynek simaképű, idősecske tulajdonosa a
whose fresh.complexioned elderly.DIM owner.POSS.3SG the
gyomra fölött paposan összefont kézzel
stomach.POSS.3SG above priest.ADJ.MOD-ESS intertwined hand.COM
követte kíváncsi tekintetünket. Ez: jó-lenne-ha-volna.
followed.3SG curious gaze.POSS.1PL.ACC this if.only.we.had.it
Az: ingyen-se-kell. *Emez*: bárcsak-ne-lenne-olyan-drága. *Amaz*:
that not.even.for.free this if.only.it.wasn't.so.expensive that
csinoska-de-nem-a-mi-esetünk.
cute-but-not-our-style
'We looked around the nice antique store a little curiously. Its elderly, fresh-complexioned owner followed our gaze with his hand crossed over his stomach. This one: if only we had it. That one: I wouldn't give it houseroom. This other one: I wish it was cheaper. That other one: it's nice, but not our cup of tea.'
(doc#1504, literary)

4.3.3.3 Anaphoric uses

We have seen in Chapter 1 that the nominal demonstratives *ez/az* play an active role in anaphoric relations across sentence boundaries. Interpreting these anaphors is not always an easy task, since their use is governed by syntactic, semantic, and pragmatic factors. The basic insights outlined on the anaphoric use of *ez/az* in Chapter 1 serve as a background to the discussion of anaphoric *emez/amaz*. In this section, I will provide some relevant examples taken from the HNC and attempt to characterise this type of usage.

Before turning to the Hungarian data itself it is worth mentioning that cross-linguistically, anaphoric demonstratives often take non-topical antecedents, thus their referent is not in the focus of attention and their function is to signal a change of topic. This tendency has been observed in German, Dutch and Russian, among others (see Diessel 1999), and we have seen that anaphoric *ez/az* might also indicate a topic shift.

There is not much information to be found about the anaphoric uses of *emez/amaz* in Hungarian descriptive grammars. As we have seen in Section 4.3.1, the *ÉrtSz.* notes that the antecedent of *emez* is the last mentioned referring expression, while regarding *amaz*, the *NSz.* points out that the antecedent of *amaz* is the NP mentioned first. Turning to the corpus data, most occurrences of *emez* and *amaz* are anaphoric in the HNC, their relative frequency being 69.32% and 57.90%, respectively. This fact is especially interesting in light of Egedi's (2014, 2015) observation that *imez/amaz* were not used anaphorically in Middle Hungarian. In what follows I will explore anaphoric *emez/amaz* in the corpus.[15] It must be noted, however, that this section only offers some observations, and I will not attempt to provide a proper analysis.

First, the examples below show that both demonstratives can co-refer with their antecedent intrasententially and across sentence boundaries. *Emez* and *amaz* are used as subject anaphors below:

(38) Legjobb esetben a vers uralja <u>lejegyzőjét</u> és
best case.INE the poem dominate.3SG writer.POSS.3SG.ACC and
emez is a verset.
this too the poem.ACC
'At best the poem dominates its writer, and he also dominates the poem.'
(doc#1734, literary)

---

15 Cataphoric uses are less frequent. As in Section 1.3.2.2.1, the analysis focuses on cases of anaphora.

(39) Bajnai feldobta a magas labdát Mesterházynak, *amaz* meg
Bajnai PRT.threw.3SG the high ball.ACC Mesterházy.DAT that and
leütötte.
PRT.hit.3SG
'Bajnai has thrown up a lob for Mesterházy and he has hit it.'
(doc#2746, social media)

(40) A hajós int a férfinak, hogy siessen. *Emez*
the sailor wave.3SG the man.DAT COMP hurry.SUBJ.3SG this
meggyorsítja lépteit.
PRT.quicken.3SG step.POSS.PL.ACC
'The sailor motions the man to hurry up. He is quickening his steps.'
(doc#706, literary)

(41) Zhang Fenget küldte, hogy fogadja a kihívást. *Amaz*
Zhang Feng.ACC sent.3SG COMP accept.SUBJ.3SG the challenge that
lovának teljes erejéből vágtatva, kész
horse.POSS.3SG.DAT entire strength.POSS.3SG.ELA gallop.GER ready
lándzsájával támadásba lendült.
spear.POSS.3SG.INST attack.ILL started.3SG
'Zhang sent Feng to accept the challenge. He rode hell for leather as he charged, holding his spear ready.'
(doc#2796, personal forum)

It is also important to note that in the examples above both demonstratives have animate antecedents, but in (42) and (43) the antecedents are inanimate.

(42) A GTX 550 Ti a Crysis 2-ben, a Just Cause 2-ben, a
the GTX 550 Ti the Crysis 2-INE the Just Cause 2-INE the
DiRT 3-ban, lepipálja a HD 6790-et, *emez* pedig a Crysisban
DiRT 3-INE outdo.3SG the HD 6790-ACC this in.turn the Crysis.INE
és a Battlefield 3-ban vágott vissza árriválisának.
and the Battlefield 3-INE retaliated.3SG PRT price.rival.DAT
'GTX 550 Ti is much better in Crysis 2, Just Cause 2, and DiRT 3 than HD 6790, but the latter has retaliated against his rival in Crysis and Battlefield 3.'
(doc#2247, journalism)

(43) Legutoljára Nintendo DS-re adták ki a
last.time Nintendo DS-SUBL released.3PL PRT the
Dragon Quest IX-et, s *amaz* 3.7 millió példányban fogyott.
Dragon Quest IX-ACC and that 3.7 million copy.INE sold.3SG
'Dragon Quest IX was last released for Nintendo DS, and it sold 3.7 million copies.'
(doc#2245, personal forum)

Finally, a common feature of the anaphoric uses exemplified above is that both *emez* and *amaz* refer to non-topic antecedents. It is also interesting to note that in (42) *emez* occurs in a clause with a contrastive sense. There are several such examples in the corpus, especially in the case of inanimate antecedents. Two further examples are presented below:

(44) az OMV, amely egyik nagy tulajdonosa a hazai
the OMV which one big owner.POSS.3SG the domestic
olajvállalatnak, már tavaly június óta közeledni próbál
oil.company.DAT already last June since approach.INF try.3SG
a MOL-hoz, *emez* viszont kézzel-lábbal tiltakozik a
the MOL-ALL this however hand.INS-foot.INS oppose.3SG the
kéretlen házasság ellen.
unwanted marriage against
'OMV, which is one of the big owners of the domestic oil company, has been trying to approach MOL since last June, which, however, opposes the unwanted marriage tooth and nail.'
(doc 2627, spoken)

(45) De merre is terítse el képzeletünk ezt a
but where too lay.IMP.3SG PRT imagination.POSS.1PL this.ACC the
híres-neves Zsanócot? Modern, a technika vívmányaival
famous Zsanóc.ACC modern the technology advances.POSS.PL.COM
jó kapcsolatot ápoló olvasóként először a Google
good connection.ACC treat.PRTC reader.ESS-FORM first the Google
Earthhöz fordulunk, de *emez* ahelyett, hogy közelebb
Earth.ALL turn.1PL but this instead.of COMP closer
vinne a tájhoz, arra szólít föl,
take.COND.3SG the landscape.ALL that.SUBL request.3SG PRT
nézzük meg, helyesen írtuk-e a helynevet.
look.IMP.1PL PRT correctly wrote.1PL-QPRT the place.name.ACC
'But where is this famous Zsanóc? As a modern reader, who is aware of technical advances, we first turn to Google Earth, but it, instead of taking us closer to the landscape, requests us to check the spelling.'
(doc 1356, journalism)

It has been pointed out in Chapter 1 that proximal *ez* acts as an anaphor only under special circumstances, for example, when its use conveys something unexpected. In the examples above there is a kind of contrast, the information carried by the clause is contrary to expectation. Thus it might be assumed that a contrast renders the use of *emez* more appropriate in these examples. However, *amaz* can also occur with a contrastive conjunction, as illustrated by (46) from the corpus. Interestingly, the animacy feature cannot explain this type of usage, since *emez* can also take animate antecedents, and it would also be acceptable in the same context.

(46) Zsuzsa ugyanis elhatározta, hogy hétfőn megmondja a
Zsuzsa namely PRT.decided.3SG COMP Monday.SUP PRT.tell.3SG the
férfinak, *amaz* azonban váratlanul, abban az időpontban, amikor
man.DAT that however unexpectedly that.INE the time.INE when
nem lehetett rá számítani, szombat éjjel becsöngetett
no was.POSSIB on.it count.INF Saturday night PRT.rang.3SG
hozzá.
she.ALL
'Zsuzsa had decided to fill the man in on Monday, but he turned up unexpectedly at a time when she wasn't expecting him, on Saturday night.'
(doc#2288, journalism)

A minor difference between *emez* and *amaz* is that in (47) below, *emez* emphasizes a change of perspective in the third person narrative. This is strengthened by the use of psych verbs (*észrevesz* 'notice' and *ért* 'understand'), which describe the mental state of the electrician.

(47) A 'vonal' az volt benne, hogy a válni
the line that COP.PST.3SG it.INE COMP the divorce.INF
készülő orvosnő beleszeret a lakásában napok
prepare.PRTC doctor.woman fall.in.love.3SG the flat.POSS.3SG.INE days
óta dolgozó villanyszerelőbe. *Emez* észreveszi, hogy valami
since work.PRTC electrician.ILL this notice.3SG COMP something
baj van az asszony házassága körül (a férj
problem COP.3SG the woman marriage.POSS.3SG around the husband

egy részeges színész), ám nem egészen érti a
a drunken actor) though no completely understand.3SG the
viselkedését.
behaviour.POSS.3SG.ACC
'The story line was that a female doctor, about to divorce, falls in love with the electrician who has been working in her flat for days. The latter notices that something's wrong with her marriage (the husband is a drunken actor), but he doesn't understand her behaviour.'
(doc#1106, journalism)

In a similar fashion, writers also use *emez/amaz* as pronominal anaphors in literary dialogues to refer to the interlocutors. Both demonstratives can fulfil this function:[16]

(48) Hát az úr kiféle volna, ha meg nem sérteném?,
well the sir who.kind COP.COND.3SG if PRT no offend.COND.1SG
lépett a doktor az idegen elé.
stepped.3SG the doctor the strange in.front
'And may I ask you what do you do?' said the doctor stepping in front of the stranger.
Íróféle, ha nem bánja, felelte az elegáns jövevény.
writer.kind if no mind.3SG replied.3SG the elegant newcomer
'I'm a writer if you don't mind' said the elegant newcomer.
Író?, csóválta meg *emez* a fejét, azok nem
writer shook.3SG PRT this the head.POSS.3SG.ACC those no
csapatostul járnak.
group.SOC go.3PL
"A writer?' the other shook his head, 'they do not travel in groups'.
(doc#2212, literary)

(49) Csak nekem nem megy ki a fejemből?
only I.DAT no go.3SG PRT the head.POSS.1SG.ELA
'Am I the only one who cannot forget it?'
Nem csak – felelte komoran *amaz.*
no only replied.3SG sombre.MOD-ESS that
"No, you're not' said the other.'
(doc#2662, social media)

16 A detailed analysis of how *emez/amaz* might represent different narrative points of view lies outside the scope of this work.

Turning to demonstrative plus lexical noun combinations it is interesting to notice that there is another special use of *emez* where it cannot be substituted by *amaz*. Namely, when a demonstrative noun phrase anaphor includes a kind of evaluative comment by the speaker or when it adds further information to the antecedent, only *emez* is grammatical. This type of usage is more common in the literary and journalism subcorpora. Consider the example below, where the anaphor contributes a new feature to the antecedent:

(50) Elkerülhetetlen, hogy itt, az 1130 méter magas, monstruózus
unavoidable COMP here the 1130 meter high monstrous
tömböt képező Székelykövön, a világnak *emez egyik*
rock.shoulder.ACC form.PRTC Székelykő.SUP the world.DAT this one
szerény magaslatán ki-ki szembe ne kerüljön azzal
modest height.POSS.3SG.SUP who-who opposite.ILL no become.IMP.3SG that.COM
a meghatározottsággal, hogy magyar.
the determination.COM COMP Hungarian
'It is unavoidable to face one's Hungarian identity here, on this 1130 m high rock shoulder of Székelykő, one of the world's more modest heights.'
(doc#1045, journalism)

In a similar fashion, *emez* plus noun constructions can also refer to propositions, thus they can serve as complex anaphors in Kocsány's (2018) terms:

(51) Ő, valahányszor rajta ért, hogy már megint a
He whenever on.it caught.3SG COMP already again the
gyermeket vigyázom, ingerülten rám szólt, mondván, minden
child.ACC watch.over.1SG irritably rebuked.me.3SG say.GER every
egyéb kötelességemet elhanyagolom *emez esztelen*
other responsibility.POSS.1SG.ACC PRT.neglect.1SG this mindless
őrködés kedvéért.
guarding sake. POSS.3SG.CAUS-FIN
'Whenever he caught me watching over the kid, he told me irritably that I was neglecting all my other chores for the sake of this mindless attending to the child.'
(doc#637, literary)

Finally, it is worth noting that in the example below, *amaz* is an indirect anaphor, its antecedent is not directly recoverable from the context, but it clearly refers to the other one out of two, which supports the assumption about its core meaning being 'that other one'.

(52) volt belőle kettő, egy száraz a vízen kívüli
COP.PST.3SG from.it two one dry the water.SUP outside.ATTR
tevékenységre, míg *amaz* megszárad
activity.SUBL while that PRT.dry.3SG
'there were two, a dry one for beach activities, while the other one was drying'
(doc#2657, personal forum)

emez can also act as an indirect anaphor; in (53) below it refers back to our Gmail account, which only occurs under negation in the first clause.

(53) És természetesen csak a nem Gmailes fiókjainkat
and naturally only the no Gmail.ADJ account.POSS.PL.1PL.ACC
kell megadogatni, mert ugyebár *emez* beállítódott
have.to PRT.give.FREQ.INF because of.course this PRT.set.up.PST.3SG
az első 2 percben és azóta jönnek is a
the first 2 minute.INE and since.then come.3PL too the
leveleink.
letter.POSS.PL.1PL.
'Naturally, we have to indicate only email accounts that are different from Gmail, since that one has already been created in the first two minutes and emails have been coming since then.'
(doc#2247, journalism)

As an interim summary, we can conclude that both *emez* and *amaz* fulfil anaphoric functions in Hungarian. Some emerging generalizations about anaphoric *emez*/*amaz* are as follows:

- *emez*/*amaz* can act as anaphors both intrasententially and across sentence boundaries;
- both demonstratives can refer to animate and inanimate antecedents;
- when used as subject anaphors, both can refer to a non-topic antecedent.

The analysis also revealed minor differences between anaphoric *emez* and *amaz*. In the next section, we will turn to contrastive anaphoric uses in order to further examine their role in anaphora.

4.3.3.4 Contrastive anaphoric uses

In the following examples, *emez* and *amaz* occur as anaphors within the same sentence, and in these cases they cannot substitute for each other.

(54) Két réve volt a Balatonnak. Az egyik a
two ferry.POSS.3SG COP.PST.3SG the Balaton.DAT the one the
tihanyi$_i$, a másik a fülöpi$_j$. *Amaz*$_i$ keskeny, *emez*$_j$ széles
Tihany.ATTR the other the Fülöp.ATTR that narrow this broad
víziút.
waterway
'Balaton used to have two ferries, one at Tihany and another at Fülöp. The former waterway was narrow, the latter broad.'
(doc#169, literary)

(55) Azt hiszem megállapodhatunk abban, hogy a
that.ACC think.1SG PRT.agree.COND.1PL that.INE COMP the
robbanómotor$_i$ kábé annyira szakszerű, mint az én
combustion.engine about that.amount professional as the I
közelebbi szakmámban a lökhajtásos$_j$. *Amaz*$_i$ nem
closer profession.POSS.1SG.INE the jet.engine that no
robban, *emez*$_j$ nem lök.
combust.3SG this no jet.3SG
'I think we all agree that the term combustion engine is as professional as the term jet engine in my own field of interest. The former does not combust, the latter does not jet.'
(doc#1002, personal forum)

The meaning of proximal *emez* in these examples is 'the latter', while distal *amaz* stands for 'the former'.[17] The order of mention varies, as illustrated below, but only pronominal forms are used in this manner.

(56) olyan ragaszkodásom van a szénhez$_i$, akár a búzához$_j$.
such attachment.POSS.1SG COP.3SG the coal.ALL even the wheat.ALL
Emez$_j$ gyomromat, *amaz*$_i$ bőrömet melegítette.
this stomach.POSS.1SG.ACC that skin.POSS.1SG.ACC warmed.3SG
'I gravitate to coal just as I gravitate to wheat. The latter heated my stomach, the former my skin.'
(doc#158, literary)

Lyons (1977) argues that anaphora can be considered as reference to entities already introduced into the universe of discourse. More specifically, he claims that 'anaphora involves the transference of what are basically spatial notions to the

17 It is interesting to note that anaphoric pronominal *emez* does not always refer to 'the latter' in these contrastive uses. Two relevant examples are given below:

temporal dimension of the context-of-utterance and the reinterpretation of deictic location in terms of what may be called location in the universe-of-discourse' (Lyons 1977: 670). This means that an anaphoric expression directs the attention of the addressee to a given part of the text where he will not find the exact location

---

(i) Piroska$_i$ is jó volt, nevettünk, élveztük, játék volt, és
Piroska too good COP.PST.3SG laughed.1PL enjoyed.1PL play COP.PST.3SG and
nem bántott. Azért jobb lett volna, ha a Szkéné körüli
no hurt.PST.3SG but better COP.COND.PST.3SG if the Szkéné around.ATTR
előadások közül inkább valami új kap meghívást: mondjuk
plays among instead something new get.3SG invitation.ACC say.1PL
Kórház-Bakony$_j$. Annak$_j$ itt lett volna a helye, *emez*$_i$
Kórház-Bakony that.DAT here COP.COND.PST.3SG the place.POSS.3SG this
viszont kissé kilógott a menüből.
however a.bit PRT.hung.3SG the menu.ELA
'Piroska was also good, we could laugh, we enjoyed it, it was a play and didn't hurt. But it would have been better if a new performance, for example Kórház-Bakony, had been invited from Szkéné's repertoire. That would have fit in; the former was a bit out of place.'
(doc#1071, journalism)

(ii) Ez a vén banya$_i$, rosszabb, mint az ura$_j$ volt. Az$_j$
this the old hag worse than the husband.POSS.3SG COP.PST.3SG that
számított politikusnak, *emez*$_i$ viszont csak makacskodik.
counted.3SG politician.DAT this however only being.stubborn
'This old hag is worse than her husband used to be. He was a real politician, but she is just being stubborn.'
(doc#2933, social media)

In both cases the antecedent of distal *az* is the immediately preceding NP. A potential explanation is that *emez* takes up the topic again after an interjection. This assumption is strengthened by the following examples, where anaphoric *emez* refers to the topic of a sentence that was introduced into the discourse earlier, i.e. there is always at least one intervening clause between *emez* and its antecedent:

(iii) Orosz zászló leng Groznij felett. Más ez a lobogó$_i$, mint amelyet
Russian flag fly.3SG Groznij above different this the banner than what.ACC
Berlin fölött lengetett a szél azon a májuson$_j$. És nemcsak
Berlin above swayed.3SG the wind that.SUP the May.SUP and not.only
azért más, mert az a zászló$_j$ a Szovjetunióé
that.CAUS-FIN different because that the flag the Soviet.Union.POSS
volt, *emez*$_i$ pedig Oroszországé.
COP.PST.3SG this in.turn Russia.POSS
'The Russian flag is flying over Groznij. This is not the flag that was flying over Berlin that May. And the only difference is not that the latter was the flag of the Soviet Union, and this is the flag of Russia.'
(doc#1095, journalism)

of the referent, since it is only in the universe of discourse; instead, he will be guided to the textual location of the referent, which serves as a guide to the location of the referent in the temporally structured universe of discourse with respect to the moment of utterance. In that way, contrastive anaphoric demonstratives encode the relation of temporal proximity, i.e. deictic considerations help in identifying the antecedents, and in turn, the referents: a proximal anaphoric expression directs the attention of the addressee to the temporally most proximate referent in the universe-of-discourse, while a distal term refers to a more remote entity in the discourse.[18] In fact, this is exactly what we can see in the examples above. The line of thought presented here also serves as evidence that this type of anaphora stems from deictic considerations. Moreover, I assume that the use of the two demonstratives to refer to entities introduced earlier into the universe of discourse creates a contrast under the broad definition of contrastiveness. Hence, just as in the case of exophoric use, a difference can be made between contrastive and non-contrastive anaphoric references. The examples presented below, which represent boundary cases between anaphoric and transposed uses, provide further evidence for this assumption:

(iv) A képernyő$_i$ ebben már szigorúan csak Super LCD, ami nem tudom,
the screen this.INE already strictly only Super LCD that no know.1SG
mitől szuper. Persze talán az elébiggyesztett fellengzős szó csak
what.ABL super of.course maybe the in.front.placed pompous word only
ellensúlyozása a konkurencia Super AMOLED-jének$_j$. Na az$_j$
counterbalancing.POSS.3SG the competitor Super AMOLED-POSS.3SG.DAT well that
tényleg szuper. *Emez*$_i$ meg átlagos, fakó.
really super. this and average faint
'The screen in this one is always Super LCD; I don't know what makes it super. Perhaps this pompous word is supposed to counterbalance the competitor's Super AMOLED. Well, that is indeed super. The former is just average, faint.'
(doc 2447 journalism)

18 In a similar fashion, Tátrai (2017) claims that in the case of discourse deixis, proximal *ez* points at a place that is closest to the time of speaking in the discourse.

(57) a tétovázást, hogy a rászabott tebennoszt$_i$ felpróbálja,
the hesitation.ACC COMP the onto.him.tailored tebenos.ACC on.try.3SG
meghosszabbította, hogy nem volt bizonyos benne, a
PRT.extended.3SG COMP no COP.PST.3SG sure it.INE the
melléhelyezett palástforma körgallér$_j$ alulra kerül-e – vagy
next.to.it.placed cloak.shaped cape under.SUBL go.3SG-QPRT or
amaz$_i$ kerül alulra s felülre *emez*$_j$?
that go.3SG under.SUBL and above.SUBL this
'His hesitation to try on the tebenos was extended by the uncertainty that he did not know whether the cloak-shaped cape placed next to it was to be worn under (the tebenos itself) – or perhaps the former should be worn under the latter?'
(doc#338, literary)

(58) Amélie az emeletes ház elé kanyarodott – még egy
Amélie the storey.ADJ house in.front turned.3SG another one
kisebb$_i$ s egy nagyobb épület$_j$ állt a tanyaudvar
smaller and one bigger building stood.3SG the farm
túlfelén, *amaz*$_i$ baromfiól volt és a
other.side.POSS.3SG.SUP that chicken.coop COP.PST.3SG and the
sertések hidasa, *emez*$_j$ felerészben istálló, felerészben
pigs sty.POSS.3SG this half.part.INE stable half.part.INE
kocsiszín és magtár.
shed and granary
'Amélie pulled up in front of the house. On the other side of the farm, there were two buildings, one small and the other large. The former was a chicken coop, a stable constituted one-half of the latter, the other half was used as a shed and a granary.'
(doc#706, literary)

4.3.3.5 Discourse deictic and recognitional uses

Discourse deictic uses usually refer to another part of the discourse. Adnominal uses are prevalent here, since the descriptive content of the NP aids the identification of the referent, as in (59).

(59) Kérlek hirdesd *emez sorokat* okulására jövő
please spread.IMP.2SG this lines.ACC education.POSS.3SG.SUBL future
nemzetségek tagjainak.
generations member.POSS.3SG.PL.DAT
'Please spread these lines, future generations could learn from them.'
(doc#2731, personal)

Emez is more common in this type of usage, but *amaz* can also fulfil discourse deictic functions:[19]

(60) Ezt a verset *amaz előbbi vers* alkotáslélektani
this.ACC the poem.ACC that former poem creation.psychological
ikrének mondtam.
twin.POSS.3SG.DAT said.1SG
'I considered this verse as the creating-psychological twin of the former one.'
(doc#1376, literary)

Sometimes *emez* is used pronominally to refer to a chunk of discourse:

(61) Polar Falcon, Dayjur (legendás nevek, főleg *emez*).
Polar Falcon Dayjur legendary names particularly this
'Polar Falcon, Dayjur (legendary names, particularly the latter).'
(doc#2061, literary)

In such instances, it can be difficult to say whether this use is best considered a case of anaphora taking the prior linguistic material as its antecedent, or a case of discourse deixis taking the prior linguistic material as its referent.

Recognitional deixis is different from exophoric and discourse deixis, since the referent is not recoverable either from the physical context or from the previous discourse. When using a recognitional demonstrative, the speaker indicates that the referent is part of the shared background knowledge of the interlocutors, which is based on their common experience. The speaker expects the hearer to be successful in identifying the referent, and the descriptive content of the noun guides the hearer in this activation process. Recognitional deixis is realized only by adnominal distal demonstratives across languages (Diessel 1999). This observation is also strengthened by the corpus data, with only adnominal *amaz* occurring in this type of use:

19 The contrast created might render the use of *amaz* more appropriate here.

(62) Álmomban, akárcsak *amaz utolsó ödenburgi reggelen,*
dream.POSS.1SG.INE just.like that last Ödenburg.ATTR morning.SUP
ott szaladok megint az égő városban.
there run.1SG again the burning city.INE
'In my dream, just like that last morning in Ödenburg, I'm running again in the burning town.'
(doc#637, literary)

As Diessel (1999) notes, recognitional deixis often conveys the emotional attitude of the speaker and can create a feeling of familiarity among interlocutors. For example, in (63) below, the demonstrative signals that participants in the conversation have the same opinion about the referent:

(63) A Gyula, a választások éjszakáján, nyilatkozván *amaz*
the Gyula the elections night.POSS.3SG.SUP state.GER that
gazbitangártányossajtónak:
malicious.nefarious.media.DAT
'Gyula, on the night of the elections, said to that malicious and nefarious media:'
GBÁS: Mit szól Ön a MIÉP eredményéhez?
MNM: what.ACC say.3SG you.FORM the MIÉP result.POSS.3SG.ALL
'MNM: What is your opinion about the MIÉP results?'
Gy: Mit szólok... Nem örülök neki.
Gy: what.ACC say.1SG no be.happy.1SG it.DAT
'Gy: Well, I'm not happy about it.'
(doc#982, forum)

In the HNC, recognitional demonstratives occurred most frequently in the literary corpus. This is not surprising, since writers often use recognitional deixis to create a familiarity with the reader. Nonetheless, Consten and Averintseva-Klisch (2012) argue that recognitional deixis is basically interactional in nature, by means of which the speakers imply mutual knowledge of the referent. At the same time, hearers might accept this reference or ask for clarification. Further research is called for to study this assumption in a spoken corpus of Hungarian.

4.3.4 Contrastive uses reconsidered

Finally, let us again turn to a use that is of special interest for the present analysis, namely, to contrastive uses. It was mentioned in Section 4.3.3.2 that *emez/amaz* have been described as having a special contrastive function, their core meaning being 'this other one' and 'that other one' when used exophorically (Laczkó 2009), and in Section 4.3.3.4 we have seen that they also create a contrast between 'the latter' and 'the former' in anaphoric uses. To further explore the notion of contrastiveness, I identified each contrastive occurrence of *emez*/*amaz* within exophoric and anaphoric uses.[20] Tables 4.12 and 4.13 show the frequencies and proportions of contrastive *emez* and *amaz* with respect to the number of occurrences in each cell. For example, in the literary subcorpus there were 126 anaphoric contrastive examples out of 229 anaphoric occurrences of *emez*, which constitutes 55.02% of anaphoric uses. Within the same subcorpus, the total number of contrastive cases (expohoric and anaphoric) is 154 out of 363, which is 42.42%.

In Table 4.12 we can see that *emez* can be used contrastively both exophorically and anaphorically, and in both cases more than half of the total occurrences are

Table 4.12: The absolute and relative frequency of contrastive *emez*

					personal			
emez	**journalism**	**literature**	**science**	**official**	forum	social media	spoken	**Total**
exophoric	0	28	2	0	3	0	0	33
	(0)	(66.66)	(100)	(0)	(100)	(0)	(0)	(63.46)
anaphoric	29	126	15	0	10	21	1	202
	(36.07)	(55.02)	(42.85)	(0)	(66.66)	(70)	(50)	(51.39)
Total	29	154	17	0	13	21	1	235
	(35.8)	(42.42)	(36.95)	(0)	(39.39)	(60)	(25)	(41.44)

Table 4.13: The absolute and relative frequency of contrastive *amaz*

					personal			
amaz	**journalism**	**literature**	**science**	**official**	forum	social media	spoken	**Total**
exophoric	12	50	1	0	0	0	2	65
	(100)	(98.03)	(25)	(0)	(0)	(0)	(100)	(89.04)
anaphoric	39	123	18	1	29	34	2	246
	(35.77)	(19.3)	(18.75)	(50)	(42.64)	(40.47)	(50)	(24.6)
Total	51	173	19	1	29	34	4	311
	(32.9)	(17.36)	(9.94)	(2.12)	(26.36)	(24.11)	(4.59)	(18)

20 Contrastive uses also include cases where the contrast is created between the referents of a demonstrative and a referential NP. Relevant examples will be provided later on (see for example (64)).

contrastive (63.46 and 51.39%, respectively). *Amaz* can be described in a similar manner, although the proportions are slightly different, i.e., almost 90% of the exophoric uses are contrastive, while the ratio is smaller in the case of anaphora, 24.6% (see Table 4.13).

Overall, these findings strengthen the hypothesis regarding the contrastive nature of *emez/amaz*. It is worth noting that for both demonstratives, the most frequent uses are anaphoric contrastive uses in the literary subcorpus, but there is also a high proportion of exophoric contrastive uses in the same subcorpus. Within contrastive uses, various subtypes can be differentiated; in what follows, I will describe these briefly.

Regarding exophoric use, *emez* and *amaz* are often used to call the attention of the addressee to an entity by contrasting it to another entity identified by an NP. This usage was already attested in Middle Hungarian, as it was mentioned in Section 4.3.1 (D. Mátai 1999). Hence, such examples strengthen the hypothesis about the core meaning of *emez/amaz*:

(64) itt egy kis hevítő; *Emez* pedig nénédnek altató.
here a little stimulant this in.turn aunt.POSS.2SG.DAT sedative
'here is a stimulant, and this (other) one is a sedative for your aunt.'
(doc#1527, literary)

(65) AbdulAziz is szeret lógni, meg *amaz* is, a rongyos kék kabátban.
AbdulAziz too like.3SG hang.INF and that too the shabby blue coat.INE
'AbdulAziz likes to play truant, just like that (other) one, in the shabby blue coat.'
(doc#2704, social media)

(66) Jellemző, hogy később a sörösüveget a másik kezével tartotta, *emez* élettelnül lifegett.
typical COMP later the beer.bottle.ACC the other hand.POSS.3SG.COM held.3SG this lifelessly hung.3SG
'It is typical that later on he was holding the beer bottle in his other hand; this one was hanging lifeless.'
(doc#1419, literary)

In many instances, in 72 cases, *emez* and *amaz* co-occur within the same utterance; such contrastive uses mostly contain pronominals. The examples below illustrate the exophoric contrastive use from the literary subcorpus:

(67) *Emez* hortyog, *amaz* szemrehúzta a süvegjét… Hé,
this snore.3SG that eye.SUBL.pulled.3SG the hat.POSS.3SG.ACC hey
te bojtár!
you shepherd
'This one is snoring, that other one has drawn his hat over his eyes… Hey, you shepherd boy!'
(doc#1513 literary)

(68) Itt két szoba van egymás mellett. Ezek voltak az
here two room COP.3SG each.other next.to these COP.PST.3PL the
öltözők: *emez* a férfiaké, *amaz* a nőké. Velük
changing.rooms this the men.POSS that the women.POSS with.them
szemben pedig a jelmeztár.
opposite but the costume.storage
'There are two rooms next to each other. These used to be the changing rooms: this one used to belong to men, that (other) one to women. And opposite them was the costume storage.'
(doc#131, literary)

Such uses are relatively rare in the corpus. Nevertheless, since the referents are located next to each other in the case of (68), we can assume that relative distance from the speaker is overwritten by the contrast invoked by the demonstratives.

Anaphoric contrastive examples have been discussed in Section 4.3.3.4 above. Another example is given below:

(69) Közülük ketten <u>Gróf István</u>$_i$ és <u>Kovács Koródi Ferenc</u>$_j$ – a
among.them two Gróf István and Kovács Koródi Ferenc the
fegyenczruhát le sem vetve magukról – Komárom
convict.clothes.ACC PRT not take.PRTC themselves.DEL Komárom
felé vették utjokat. *Amaz*$_i$ gyilkosságért 12
toward took.3PL journey.POSS.3PL.ACC that murder.CAUS-FIN 12
évre, *emez*$_j$ rablásért öt évi fegyházra
year.SUBL this robbery.CAUS-FIN five year.ATTR jail.SUBL
volt ítélve.
COP.PST.3SG sentence.PRTC
'Two of them, István Gróf and Ferenc Kovács Koródi had not even taken off their convict's clothes, but turned to Komárom. The former was sentenced to 12 years for murder, and the latter to 5 years for robbery.'
(doc#1109, journalism)

Table 4.14: Contrastive patterns in the HNC

pattern	absolute frequency	relative frequency
emez-amaz	72	24.32%
ez-emez	17	5.75%
ez-amaz	180	60.82%
az-emez	21	7.09%
az-amaz	6	2.02%
Total	296	100

Not only do *emez* and *amaz* occur in contrastive contexts together, the other nominal demonstratives *ez*/*az* can also combine with *emez*/*amaz* intrasententially. The various combinations and the relative frequency of the individual patterns are given in Table 4.14.[21]

The most frequent pattern, which constitutes almost 61% of the total number of cases, is formed by *ez-amaz*. This pattern surfaces in both exophoric (70) and anaphoric (71) uses:

(70)

Csiribű, csiribá,	*ez*	ide	az	ágy	alá,	*amaz*	meg	a
bibbidi-bobbidi	this	to.this.place	the	bed	under	that	and	the

polcra –	jó	lesz	karácsonyra.
shelf.SUBL	good	COP.FUT.3SG	Christmas.SUBL

'Bibbidi-bobbidi, this comes here below the bed, that (other) one goes to the shelf – for Christmas!'
(doc#1345, literary)

(71)

Szeretem	az	őszi	hideg	szobákat,	ülni	kora	reggel
like.1SG	the	autumn.ATTR	cold	rooms.ACC	sit.INF	early	morning

összehúzott	köntösben	a	kitárt	ablaknál,	vagy	a	tetőn,
together.pulled	robe.INE	the	open	window.ADE	or	the	roof.SUP

párolog	a	völgy$_i$	meg	a	csésze	kávé$_j$ –	*ez*$_j$	hűl,	*amaz*$_i$
steam.3SG	the	valley	and	the	cup	coffee	this	cool.3SG	that

melegszik.
warm.3SG

'I like cold autumn rooms, sitting early morning in a nightgown in front of the open window or on the roof; the valley and my cup of coffee are steaming – the latter is cooling, the former is warming.'
(doc#2775, social media)

21 Here only those patterns are mentioned in which one of the demonstratives is either *emez* or *amaz* (nominative cases). Patterns involving only *ez-az* are not discussed here.

In (70), the exact location of the referents cannot be recovered, they might be located in a way that mirrors the proximal/distal distinction between the demonstratives, but the entities being referred to could also be equidistant from the speaker. In the anaphoric case, in (71), the proximal/distal distinction appears in a different form, with *amaz* retaining the role we have seen in Section 4.3.3.4; it co-refers with the phrase that has been introduced earlier into the discourse, therefore, it is further away from the origo, the time of speaking.

The second most frequent pattern, *emez-amaz*, occurs in 24% of the cases. Such examples have already been discussed above. Interestingly, the two patterns mentioned so far cover roughly 85%, i.e., the overall majority, of contrastive uses. Of the more marginal patterns, *az-emez* occurs in 7% of contrastive uses, but only anaphorically:

(72) Magyar ajkúnak nem kell nagy fejtörés ahhoz, hogy
Hungarian lipped.DAT no need big puzzle that.ALL COMP
megkülönböztesse fában a szút$_i$ a serpenyőbeli
PRT.differentiate.SUBJ.3SG wood.INE the beetle the pan.ATTR
zsírtól$_j$: *az*$_i$ perceg, *emez*$_j$ meg serceg.
fat.ABL that tick.3SG this and crackle.3SG
'It is not difficult for a Hungarian to differentiate the sound of a wood beetle from that of cooking fat: the former ticks, the latter crackles.'
(doc#1079, journalism)

The exceptional use of anaphoric *emez*, when it does not refer to 'the latter', is often realized within this pattern (see footnote 61).

It was pointed out above in Section 4.3.3.2 that there is a preferred order of mention in the contrastive exophoric use of *ez-emez*. This pattern with two proximal demonstratives is much less frequent than the one with one proximal and one distal: *ez-amaz*. A possible reason for this observation is that speakers prefer to combine one proximal and one distal demonstrative in contrastive use. There are even fewer examples in which the distal demonstratives *az* and *amaz* occur together. Two relevant examples are given below:

(73) Gyakran jártuk együtt az erdőt, s apám
often wandered.1PL together the forest.ACC and father.POSS.1SG
sorra megmutogatta: *ez* a sötétzöld, kard alakú levél
line.SUBL PRT.showed.3SG this the dark.green sword shaped leaf
a gyöngyvirágé, *emez* a fénytelen szürkés a
the lily.of.the.valley.POSS.3SG this the pallid grayish the
salamonpecsétė.
whorled.Solomon's.seat.POSS.3SG
'We often wandered in the forest, and my father showed me different things: this, the dark green, sword-shaped leaf, belongs to the lily of the valley; this, the pallid greyish one, is that of the whorled Solomon's seat.'
(doc#637, literary)

(74) *az* pedig, jé, a barátom, *amaz* meg, akinek
that in.turn look the friend.POSS.1SG that and who.DAT
részigazsága mindennél világosabb, az az a szemét…
part.truth.POSS.3SG everything.ADE clearer that that the creep
'look, that one is my friend, and that other one, whose half-truths are so apparent, that one is the nasty little creep…'
(doc#1409, literary)

To sum up, the broadly contrastive patterns attested in the corpus usually combine one proximal and one distal form. Examples with *ez-emez* and *az-amaz* occur less frequently, but when they do, they typically belong to spatial deixis. There are no hits for *emez-emez, amaz-amaz*. This is indirect evidence in favour of the claim that the meaning of *emez* is 'this other one', while that of *amaz* is 'that other one'.

As mentioned above, one disadvantage of corpus-based studies is the lack of contextual clues. Therefore, while the contrastive patterns mentioned above support the hypothesis regarding the inherent contrastive function of *emez-amaz*, it is not possible to decide whether relative distance can be overwritten by contrastiveness in those cases where the referents are equidistant from the speaker. The use of *amaz* in proximal scenarios and the use of *emez* in distal space would support this claim. However, it is reasonable to assume that in the case of contrastive situations where the two entities are not equidistant from the speaker and *ez-amaz* or *emez-amaz* are used, the proximal terms refer to the objects that are closer to the speaker.

4.3.5 Phraseologisms and other uses

Finally, let us turn to the last category to wrap up the corpus-based study aimed at exploring the pragmatic uses of *emez/amaz* in the HNC. This concerns the category of phraseologisms or fixed phrases, which comprises vague category markers in the corpus. In English, for example, *this and that* means 'different, unspecified matters' in the example below:

(75) I mean the post office is one of our meeting places where the people would go along and inquire about *this and that* or another thing. (O'Keeffe et al. 2011: 38)

In Hungarian, there are similar vague category markers; 263 examples were detected in the HNC. The demonstratives in these phrases no longer preserve their deictic meaning; instead, they refer to unspecified things or to nothing special at all, i.e., they function as umbrella terms for individuals or things that do not need to be identified. *Amaz* is much more frequent in these fixed phrases than *emez* (249 vs 14 occurrences).

It is worth noting that such phrases were attested in Middle Hungarian, too. Consider the example below (*A magyar nyelv történeti-etimológiai szótára*, henceforth *TESz.*, cited by D. Mátai 1999: 460):

(76)

imilyen	amolyan	dolgoc	történtenec,	*emezt*	*amazt*	végezték,
of.this.kind	of.that.kind	things	happened.3PL	this.ACC	that.ACC	did.3PL

imigy	amúgy	voltak	az	emberek
like.this	like.that	cop.PST.3PL	the	people

'such and such things happened, this and that were done, and people were such and such'

It is beyond the scope of this work to analyse these expressions in a detailed fashion, but some illustrative examples from the HNC are given below:

(77)

minden	ami	porrá	égett,	*emez*	*vagy*	*amaz*	gyújtotta	is
everything	that	dust.TRA	burned.3SG	this	or	that	torched.3SG	too

fel
PRT

'everything that burned, whoever set it on fire'
(doc#644 literary)

(78) Egyebet nem mondanak?
else.ACC no say.3PL
'Do they say anything else?'
De mondanak egyebet is.
but say.3PL else.ACC too
'Well, they say other things, too.'
Mi az az egyéb?
what that the else
'What kind of other things?'
Az egyéb? Hát *ez is meg amaz is.*
the else well this too and that too
'Other things? Well, this and that.'
(doc#1923, literary)

(79) Joe-nak *hol ez, hol amaz* a véleménye.
Joe-DAT where this where that the opinion.POSS.3SG
'Joe's opinion is sometimes this, sometimes that.'
(doc#2037, literary)

(80) Ez fáj, az fáj, csontjaim, lábaim, *ez, az,*
this hurt.3SG that hurt.3SG bone.POSS.1SG.PL leg.POSS.1SG.PL this that
amaz, ehhez nincs kedvem, ahhoz nincs
that this.ALL COP.NEG.3SG mood.POSS.1SG that.ALL COP.NEG.3SG
kedvem.
mood.POSS.1SG
'This hurts, that hurts, my bones hurt, my legs hurt, one thing and another, I don't feel like doing this, I don't feel like doing that.'
(doc#1018, personal forum)

(81) Akkor az államtitkár úr elmondta, hogy *ez meg*
then the secretary.of.state mister said COMP this and
az meg amaz fog épülni.
that and that COP.FUT.3SG build.INF
'Then the secretary of state said that this would be built and that would be built.'
(doc#2181, official)

4.4 Summary

This chapter first presented an elicitation study that explored the contrastive use of Hungarian nominal demonstratives, then summarized the results of a corpus-based analysis exploring the pragmatic functions of the reinforced demonstratives *emez*/*amaz* across the registers of the HNC.

It was revealed that in the case of contrastive demonstrative reference in table-top space relative distance from the speaker was neutralized, and distal demonstratives occurred even when speakers referred to entities within easy arm's reach, that is, elicited data on the contrastive use of Hungarian demonstratives supports the generalization made by Levinson (2018a) that contrastive uses are different from non-contrastive uses across languages. The reinforced demonstratives *emez*/*amaz* 'this/that', which are considered marginal in present day Hungarian, were also spontaneously used during the elicitation sessions. A follow-up corpus-based study examined their occurrence in the Hungarian National Corpus. The findings show that both pronominal and adnominal forms occur in the corpus, although in general the pronominal form is more common. Exophoric and anaphoric uses favour pronominal demonstratives, but the adnominal form dominates in recognitional and discourse deictic uses. It was also demonstrated that both forms occur in each register and both fulfil diverse pragmatic functions.

A detailed analysis of the data supports Laczkó's (2009) and Kleiber et al.'s (2018) suggestion that within deictic use, the basic function of *emez* is to call attention to an entity located close to the speaker in relation to (at least) another entity that is also close to the speaker; accordingly, the meaning of *emez* can be paraphrased as 'this other one', but no evidence was found in favour of the claim that *emez* creates a further distinction within 'near' with respect to *ez*.

For *amaz*, the emerging picture is slightly different: it can be argued that *amaz* makes a further distinction within 'far' with respect to *az* and refers to objects that are located further away from the speaker. At the same time, *amaz* can also be used to emphasize that there is another alternative and can refer to the entity competing to be in the centre of joint attention, meaning 'that other one there'.

Both *emez* and *amaz* can act as anaphors. In accordance with the cross-linguistic generalization that demonstrative anaphors refer to non-topical antecedents, both can signal a topic shift. In the case of contrastive anaphoric use, they create a contrast between 'the latter' and 'the former'. Overall, the empirical generalizations support the claim that *emez* and *amaz* have an inherent contrastive function.

CHAPTER 5

Conclusion

Current research on deixis relies on a wide range of empirical research methods and strives to incorporate novel types of data. The ultimate goal of the work reported here was to develop a deeper understanding of Hungarian demonstrative practice from a novel perspective, and to provide a systematic analysis of the use of Hungarian nominal demonstratives in an empirical framework. The research presented was aimed at answering two related research questions. First, to understand and explain the choice a speaker makes between proximal and distal demonstrative expressions upon any instance of demonstrative use, second, to investigate the factors and their potential interaction that have an effect on this choice in any communicative event.

In Chapter 1, first the notions of deixis and demonstratives were introduced, then, after a cross-linguistic overview of demonstrative practice, a taxonomy of demonstrative uses was put forward. Finally, previous research on Hungarian demonstratives was briefly discussed, while introducing the relevant Hungarian data. The analysis, due to time and space limitations, focused on exophoric uses of demonstratives in general, although non-deictic uses were also investigated to a certain extent.

Chapter 2 provided a critical discussion, revision and elaboration of various approaches pertaining to demonstrative choice, with particular emphasis on empirical approaches. Among others, I gave an overview of different cognitive theories of referring expressions in general. Each of these argues that reference is a collaborative process, where not only the speaker but also the hearer takes an active part. Current empirical findings were also reviewed, which, in line with the cognitive approaches, argue that the traditional, speaker-anchored view cannot adequately describe demonstrative selection across different languages.

Chapter 3 presented two empirical studies exploring the factors influencing the choice between the Hungarian proximal/distal demonstratives: *ez* and *az*. First, I presented the findings of a production study, which used data gained from natural conversations that were video recorded in a controlled dialogue game setting where two interlocutors worked to reach a common goal (cf. Piwek et al. 2008). A detailed analysis of nominal demonstrative occurrences revealed that the choice between proximal and distal gestural demonstratives in Hungarian is influenced by relative distance from the speaker; however, accessibility, which was defined in terms of the processing effort required on the part of the addressee in identifying the intended referent, was not a decisive factor.

A follow-up qualitative analysis showed that relative distance on its own cannot always explain the selection of demonstratives, hence the use of demonstratives can only be described as a dynamic process affected by the interaction of several factors, such as perceptibility, visibility, pointing, manipulation, and change of perspective or attitude. The results obtained in this preliminary study also showed that contrastive uses of demonstratives might be subject to different constraints, thus further studies based on different methodologies are called for to understand the subtleties of Hungarian demonstrative practice.

Second, the results on an online production task were reported. The experiment, which was motivated by the work of Peeters et al. (2014) on Dutch, aimed to examine the role of other factors in Hungarian demonstrative practice. More specifically, it investigated whether distance, joint attention, and the presence or absence of a manual pointing gesture influence the selection of demonstratives; moreover, the potential interactions of these factors were also explored. The findings of the online production task indicate that each of the factors investigated influence the use of Hungarian nominal demonstratives, and are compatible with similar findings for English (Stevens & Zhang 2013), Dutch (Peeters et al. 2014) and Jordanian Arabic (Jarbou 2010). Moreover, it was shown that the traditional analysis based on proximal/distal opposition presents an oversimplified picture, and the use of demonstratives in Hungarian cannot be described adequately from a solely speaker-anchored perspective.

Chapter 4 focused on contrastive uses of Hungarian nominal demonstratives. A controlled elicitation task (Wilkins 1999), which was conducted with five native speakers of Hungarian, explored the contrastive exophoric uses of Hungarian demonstratives, thus collecting data that are not easy to come across by other methods. It was shown that in the case of non-contrastive uses, physical proximity to the speaker is crucial regarding the choice of demonstratives in table-top space, but in the case of contrastive uses, the pattern of demonstratives changed, relative distance from the speaker was neutralized, and distal demonstratives occurred even when speakers referred to entities within reaching space. The study yielded complementary data and offered novel insights not only on the use of basic nominal demonstratives, but also on the use of the previously understudied reinforced demonstratives (*emez*/*amaz*).

Finally, in a follow-up study I collected further data and explored the use of *emez*/*amaz* in the Hungarian National Corpus. A detailed analysis of the data revealed that *emez*/*amaz* fulfil various deictic and non-deictic functions. First, it was argued that within exophoric use, the basic function of these reinforced demonstratives is to call attention to an entity located close/far to the speaker in relation to (at least) another entity that is also close/far to the speaker. Therefore, *emez* and *amaz* are inherently contrastive in nature, their core meaning being 'this/that other one.' The corpus-based study also provided novel insights about other, non-deictic uses of *emez*/*amaz*. Namely, both reinforced demonstratives might signal topic shift when they occur as subject anaphors. Moreover, their contrastive anaphoric use presents further evidence in favour of the assumption that *emez*/*amaz* have an inherent contrastive function.

Overall, the aim of the work reported was to provide an in-depth analysis of the use of Hungarian nominal demonstratives by the application of multiple methods. The analysis presented was based on the findings of two corpus-based studies, an elicitation study and an online experiment. In line with previous findings on demonstrative use in English (Coventry et al. 2008, Stevens & Zhang 2013), Dutch (Peeters et al. 2014, 2015), and Finnish (Etelämäki 2009), it was shown that in addition to relative distance from the speaker, other factors influence the selection of Hungarian demonstratives. The analysis described here emphasized the importance of differentiating contrastive and non-contrastive uses of demonstratives. It was shown that

- (i) patterns of demonstrative selection depend on the type of use: non-contrastive vs contrastive;
- (ii) in the case of non-contrastive uses physical proximity to the speaker matters considerably, but spatial considerations only do not provide an adequate description of Hungarian demonstrative practice;
- (iii) in the case of non-contrastive uses, besides relative distance from the speaker other factors (for example, manipulation, perceptibility, visual joint attention, the presence or absence of a pointing gesture) also have an effect upon demonstrative choice;
- (iv) in contrastive contexts spatial constraints are overwritten, and a subtle interplay of interactional factors can be observed;
- (v) Hungarian reinforced demonstratives (*emez*/*amaz*) have an inherent contrastive function.

In this study I hope to have shown that exploring the pragmatic uses of demonstratives is an intriguing field of research; however, there is much left for future work. Regarding exophoric use, I have pinned down several factors that play a crucial role in demonstrative selection in Hungarian, but it is left for future research to explore the interaction of these factors in a subtler manner. However, even at this point of research it can be concluded that demonstrative reference in Hungarian is a joint action, and the use of demonstratives cannot be described adequately from a solely speaker-anchored perspective. The empirical findings reported above contribute to a better understanding of the semantics and pragmatics of nominal demonstratives not only in Hungarian, the emerging data and the findings advance the formulation of cross-linguistic generalisations on demonstrative systems and demonstrative practice per se; the analysis leads to a more adequate characterisation of demonstrative reference as an interactional process between the speaker and the addressee. Considering non-deictic uses of demonstratives, however, I have only begun to explore the tip of the iceberg. It is left for future research to provide a more detailed analysis of anaphoric and discourse deictic uses of Hungarian nominal demonstratives.

References

A magyar nyelv értelmező szótára I–VII. (*ÉrtSz.*) [Explanatory Dictionary of Hungarian]. 1959–1962. Chief editors: Bárczi, G. & L. Országh. Budapest: Akadémiai Kiadó.

A magyar nyelv történeti-etimológiai szótára. (*TESz.*) [Etymological Dictionary of Hungarian]. 1967–1984. Chief editor: Benkő, L. Budapest: Akadémiai Kiadó.

A magyar nyelv nagyszótára. (*NSz.*) [Comprehensive Dictionary of Hungarian]. 2006–2019. Chief editor: Ittzés, N. Budapest: MTA Nyelvtudományi Intézet. http://nagyszotar.nytud.hu

Allen, S. E. M. 1996. *Aspects of Argument Structure Acquisition in Inuktitut.* Amsterdam: John Benjamins.

Anderson, S. R. & E. L. Keenan. 1985. Deixis. In Shopen, T. (ed.) *Language Typology and Syntactic Description.* Cambridge: Cambridge University Press: 259–308.

Ariel, M. 1990/2014. *Accessing Noun-Phrase Antecedents.* London, New York: Routledge.

Ariel, M. 2001. Accessibility theory: An overview. In Sanders, T., J. Schilperoord & W. Spooren (eds.) *Text Representation: Linguistic and Psycholinguistic Aspects.* Amsterdam: John Benjamins: 29–87.

Ariel, M. 2004. Accessibility marking: Discourse functions, discourse profiles, and processing cues. *Discourse Processes* 37(2): 91–116.

Bangerter, A. 2004. Using pointing and describing to achieve joint focus of attention in dialogue. *Psychological Science* 15(6): 415–419.

Bar-Hillel, Y. 1954. Indexical expressions. *Mind* 63: 359–379.

Benkő, L. (ed.) 1993. *Etymologischen Wörterbuch des Ungarischen. Vol 1 & Vol 2.* [Etymological Dictionary of Hungarian]. Budapest: Akadémiai Kiadó.

Biber, D., S. Conrad & R. Reppen. 1998. *Corpus Linguistics: Investigating Language Structure and Use.* Cambridge: Cambridge University Press.

Blakemore, D. 2002. *Relevance and Linguistic Meaning: The Semantics and Pragmatics of Discourse Markers.* Cambridge: Cambridge University Press.

Bohnemeyer, J. 2018. Yucatec demonstratives in interaction: Spontaneous vs. elicited data. In Levinson, S. C., S. Cutfield, M. J. Dunn, N. J. Enfield & S. Meira (eds.) *Demonstratives in Cross-Linguistic Perspective*. Cambridge: Cambridge University Press: 176–205.

Boronkai, D. 2010. A deixis szerepe a nézőpont jelölésében. [The role of dexis in marking perspective]. *Magyar Nyelv* 134(4): 436–452.

Bui, L. T. 2014. *Vietnamese Demonstratives: A Spatially-based Polysemy Network*. Ms. Doctoral dissertation. The University of Queensland.

Burenhult, N. 2003. Attention, accessibility, and the addressee: The case of the Jahai demonstrative *ton*. *Pragmatics* 13(3/4): 363–379.

Bühler, K. 1934. *Sprachtheorie: Die Darstellungsfunktion der Sprache*. [Theory of Language: The Representational Function of Language]. Jena: Fischer.

Bühler, K. 1965. *Sprachtheorie*. [Theory of Language]. 2nd edition. Stuttgart: Fischer.

Chafe, W. L. 1976. Givenness, contrastiveness, definiteness, subjects, topics, and point of view. In Li, C. N. (ed.) *Subject and Topic*. New York: Academic Press: 25–55.

Chafe, W. L. 1994. *Discourse, Consciousness, and Time: The Flow and Displacement of Conscious Experience in Speaking and Writing*. Chicago, London: University of Chicago Press.

Clark, E. V. 1978. From gesture to word: On the natural history of deixis in language acquisition. In Bruner, J. S. & A. Garton (eds.) *Human Growth and Development*. Oxford: Oxford University Press: 85–120.

Clark, H. H. 1996. *Using Language*. Cambridge: Cambridge University Press.

Clark, B. 2013. *Relevance Theory*. Cambridge: Cambridge University Press.

Clark, H. H. & A. Bangerter. 2004. Changing conceptions of reference. In Noveck, I. & D. Sperber (eds.) *Experimental Pragmatics*. Basingstoke, England: Palgrave Macmillan: 25–49.

Clark, H. H., R. Schreuder & S. Buttrick. 1983. Common ground and the understanding of demonstrative reference. *Journal of Verbal Learning and Verbal Behavior* 22: 245–258.

Comrie, B., M. Haspelmath & B. Bickel. 2008. The Leipzig Glossing Rules: Conventions for interlinear morpheme-by-morpheme glosses. Max Planck Institute for Evolutionary Anthropology. https://www.eva.mpg.de/lingua/resources/glossing-rules.php

Consten, M. & M. Averintseva-Klisch. 2012. Tentative reference acts? 'Recognitional demonstratives' as means of suggesting mutual knowledge – or overriding a lack of it. *Research in Language* 10(3): 257–277.

Cornish, F. 2001. Modal *that* as determiner and pronoun: The primacy of the cognitive interactive dimension. *English Language and Linguistics* 5(2): 297–315.

Coventry, K. R. 2015. Space. In E. Dabrowska & D. Divjak (eds.) *Handbook of Cognitive Linguistics*. Berlin: Mouton De Gruyter: 489–507.

Coventry, K. R., B. Valdés, A. Castillo & P. Guijarro-Fuentes. 2008. Language within your reach: Near-far perceptual space and spatial demonstratives. *Cognition* 108: 889–895.

Coventry, K. R., D. Griffiths & C. J. Hamilton. 2014. Spatial demonstratives and perceptual space: Describing and remembering object location. *Cognitive Psychology* 69: 46–70.

Diessel, H. 1999. *Demonstratives. Form, Function and Grammaticalization*. Amsterdam: John Benjamins.

Diessel, H. 2012. Deixis and demonstratives. In Maienborn, C., K. von Heusinger & P. Portner (eds.) *An International Handbook of Natural Language Meaning. Vol. 3*. Berlin: Mouton de Gruyter: 2407–2431.

Diessel, H. 2013. Where does language come from? Some reflections on the role of deictic gesture and demonstratives in the evolution of language. *Language and Cognition* 5(2–3): 239–249.

Diessel, H. & M. Breunesse. 2020. A typology of demonstrative clause linkers. In Næss, A., A. Margetts & Y. Treis (eds.) *Demonstratives in Discourse*. Berlin: Language Science Press: 305–341.

Diessel, H. & K. Coventry. 2021. Demonstratives in spatial language and social interaction: An interdisciplinary review. In Diessel, H., K. Coventry, H. Gudde & O. Capirci (eds.) *Demonstratives, Deictic Pointing and the Conceptualization of Space*. Lausanne: Frontiers Media SA: 133–146.

Dömötör, A. 2008. A főnévi névmási kijelölő jelző a középmagyar korban. [Adnominal demonstratives in Middle Hungarian]. In Büky, L., T. Forgács & B. Sinkovics (eds.) *A nyelvtörténeti kutatások újabb eredményei V.* Szeged: Szegedi Tudományegyetem Magyar Nyelvészeti Tanszék: 17–25.

Dömötör, É. 2012. Mutató névmások a grammatikalizációs ösvényen. [On the grammaticalization of demonstrative pronouns]. In Parapatics, A. & D. Csernák-Szuhánszky (eds.) *Félúton 7*. Budapest: ELTE BTK Nyelvtudományi Doktori Iskola: 1–13.

Dömötör, É. 2022. Demonstratívumok pragmatikai és pragmatikalizálódott használatai konstrukciós megközelítésben: az *azért* konstrukciói. [A pragmatic approach to demonstratives involving pragmaticalized constructions of use: Constructions of *azért* 'for that']. *Nyelvtudományi Közlemények* 118: 231–255.

D. Mátai M. 1999. A névmások története a középmagyar kor végéig. [The history of pronouns up to the end of the Middle Hungarian period]. *Magyar Nyelvőr* 123(4): 438–464.

Egedi, B. 2014. The DP-cycle in Hungarian and the functional extension of the noun phrase. In: É. Kiss, K. (ed.) *The Evolution of Functional Left Peripheries in Hungarian Syntax. Oxford Studies in Diachronic and Historical Linguistics 11*. Oxford: Oxford University Press: 56–82.

Egedi, B. 2015. Változó struktúrák, versengő stratégiák: a mutató névmási módosítók esete. [Changing structures, competing strategies: the case of demonstratives]. *Általános Nyelvészeti Tanulmányok* 27: 107–132.

Enfield, N. J. 2003. Demonstratives in space and interaction: Data from Lao speakers and implications for semantic analysis. *Language* 79(1): 82–117.

Enfield, N. J. 2009. *The Anatomy of Meaning: Speech, Gesture, and Composite Utterances*. Cambridge: Cambridge University Press.

Etelämäki, M. 2009. The Finnish demonstrative pronouns in light of interaction. *Journal of Pragmatics* 41(1): 25–46.

É. Kiss, K. 1998. Informational focus vs. identification focus. *Language* 74: 245–273.

É. Kiss, K. 2002. *The Syntax of Hungarian*. Cambridge: Cambridge University Press.

É. Kiss K. 2012. Patterns of agreement with coordinate noun phrases in Hungarian. *Natural Language and Linguistic Theory* 30: 1027–1060.

Farkas, J. & G. Alberti. 2018. Characterization. In Alberti, G. & T. Laczkó (eds.) *Syntax of Hungarian, Nouns and Noun Phrases. Vol. 1*. Amsterdam: Amsterdam University Press: 5–151.

Fillmore, C. J. *Towards a Theory of Deixis*. 1971/1997. The PCCLLU Papers 3.4. Hawaii: Department of Linguistics, University of Hawaii, 1971. Reprinted in Fillmore, C. J. *Lectures on Deixis*. Stanford: CSLI Publications, 1997.

Fillmore, C J. 1975. *Santa Cruz Lectures on Deixis 1971*. Bloomington, IN: Indiana University Linguistics Club.

Fillmore, C. J. 1982. Towards a descriptive framework for spatial deixis. In Jaravella, R. J. & W. Klein (eds.) *Speech, Place and Action*. New York: John Wiley and Sons: 31–59.

Green, M. G. 2011. Meaning in language use. In Maienborn, C., K. von Heusinger & P. Portner (eds.) *An International Handbook of Natural Language Meaning. Vol. 1*. Berlin: Mouton de Gruyter: 74–95.

Grice, H. P. 1975. Logic and conversation. In Cole, P. & J. L. Morgan (eds.) *Syntax and Semantics. Vol. 3*. New York: Academic Press: 41–58.

Grice, H. P. 1989. *Studies in the Way of Words*. Cambridge, MA: Harvard University Press.

Gries, S. Th. 2008. Phraseology and linguistic theory: a brief survey. In Granger, S. & F. Meunier (eds.) *Phraseology: An Interdisciplinary Perspective*. Amsterdam: John Benjamins: 3–25.

Gundel, J. K., N. Hedberg & R. Zacharski 1993. Cognitive status and the form of referring expressions in discourse. *Language* 69(2): 274–307.

Gyuris, B., K. Varasdi & M. Maleczki. 2008. *Formális szemantika*. [Formal semantics]. Második kiadás. [Second edition]. Szeged: JatePress.

Halácsy, P., A. Kornai, L. Németh, A. Rung, I. Szakadát & V. Trón. 2004. Creating open language resources for Hungarian. In *Proceedings of the 4th International Conference on Language Resources and Evaluation (LREC2004)*.

Hanks, W. F. 1990. *Referential Practice: Language and Lived Space among the Maya*. Chicago, IL: University of Chicago Press.

Hanks, W. F. 2009. Fieldwork on deixis. *Journal of Pragmatics* 41: 10–24.

Hanks, W. F. 2011. Deixis and indexicality. In Bublitz, W. & N. R. Norrick (eds.) *Foundations of Pragmatics, Vol. 1 of Handbooks of Pragmatics*. Berlin: Mouton de Gruyter: 315–346.

Hedley, P. 2005. Pronouns, procedures and relevance theory. *Durham Working Papers in Linguistics* 11: 41–55.

Himmelmann, N. 1996. Demonstratives in narrative discourse: A taxonomy of universal uses. In Fox, B. (ed.) *Studies in Anaphora*. Amsterdam: John Benjamins: 205–254.

Huddleston, R. & G. K. Pullum. 2002. *The Cambridge Grammar of the English Language*. Cambridge: Cambridge University Press.

Imai, S. 2003. *Spatial Deixis*. Ms. Doctoral dissertation. State University of New York.

Jarbou, S. O. 2010. Accessibility vs. physical proximity: An analysis of exophoric demonstrative practice in Spoken Jordanian Arabic. *Journal of Pragmatics* 42: 3078–3097.

Jungbluth, K. 2003. Deictics in the conversational dyad: Findings in Spanish and some cross-linguistic outlines. In Lenz, F. (ed.) *Deictic Conceptualisation of Space, Time and Person*. Amsterdam: John Benjamins: 13–40.

Kahneman, D. 2003. A perspective on judgement and choice: Mapping bounded rationality. *American Psychologist* 58(9): 697–720.

Kaplan, D. 1989a. Demonstratives. In Almog, J., J. Perry & H. Wettstein (eds.) *Themes from Kaplan*. Oxford: Oxford University Press: 481–563.

Kaplan, D. 1989b. Afterthoughts. In Almog, J., J. Perry & H. Wettstein (eds.) *Themes from Kaplan*. Oxford: Oxford University Press: 565–614.

Kemmerer, D. 1999. *Near* and *far* in language and perception. *Cognition* 73: 35–63.

Kenesei, I. 1994. Subordinate clauses. In Kiefer, F. & K. É. Kiss (eds.) *Syntax and Semantics. Volume 27. The Syntactic Structure of Hungarian*. San Diego & New York: Academic Press: 275–354.

Kibrik, A. A. 2011. *Reference in Discourse*. Oxford: Oxford University Press.

Kleiber, J., V. Szabó & A. Viszket. 2018. Articles and demonstratives. In Alberti, G. & T. Laczkó (eds.) *Syntax of Hungarian. Nouns and Noun Phrases. Vol. 2*. Amsterdam: Amsterdam University Press: 976–1044.

Kocsány, P. 1995. Műhelytanulmány az „ő" névmásról. [A working paper on the pronoun 'ő']. *Magyar Nyelvőr* 119(1): 285–93.

Kocsány, P. 2009. A közelre mutató névmás szövegalkotó szerepben. [The proximal demonstrative in text construction]. *Acta Academia Paedagogicae Agriensis. Sectio Linguistica Hungarica* 36: 203–209.

Kocsány, P. 2018. A közelre mutató *ez* névmás anaforikus kifejtő szerkezetekben és a diszkurzív kontinuitás fokozatai. [The proximal demonstrative pronoun *ez* in anaphoric constructions and the degrees of discourse continuity]. *Jelentés és Nyelvhasználat* 5: 117–158.

Kornai, A., P. Halácsy, V. Nagy, Cs. Oravecz, V. Trón & D. Varga. 2006. Web-based frequency dictionaries for medium density languages. In Kilgarriff, A. & M. Baroni (eds.) *Proceedings of the 2nd International Workshop on Web as Corpus. ACL-06*: 1–9.

Kugler, N. & K. Laczkó. 2000. A névmások. [Pronouns]. In Keszler, B. (ed.) *Magyar grammatika*. [Hungarian Grammar]. Budapest: Nemzeti Tankönyvkiadó: 152–175.

Küntay, A. C. & A. Özyürek. 2006. Learning to use demonstratives in conversation: what do language specific strategies in Turkish reveal? *Journal of Child Language* 33: 303–320.

Laczkó, K. 2003. A mutató névmások funkcionális vizsgálata. [A functional study of demonstrative pronouns]. *Magyar Nyelvőr* 127(3): 314–325.

Laczkó, K. 2006. *A magyar névmási rendszer – nyelvtan és funkció*. [The Hungarian pronominal system – grammar and function]. Budapest: Martin Opitz Kiadó.

Laczkó, K. 2008. A mutató névmási deixisről. [On deixis and demonstratives]. *Általános Nyelvészeti Tanulmányok* XXII. Budapest: Akadémiai Kiadó: 309–347.

Laczkó, K. 2009. *Emez emitt, amaz amott*: Pontosan hol is? [*This here, that one over there*: where exactly?] In Keszler, B. & Sz. Tátrai (eds.) *Diskurzus a grammatikában – grammatika a diskurzusban*. [Discourse in grammar – grammar in discourse]. Budapest: Tinta Könyvkiadó: 235–242.

Laczkó K. 2010. Demonstrative pronouns in spatial deixis, discourse deixis, and anaphora. *Acta Linguistica Hungarica* 57(1): 99–118.

Laczkó, K. 2012. Spatial deixis and demonstrative pronouns in Hungarian. In *Selected Papers from UK-CLA Meetings*. Vol. 1: 289–301.

Laczkó, K. 2014. Térdeixis és a mutató névmások a magyarban. [Spatial deixis and demonstrative pronouns in Hungarian]. In Laczkó, K. & Sz. Tátrai (eds.) *Elmélet és módszer*. [Theory and method]. Budapest: ELTE Eötvös József Collegium: 223–236.

Laczkó, K. & Sz. Tátrai. 2012. Személyek és/vagy dolgok. A harmadik személyű és a mutató névmási deixis a magyarban. [People and/or things. Deictic uses of 3rd person personal pronouns and demonstrative pronouns in Hungarian]. In Tolcsvai Nagy, G. & Sz. Tátrai (eds.) *Konstrukció és jelentés. Tanulmányok a magyar nyelv funkcionális kognitív leírására*. [Construction and Meaning. Papers on the Functional-cognitive Description of Hungarian]. Budapest: ELTE: 231–258.

Lakoff, R. 1974. Remarks on *this* and *that*. CLS 10. Chicago, IL: Chicago Linguistic Society: 345–356.

Laury, R. 1997. *Demonstratives in interaction. The emergence of a definite article in Finnish*. Amsterdam: John Benjamins.

Leech, G., P. Rayson & A. Wilson. 2001. *Word Frequencies in Written and Spoken English: Based on the British National Corpus*. New York: Routledge.

Levinson, S. C. 1983. *Pragmatics*. Cambridge: Cambridge University Press.

Levinson, S. C. 2000. *Presumptive Meanings: The Theory of Generalized Conversational Implicature*. Cambridge, MA: The MIT Press.

Levinson, S. C. 2004. Deixis. In Horn, L. & G. Ward (eds.) *The Handbook of Pragmatics*. Oxford: Blackwell: 97–121.

Levinson, S. C. 2018a. Introduction: Demonstratives: Patterns in diversity. In Levinson, S. C., S. Cutfield, M. J. Dunn, N. J. Enfield & S. Meira (eds.) *Demonstratives in Cross-Linguistic Perspective*. Cambridge: Cambridge University Press: 1–42.

Levinson, S. C. 2018b. Yélî Dnye demonstratives. In Levinson, S. C., S. Cutfield, M. J. Dunn, N. J. Enfield & S. Meira (eds.) *Demonstratives in Cross-Linguistic Perspective*. Cambridge: Cambridge University Press: 318–342.

Lipták, A. 2012. Correlative topicalization. *Acta Linguistica Hungarica* 59(3): 245–302.

Luz, S. & I. Van der Sluis. 2011. Production of demonstratives in Dutch, English and Portuguese dialogues. In Gardent, C. & K. Striegnitz (eds.) *Proceedings of the 13th European Workshop on Natural Language Generation*. Association for Computational Linguistics: 181–186.

Lyons, J. 1977. *Semantics. Vol. 2*. Cambridge: Cambridge University Press.

Maes, A. & C. de Rooij. 2007. (How) Do demonstratives code distance? In Branco, A., T. McEnery, R. Mitkov & F. Silva (eds.) *Proceedings of DAARC 2007*. Lagos Portugal: Centro de Linguistica da Universidade de Porto: 83–89.

Margetts, A. 2018. Saliba-Logea: Exophoric demonstratives. In Levinson, S. C., S. Cutfield, M. J. Dunn, N. J. Enfield & S. Meira (eds.) *Demonstratives in Cross-Linguistic Perspective*. Cambridge: Cambridge University Press: 257–281.

Meibauer, J. 2012. What is a context? Theoretical and empirical evidence. In Finkbeiner, R., J. Meibauer & P. B. Schumacher (eds.) *What is a Context? Linguistic Approaches and Challenges*. Amsterdam: John Benjamins: 9–32.

Meira, S. & A. Terril. 2005. Contrasting contrastive demonstratives in Tiriyo′ and Lavukaleve. *Linguistics* 43(6): 1131–1152.

O'Keeffe, A., B. Clancy & S. Adolphs. 2011. *Introducing Pragmatics in Use*. New York: Routledge.

Olson, D. R. 1970. Language and thought: Aspects of a cognitive theory of semantics. *Psychological Review* 77(4): 257–273.

Oravecz, Cs., T. Váradi & B. Sass. 2014. The Hungarian Gigaword Corpus. In *Proceedings of LREC 2014*. European Language Resources Association: 1719–1723.

Pederson, E. 2012. The expression of space across languages. In Maienborn, C., K. von Heusinger & P. Portner (eds.) *An International Handbook of Natural Language Meaning. Vol. 3*. Berlin: Mouton de Gruyter: 2608–2624.

Pederson, E. & D. Wilkins. 1996. A cross-linguistic questionnaire on 'demonstratives'. In Levinson, S. C. (ed.) *Manual for the 1996 Field Season*. Nijmegen: Max Planck Institute for Psycholinguistics: 1–11.

Peeters, D. & A. Özyürek. 2016. *This* and *that* revisited: A social and multimodal approach to spatial demonstratives. *Frontiers in Psychology* 7. Article 222: 1–4.

Peeters, D., A. Zeynep & A. Özyürek. 2014. The interplay between joint attention, physical proximity, and pointing gesture in demonstrative choice. In Bello, P., M. Guarini, M. McShane & B. Scassellati (eds.) *Proceedings of the 36th Annual Meeting of the Cognitive Science Society. Cognitive Science Meets Artificial Intelligence: Human and Artificial Agents in Interactive Contexts*. Austin, TX: Cognitive Science Society: 1144–1149.

Peeters, D., P. Hagoort & A. Özyürek. 2015. Electrophysiological evidence for the role of shared space in online comprehension of spatial demonstratives. *Cognition* 136: 64–84.

Pete, I. 2012. Nem- és fajfogalom – névmási jelentés. [Hypernym, hyponym – meaning of pronouns]. *Magyar Nyelvőr* 136(3): 336–340.

Piwek, P. & A. Cremers. 1996. Dutch and English demonstratives: A comparison. *Language Sciences* 18(3–4): 835–851.

Piwek, P., R.-J. Beun & A. Cremers. 2008. 'Proximal' and 'distal' in language and cognition: Evidence from deictic demonstratives in Dutch. *Journal of Pragmatics* 40: 694–718.

Pléh, Cs. 1982. Subject and topic in Hungarian: some psycholinguistic evidence to increase the confusion. In Kiefer, F. (ed.) *Hungarian General Linguistics*. Amsterdam: John Benjamins: 447–465.

Pléh, Cs. 1998. *A mondatmegértés a magyar nyelvben: Pszicholingvisztikai kísérletek és modellek*. [Sentence Processing in Hungarian. Psycholinguistic Experiments and Models]. Budapest: Osiris Kiadó.

Pléh, Cs. & K. Radics. 1976. Hiányos mondat, pronominalizáció és a szöveg. [Elliptical sentences, pronominalization and the text]. In Telegdi, Zs. & Gy. Szépe (eds.) *Általános Nyelvészeti Tanulmányok XI. A szöveg megközelítései*. [Approaches to text]. Budapest: Akadémiai Kiadó: 261–277.

Powell, G. 2003. *Language, Thought and Reference*. Ms. Doctoral dissertation. University College London.

Powell, G. 2010. *Language, Thought and Reference*. Hampshire: Palgrave Macmillan.

Reile, M. 2015. Space and demonstratives: An experiment with Estonian exophoric demonstratives. *Eesti ja Soome-Ugri Keeleteaduse Ajakiri* 6(2): 137–165.

Reile, M. 2019. *Estonian demonstratives in exophoric use: an experimental approach*. Dissertationes Linguisticae Universitatis Tartuensis 34. Tartu: University of Tartu.

Reile, M., P. Taremaa, T. Nakhola & R. Pajusalu. 2019. Reference in the borderline of space and discourse: A free production experiment in Estonian, Finnish and Russian. *Linguistica Uralica* 55(3): 185–208.

Reile, M., H. Plado, H. B. Gudde & K. R. Coventry. 2020a. Demonstratives as spatial deictics or something more? Evidence from Common Estonian and Võro. *Folia Linguistica* 54(1): 167–195.

Reile, M., K. Averin & N. Põldver. 2020b. Interpreting Estonian demonstratives: The effects of referent's distance and visual salience. *Frontiers in Psychology* 11. Article 553226.

Rühlemann, C. 2007. *Conversation in Context. A Corpus-driven Approach*. London: Continuum.

Rühlemann, C. 2019. *Corpus Linguistics for Pragmatics*. New York: Routledge.

Scott, K. 2013. *This* and *that*: A procedural analysis. *Lingua* 131: 49–65.

Scott, K. 2020. *Referring Expressions, Pragmatics and Style. Reference and Beyond*. Cambridge: Cambridge University Press.

Shaw, J. A., L. K. Bryant, B. F. Malle, D. J. Povinelli & J. R. Pruett Jr. 2017. The relationship between joint attention and theory of mind in neurotypical adults. *Consciousness and Cognition* 51: 268–278.

Sidnell, J. 2009. Deixis. In Verschueren, J. & J. Östman (eds.) *Key Notions for Pragmatics*. Amsterdam: John Benjamins: 114–138.

Sidnell, J. & N. J. Enfield 2017. Deixis and the interactional foundations of reference. In Huang, Y. (ed.) *The Oxford Handbook of Pragmatics*. Oxford: Oxford University Press: 217–239.

Skarabela, B., S. E. M. Allen & T. C. Scott-Phillips. 2013. Joint attention helps explain why children omit new referents. *Journal of Pragmatics* 56: 5–14.

Sperber, D. & D. Wilson. 1986/1995. *Relevance: Communication and Cognition*. Oxford: Blackwell.

Sperber, D. & D. Wilson. 1998. The mapping between the mental and the public lexicon. In Carruthers, P. & J. Boucher (eds.) *Thought and Language*. Cambridge: Cambridge University Press: 184–200.

Sperber, D. & D. Wilson. 2002. Relevance, Modularity and Mind-Reading. *Mind and Language* 17: 3–23.

Strauss, S. 1993. Why *this* and *that* are incomplete without *it*. In *Proceedings of the 29th Regional Meeting of the Chicago Linguistic Society*. Chicago Linguistic Society: 403–417.

Strauss, S. 2002. *This*, *that*, and *it* in Spoken American English: A demonstrative system of gradient focus. *Language Sciences* 24: 131–152.

Stevens, J. & Y. Zhang. 2013. Relative distance and gaze in the use of entity-referring spatial demonstratives: An event-related potential study. *Journal of Neurolinguistics* 26: 31–45.

Stevens, J. & Y. Zhang. 2014. Brain mechanisms for processing co-speech gesture: A cross-language study of spatial demonstratives. *Journal of Neurolinguistics* 30: 27–47.

Szalamin, E. 1988. Az ún. témaismétlő névmások kérdéséhez. [On resumptive pronouns]. In Kontra, M. (ed.) *Beszélt nyelvi tanulmányok*. [Spoken language studies]. Budapest: MTA Nyelvtudományi Intézet: 90–101.

Szűcs, P. 2015. On pronouns in Hungarian complex sentences. *Argumentum* 11: 292–313.

Szűcs, P. 2017a. *On Clause-initial Discourse-related Constructions in English and Hungarian*. Ms. Doctoral dissertation. University of Debrecen.

Szűcs, P. 2017b. 'Balra kihelyezések' a magyarban. [Left dislocation in Hungarian]. *LingDok* 16: 81–100.

Szűcs, P. 2019. Left Dislocation in Hungarian. In Butt, M., T. H. King & I. Toivonen (eds.) *Proceedings of the LFG'19 Conference, Australian National University*. Stanford, CA: CSLI Publications: 293–313.

Talmy, L. 2000. *Toward a Cognitive Semantics. Vol. 1. Concept Structuring Systems*. Cambridge, MA: The MIT Press.

Tanz, C. 1980. *Studies in the Acquisition of Deictic Terms*. Cambridge: Cambridge University Press.

Tátrai, Sz. 2010. Áttekintés a deixisről. [A brief survey of the issue of deixis]. *Magyar Nyelvőr* 134(2): 211–233.

Tátrai, Sz. 2017. Pragmatika. [Pragmatics]. In Tolcsvai Nagy, G. (ed.) *Nyelvtan*. [Grammar]. Budapest: Osiris Kiadó: 899–1058.

Tolcsvai Nagy, G. 2000. Vázlat az *ő* – *az* anaforikus megoszlásról. [A sketch on the anaphoric distribution of the pronouns *ő* 'he/she' vs. *az* 'that']. *Magyar Nyelv* 96(3): 282–296.

Tolcsvai Nagy, G. 2001. *A magyar nyelv szövegtana*. [Textlinguistics of Hungarian]. Budapest: Nemzeti Tankönyvkiadó.

Tomasello, M. 1999. *The Cultural Origins of Human Cognition*. Cambridge: Cambridge University Press.

Tóth, E. 2014. Gestural demonstratives in English: an experiment. *Argumentum* 10: 600–610.

Tóth, E. 2018. A production study on the choice of Hungarian demonstratives. *Argumentum* 14: 110–123.

Tóth, E. 2019. *Ez* vagy *az*? Egy produkciós kísérlet eredményei. [Demonstrative choice in Hungarian]. *Jelentés és nyelvhasználat* 6: 129–146

Tóth, E. 2020. Some insights on demonstrative use in Hungarian: results of a controlled-dialogue game. *Argumentum* 16: 209–229.

Tóth, E. & P. Csatár. 2014. A főnévi mutató névmások indexikális használatát befolyásoló tényezők a magyarban. [Indexical demonstratives in Hungarian: An experiment]. *Jelentés és nyelvhasználat* 1: 67–85.

Tóth, E. & P. Csatár. 2016. Indexical demonstratives and identificational focus in Hungarian. *Linguistica* 56(1): 281–291.

Tóth, E., P. Csatár & A. Banga. 2014. Exploring Hungarian and Dutch gestural demonstratives. In Veselovská, L. & M. Janebová (eds.) *Complex Visibles Out There. Proceedings of the Olomouc Linguistics Colloquium 2014: Language Use and Linguistic Structure*. Olomouc: Palacký University: 607–625.

Traunmüller, H. 1996. Sound symbolism in deictic words. *Speech, Music and Hearing: Quarterly Progress and Status Report. TMH-QPSR* 2: 147–151.

Veszelszki, Á. 2008. Egy beszélt nyelvi jellemző, a témaismétlő névmás csevegésszövegekben. [Resumptive structures: A spoken-language feature in chatroom texts]. *Magyar Nyelvőr* 132: 235–244.

Veszelszki, Á. 2017. *Digilect: The Impact of Infocommunication Technology on Language*. Berlin, Boston: De Gruyter Saur.

Wilkins, D. 1999. Eliciting contrastive use of demonstratives for objects within close personal space (all objects well within arm's reach). In Wilkins, D. (ed.) *Manual for the 1999 Field Season*. Nijmegen: Max Planck Institute for Psycholinguistics: 25–28.

Wilkins, D. 2018. The demonstrative questionnaire: 'THIS' and 'THAT' in comparative perspective. In Levinson, S. C., S. Cutfield, M. J. Dunn, N. J. Enfield & S. Meira (eds.) *Demonstratives in Cross-Linguistic Perspective*. Cambridge: Cambridge University Press: 43–71.

Wilson, D. & D. Sperber. 2004. Relevance theory. In Ward, G. & L. Horn (eds.) *Handbook of Pragmatics*. Oxford: Blackwell: 607–632.

Wolter, L. 2009. Demonstratives in philosophy and linguistics. *Philosophy Compass* 4(3): 451–468.

Yule, G. 1996. *Pragmatics.* Oxford: Oxford University Press.
Zaki, M. 2011. *The Semantics and Pragmatics of Demonstratives in English and Arabic.* Ms. PhD Dissertation. Middlesex University.

Corpora

Hungarian Webcorpus. http://mokk.bme.hu/resources/webcorpus/
Magyar Nemzeti Szövegtár. [Hungarian National Corpus] Available online at http://clara.nytud.hu/mnsz2-dev/
Virginia-kódex. [Virginia codex] Available online at http://mek.oszk.hu/10700/10741/#

Index